Folens

Second Edition

Technology, War and Identities

A World Study After 1900

Aaron Wilkes

James Ball

D0488314

Authors' acknowledgements

James Ball would like to thank the Hunt family for their kind permission to use the war diary of their relative Jack Folk. He would also like to thank his parents for nurturing and bankrolling his love of history for far longer than was reasonable to ask, and his girlfriend Karen for all her love, support and patience.

Aaron Wilkes wishes to acknowledge Jo Murray for all her hard work and advice. He would also like to thank Hannah and Eleanor Wilkes for all their patience and support during the preparation of this book.

© 2009 Folens Limited, on behalf of the authors.

United Kingdom: Folens Publishers, Waterslade House, Thame Road, Haddenham, Buckinghamshire, HP17 8NT.

Email: folens@folens.com

www.folens.com

Ireland: Folens Publishers, Greenhills Road, Tallaght, Dublin 24.

Email: info@folens.ie

Editors: Daniel Bottom and Joanne Murray

Layout artist: Sally Boothroyd

Picture researcher: Sue Sharp

Illustrations: Tony Randell and Clive Wakfer

Cover design: Mike Cryer at EMC Design

Cover image: Mary Evans Picture Library (left and right) and Photos.com (centre)

First published 2009 by Folens Limited.

Every effort has been made to contact copyright holders of material used in this publication. If any copyright holder has been overlooked, we should be pleased to make any necessary arrangements.

British Library Cataloguing in Publication Data. A catalogue record for this publication is available from the British Library.

ISBN 978-1-85008-347-4

Acknowledgements

Getty Images: 7 (top right); Getty/Fox Photos: 7 (bottom right); Liverpool Record Office: 7 (middle left); Corbis: 8 (top); 9, 26/27, 34, 35 (bottom right), 87 (bottom), 90, 103 (middle right); Topfoto/The Granger Collection New York: 8 (bottom); Corbis/Sygma: 10 (top left); The Art Archive/Ocean Memorabilia Collection: 10 (bottom right); Getty Images: 11; The Sinking of the Titanic by Coton, Graham (1926–2003) Private Collection/© Look and Learn/The Bridgeman Art Library: 12/13, 109; Aaron Wilkes: 14 (top); Getty/Time Life Pictures: 17, 152 (top left); Imperial War Museum: 21 (top left), 21 (middle right), 21 (bottom left), 23 (top right), 28 (top left), 28 (bottom left), 28 (right), 29 (top left), 29 (bottom left), 29 (bottom right), 35 (top right), 63 (middle), 83; 20 (top), 20 (bottom left), 20 (bottom right), 94, 77; Corbis/Hulton Deutsch: 23 (bottom left), 37 (top right), 37 (middle left), 50 (top right), 52/53, 89 (bottom), 115 (top); Corbis/Bettmann: 28 (middle), 38, 42 (top), 44, 45, 51, 57, 60 (bottom right), 88, 91 (bottom), 98, 100, 101, 103 (top), 103 (middle left), 111, 122 (top left); Alamy/Akg Images: 29 (top middle); Alamy/David Osborn: 29 (bottom middle); British Pathe Plc/ITN Archive: 30; Janet Booth: 31; Alamy/Jaxpix: 33; Getty Images/ Hulton Archive: 35 (bottom left), 41, 42 (bottom right), 58 (bottom), 59, 82 (top right), 82 (bottom right), 116 (top right), 121 (middle); Mary Evans Picture Library/ILN: 35 (top left), 113; Permission of The Royal British Legion: 37 (bottom middle); Ronald Grant Archive: 43 (bottom left), 43 (bottom right); Time Life Pictures/Getty Images: 43 (top); Mary Evans Picture Library: 50 (bottom left), 53, 62 (top left), 62 (bottom right), 63 (top left), 65 (top left), 65 (bottom right), 66, 69, 110 (top), 110 (bottom left); GettyImages/ Popperfoto: 60 (top left), 67, 138; Getty/AFP: 61; Akg images, London: 68, 71, 91 (top), 93, 130; Will Dyson, Daily Herald, 13 May 1919, British Cartoon Archive, University of Kent, www.cartoons.ac.uk: 73; Corbis/David Pollack: 75; Corbis/Reuters: 78 (top left), 133; DPA/Empics: 78 (bottom middle); Richard Seaman: 78 (bottom right); Getty Images/Fox Photos/ Hulton Archive: 78 (top right); Topfoto: 78 (bottom left); Corbis/ Hulton: 80; Still Pictures: 84; Corbis/epa: 87 (top); The Art Archive: 89 (top); Alamy/ Medical-on-Line: 96; Corbis/epa/Sergei Chirikov: 102 (top); Science Photo Library: 102 (bottom); NASA: 104; Chirikov: 102 (top); Corbis/NASA: 104; Corbis/NASA/Roger Ressmeyer: 103 (bottom left); NASA Marshall Space Flight Center: 106/107; Imagestate Media/HIP: 108, 119; Comic Relief: 116 (bottom right); Corbis/Reuters/Luis Enrique Ascui: 116 (middle left); Science & Society/NMeM Daily Herald Archive: 121 (top left); Archive of the Irish in Britain, London, Metropolitan University: 121 (middle right); Corbis/Gideon Mendel: 122 (bottom); Redferns Music Picture Library: 122 (top right); Rex Features: 122 (top middle); Alamy/Zak Waters: 123 (bottom); PA Photos: 123 (middle left); PA Photos/Empics: 123 (top right); AP/PA Photos: 124, 127, 136/137, 151 (middle top); Getty Images/Time Inc: 126; Corbis/Ricki Rosen: 128; Reuters/Abed Omar Quini: 132 (bottom); Rex Features/Alinari: 132 (top); NI Syndication: 134; Corbis/Reuters: 136 (bottom); Corbis/ Reuters/Ian Hodgson: 139; Rex Features/Michael Dunlea: 142; Corbis/ Matthew Polak/Sygma: 143; Alamy/Adrian Sherratt: 144; Alamy/Colin Underhill: 145 (bottom); Corbis/Phillipa Lewis/Edifice: 145 (top); Corbis/ Andrew Brusso: 149; The Advertising Archive: 151 (top left); McDonald's Corporation: 151 (top right), 151 (middle right); Corbis/Danny Lehman: 152 (bottom right); Rex/Simon Roberts: 153.

'Forgotten voices of the Great War', Max Arthur, Ebury Press, 2006: 21; 'A Victorian Son: An autobiography 1897–1922', Stuart Cloete, J. Day Co., 1973: 27; 'The Great War: I was there', Sir John Hammerton, Amalgamated Press, undated: 34; 'Sagittarius Rising', Cecil Lewis, Time Warner Paperbacks, 1994: 36; 'My Own Story', Emmeline Pankhurst, Virago Press Ltd, rev. ed. edition, 1979: 51; 'The Suffrage Movement: An Intimate Account of Persons and Ideals', Sylvia Pankhurst, Virago Press Ltd; New edition, 1977: 52; 'The Twentieth Century', JD Clare, Nelson Thornes, 1993: 60; 'Weimar Germany', Josh Brooman, Longman, 1985: 61; 'Hitler's Germany', Josh Brooman, Longman, 1991: 69; 'Keep Smiling Through: Women in the Second World War', Caroline Lang, Cambridge University Press, 1989: 81; 'SHP Peace and War', Shepherd, Reid and Shephard, John Murray, 1993: 81, 87; Newcastle Evening Chronicle, 1940: 82; 'Investigating History', Neil De Marco, Hodder & Stoughton, 2003: 92; 'We Never Went to the Moon', Bill Kaysing, Eden Press, 1976: 105; www.redzero.demon.co.uk/moonhoax/: 106; www.badastronomy.com: 106; 'World History (DK Pockets Full of Knowledge)', p133, Dorling Kindersley Publishers Ltd, 1996: 117; 'Bloody Foreigners – the story of immigration to Britain', Robert Winder, Little, Brown and Company, 2004: 144; 'Prince Charles to be known as Defender of Faith', Andrew Pierce, *Daily Telegraph*, 14 Nov 2008: 145.

Contents

What is history?

Before you start this book, take a few minutes to think about these questions.

- What do you think history is? What does the word mean?
- What have you learnt in history lessons before, perhaps in your primary school? Did you enjoy them or not? If you enjoyed them, say why. If you didn't enjoy them, why not?
- Have you read any history books or stories about things that happened a long time ago? Have you watched any television programmes, films or plays about things that happened in the past? If so, which ones?

History is about what happened in the past. It is about people in the past, what they did and why they did it, what they thought and what they felt. To enjoy history you need to have a good imagination. You need to be able to imagine what life was like in the past, or what it may have been like to be involved in past events.

How did people feel, think and react to events like these?

The year is 1910 and I, like every other woman in Britain, am not allowed a say in who runs the country. We make up over half the population and it is only fair that we get the vote. The politicians won't listen to our demands – so what will make them sit up and take notice?

DEEDS NOT WORDS

I volunteered to fight for King and Country in August 1914, but I didn't think it would be like this. But what would people have thought of me if I hadn't 'joined up'? How long am I going to have to stay in this muddy hellhole? And am I ever going to make it home alive?

The year is 1948 and I have come from Jamaica to start a new life in Britain. I fought in the RAF during the war, have a British passport and have been brought up to see Britain as the 'mother country'. I have been told that life in Britain is wonderful and full of opportunities, but why is everything so grey and cold? How will people treat me? And will I find work and happiness?

How to use this book

As you work through this book, you will notice a number of features that keep appearing.

——— MISSION OBJECTIVES ———

All sections of this book will start by setting your Mission Objectives. These are your key aims that set out your learning targets for the work ahead. Topics will end by trying to get you to assess your own learning. If you can accomplish each Mission Objective then you are doing well!

——— MISSION ACCOMPLISHED? ———

WISE-UP Words are key terms that are vital to help you discuss and understand the topics. You can spot them easily because they are in bold type. Look up their meanings in a dictionary or use the Glossary at the end of the book. The Glossary is a list of words and their meanings.

Some topics contain PAUSE for Thought boxes. This is an opportunity for you to stop and think for yourself.

❚❚ PAUSE for Thought

The Hungry for MORE features give you a chance to extend your knowledge and research beyond the classroom. This is a time for you to take responsibility for your own learning. You might be asked to research something in the library or on the Internet, work on a presentation, or design and make something. Can you meet the challenge?

 FACT

These are all the fascinating, amazing or astounding little bits of history that you usually don't get to hear about! But in Folens History we think they are just as important and give you insights into topics that you'll easily remember.

Historical Enquiries

There are also seven Historical Enquiries in this book. These will get you to focus on the following themes:

- **BRITAIN AT WAR (1)**
- **WHO RULES?**
- **BRITAIN AT WAR (2)**
- **BRITAIN ABROAD**
- **HOW TOLERANT IS MODERN BRITAIN?**
- **CAN YOU GET JUSTICE IN MODERN BRITAIN?**
- **HOW RELIGIOUS IS MODERN BRITAIN?**

These themes will give you a broad knowledge of medieval religion, social attitudes and rules, power and England's relations with other countries.

Work

Work sections are your opportunity to demonstrate your knowledge and understanding. You might be asked to put events in the correct chronological order. You might be asked to:

- explain how things have changed over time
- work out why two people might interpret the same event differently
- work out what triggered an event to take place in the short term or the long term.

Britain and the world in 1900

MISSION OBJECTIVES

- To understand Britain's place in the world at the turn of the century.
- To understand how other countries were catching up with Britain in terms of industry, trade and empire.

In 1900, the British people had every reason to be proud. For a start, most Brits were better fed, clothed, healthier and more educated than many of the people of other nations of the world. Cities were full of shops that contained a wide range of goods, either made in British factories or brought in from parts of their Empire. In 1900, Britain controlled over a quarter of the world (about 400 million people) and was the largest empire the world had ever seen.

The world in 1900

Britain had been the first country in the world to have an industrial revolution. As a result, Britain became a great industrial power and, by 1900, was the richest country in the world. Yet Britain's status in the world was under serious threat. The USA was now making more goods than Britain, and Germany and Japan were quickly catching up. How long could Britain hold onto its position as the country that did more trade (and made more money) than any other? And there were some serious rivals on the military front, too. Despite Britain having more battleships than any other two countries added together, several other nations were increasing the size of their armies and navies. By 1900, France had a big army and Germany's was one of the largest and best-trained that Europe had ever seen. Japan, Germany, Russia and the USA greatly expanded the number of battleships they had in the years around 1900 too. And these countries were just as proud and patriotic as the British were. So could this rivalry lead to war?

What was Britain like?

Queen Victoria died on the evening of Monday 22 January 1901. She had been Queen for 63 years. Her son, Edward, became King Edward VII. Through her marriage to Albert, and the marriages of her children, Britain's royal

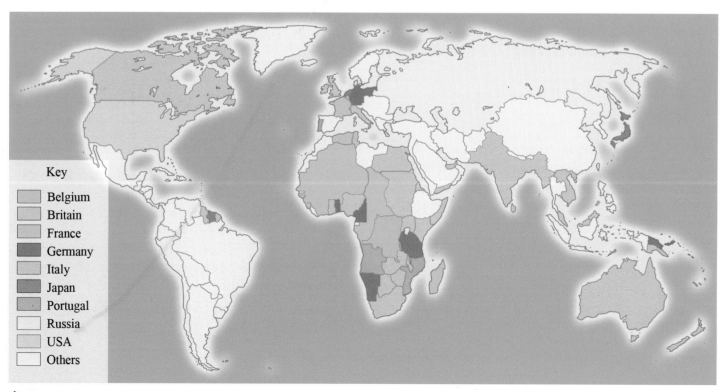

Key
- Belgium
- Britain
- France
- Germany
- Italy
- Japan
- Portugal
- Russia
- USA
- Others

↳ SOURCE A: *The empires of the world in 1900.*

family were directly connected to the rulers of Russia, Germany, Spain, Norway, Denmark, Sweden, Greece and Romania. Indeed, before the end of her reign, some people had started to call Queen Victoria the 'Grandmother of Europe'.

Britain itself, in 1900, was a very mixed nation. One writer even went so far as to claim that the lives led by the rich and poor were so different that Britain was like two nations – a poor one and a rich one. About 3% were very rich (upper class), 25% were relatively wealthy (middle class – bankers, doctors, accountants, managers, and so on) and the rest, the working class, were poor – with some being very, very poor!

The richer side of Britain enjoyed a life of luxury and ease. They owned land, homes and many didn't even have to work at all because they made so much money out of investments and rents. On the other side, the vast majority of poor people lived miserable lives – some earning only enough money to get by, others earning nowhere near enough to feed their families. There was no state sick pay, pensions or unemployment benefit. The injured and sick paid for their own medical care.

SOURCE B: *These two photographs highlight the contrast between rich and poor in 1900. They were taken only a few days and a few miles apart, yet the poor slum area is vastly different from the rich Park Lane region of London. How can you tell which one is poor and which is rich?*

SOURCE C: *Shopping habits were beginning to change in the early 1900s. Instead of shopkeepers selling just a few similar items, they would sell a wide range of different items in separate departments – the department store was born. This early photograph of a John Lewis department store on Oxford Street, London was taken in November, 1936. By 1910, the store would be able to sell Coca-Cola (arrived from the USA in 1900), Heinz Baked Beanz (1901), Marmite (1902), Gillette razors (1904), Kellogg's Corn Flakes (1906), Hoover Vacuum cleaners (1907) and Persil washing powder (1909).*

What were the latest inventions?

The start of the twentieth century saw major development in three particular areas of discovery and invention. This new technology was to have a major impact on life after 1900. One historian went so far as to write that the new discoveries turned the twentieth century into 'the age of the ordinary man'.

Transport

In 1885, Karl Benz, a German, made the first successful petrol-driven vehicle. It had three wheels and could reach speeds of up to ten miles per hour. In 1886, Gottlieb Daimler, another German, made the first four-wheeled petrol-driven car.

By 1900, car making had become a big moneymaking industry but cars were still too expensive for most people. Then, in 1908, an American called Henry Ford began making what was to become one of the best-selling cars ever – the Model T Ford. Based in Detroit, USA, the Henry Ford Motor Company had made over one million by 1915. Ford used state-of-the-art techniques in his factory to **mass-produce** them on an **assembly line**. The cars would pass in front of the workers on a conveyor belt and each person would have an individual job to do. The cars were made quickly… and cheaply. In fact, in 1908, a Model T cost $900 to buy but, by 1927, Ford was making them so efficiently that the price dropped to $290.

On 17 December 1903, in North Carolina, USA, Orville Wright made the first man-carrying powered flight. It lasted 12 seconds and he flew a distance of 37 metres. His brother, Wilbur, had helped to build the aeroplane. By 1905, the brothers had made nearly 300 flights, some lasting nearly 20 minutes. Flying became the latest craze and, in 1909, a Frenchman, Louis Bleriot, flew over the English Channel. By 1910, some countries were looking into the possibility of attaching bombs to planes so they could be dropped on an enemy!

↳ SOURCE D: *An advert for the Ford car.*

> **! FACT** Not so fast
> Along with the motor car came the motor driving offence. In 1896, Walter Arnold from Kent became the first British driver to be fined for speeding. He was caught doing eight miles per hour in a two miles per hour zone.

SOURCE E: *Wright Brothers' 'Baby Grand' plane.* ↴

Communications

The telephone, invented in 1876, rapidly grew in use between towns (and even countries) in the early 1900s. Radio would also become very popular after 1900 and by the 1920s would be the 'must have' household appliance. These inventions sped up the spread of news and enabled business to be done more quickly.

Consumer goods

New inventions, such as vacuum cleaners and electric irons, were based on the growing use of electricity. Other consumer goods, such as wristwatches, gramophones (ask your teacher!), telephones and cameras became popular after 1900, each helping to turn the old way of life upside down.

How did people amuse themselves?

Sport remained a popular activity, as it had been in the previous century. Football, cricket, rugby, tennis and golf continued to attract thousands of spectators and participants. Going to the pub was as popular as ever, too! The early 1900s also saw the growth of the cinema and 'movie stars' such as Charlie Chaplin, Laurel and Hardy and Buster Keaton became household names. It wouldn't be long before people were familiar with the likes of Mickey Mouse, Donald Duck and Pluto.

↵ **SOURCE F:** *A film poster for a famous Charlie Chaplin comedy.*

CHARLIE CHAPLIN *in* The VAGABOND

All Rights Controlled by EXPORT & IMPORT FILM CO. Inc.

⭐ **WISE-UP** Words

assembly line
mass-produce

Work

1 a Why do you think many Britons were proud of their nation in 1900?

b For what reasons might some Britons have been worried about their nation's status by 1900?

2 Look at Source B.

a Write a sentence or two describing each of the photographs.

b What details in the photographs helped you to decide which area was rich and which was poor?

3 a Design a poster that describes Britain and the world at the start of the twentieth century. Your poster should:

• be aimed at a Year 6 pupil who has never studied Britain in the early 1900s

• include no more than 50 words

• mention the rich/poor divide, shopping, the media, sport and transport developments.

b Using the same guidelines, design another poster that describes Britain and the world at the start of the twenty-first century (the year 2000).

c In what areas and categories are the two posters similar and how are they different?

MISSION ACCOMPLISHED?

• If a Year 7 student asked you what the world was like in 1900, do you think you could describe it to them in five minutes?

Why is the *Titanic* so famous?

MISSION OBJECTIVES

- To be able to explain why the *Titanic* is such a famous ship.
- To decide if women and children really were rescued first.

If you were to ask somebody to name a famous shipping disaster, they would probably answer: 'the *Titanic*'. In fact, they would probably struggle to name another one! The *Titanic* is famous all over the world – and not just because of the Hollywood film that was set around its sinking. So just why is the *Titanic* so famous? What makes it different from the thousands of other shipping tragedies? And what does the disaster tell us about how poor people were treated in the early twentieth century?

Titanic technology!

One of the most impressive – and staggering – things about *Titanic* was its sheer size. At more than three football pitches long, weighing 46,000 tons and being taller than a 17-storey building, it was the biggest moving, manufactured object the world had ever seen. Its **hull** was made from 16 watertight compartments – which its owners claimed made it 'practically unsinkable'. On top of all that, it was widely tipped to beat the **transatlantic** speed record. What could possibly go wrong?

SOURCE A: *The* Titanic's *very famous 'grand staircase', which led to the first-class dining area (Source B).*

SOURCE B: *The first-class passengers enjoyed every luxury of a five-star hotel.*

Passengers – posh and poor

When the *Titanic* set sail on 10 April 1912, some of the richest people in the world were on board. To keep them comfortable, the first-class cabins were fitted out like rooms in a five-star hotel. To keep them entertained, there was a state-of-the-art gymnasium, a swimming pool, a tennis court and a Parisian café. As you can imagine, a first-class ticket was very expensive. In fact, a top-of-the-range ticket from Southampton to New York would have cost £870 – about £27,000 in today's money! But the rich passengers were in the minority (there were only 322 in first class). The vast majority of passengers (709) were poor people who had bought a one-way ticket to a new life in the USA. They weren't just British and Irish working-class people, but Russians, Italians, Swedes, Germans, Spaniards, French people and many other nationalities were on board too. Some had paid as little as £3 (about £95 today) for a space in a basic third-class compartment deep inside the ship.

The icy end?

Just four days into its **maiden** voyage, on the evening of Sunday 14 April, the *Titanic* moved into the freezing waters in the middle of the Atlantic. As the temperature dropped below zero, hitting one of the giant, silent icebergs in the inky-black night became a real possibility. Just before midnight, one of the lookouts spotted the outline of an iceberg 'dead ahead'. Despite desperately turning to avoid it and putting the engines in full reverse, the *Titanic* struck the iceberg at speed and was holed below the waterline. Five of the watertight compartments had been gashed open and water flooded in. The ship could only stay afloat with four compartments filled with water and, less than three hours later, *Titanic* sank beneath the waves. The order went out for women and children to get in the lifeboats first, but of the 2206 people on board, only 704 were rescued from the icy waters.

First class

	On board	Rescued	% Rescued
Men	173	58	34
Women	144	139	97
Children	5	5	100
Total	**322**	**202**	**63**

Second class

	On board	Rescued	% Rescued
Men	160	13	8
Women	93	78	84
Children	24	24	100
Total	**277**	**115**	**42**

Third class

	On board	Rescued	% Rescued
Men	454	55	12
Women	179	98	55
Children	76	23	30
Total	**709**	**176**	**25**

Total passengers and crew

	On board	Rescued	% Rescued
Men	1 662	315	19
Women	439	338	77
Children	105	51	49
Total	**2 206**	**704**	**32**

⤶ **SOURCE C:** *Casualty figures issued shortly after the sinking.*

SOURCE D: *A painting of the* Titanic *sinking.* ⤶

SOURCE D: *The ship's captain, E J Smith, said this in an interview in 1910. The captain was a very well respected sailor who'd had a successful and accident-free career.* ⤶

'When anyone asks me to describe my career at sea, I just say – uneventful. Of course there have been winter gales, storms and fog, but in all my years, I have never been in an accident. I've only seen one ship in trouble in all my years at sea. I've never seen a wreck, have never been wrecked, and I have never been in a situation that threatened to end in disaster.'

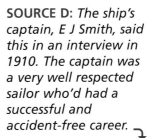

WISE-UP Words

hull
maiden
transatlantic

Work

1 There are a number of factors that explain why the *Titanic's* sinking is such a famous event. Put the following factors in the order that you think are most important:

It was the *Titanic's* maiden voyage. • The owners said it was practically unsinkable. • It was the biggest ship in the world. • A very successful film was called *Titanic*. • So many people died.

2 Look at Source C.
   a Draw three separate bar graphs to show the percentage of men, women and children rescued from each class of passengers.
   b Which class of passengers suffered the most?
   c Do you think the order for women and children to get on the lifeboats first was followed? Explain your answer carefully.
   d What does this evidence tell you about the attitude that rich people had towards poor people in 1912?
   e Do you think the same thing would happen today? You may want to discuss this as a class.

3 Write a 'Fact File' on *Titanic*, including your Top Ten facts about the ship and the sinking. Why not use a computer to design your 'Fact File', including any pictures you can find on the Internet too.

MISSION ACCOMPLISHED?

- Could you tell someone why the *Titanic* is probably the most famous ship in history?
- Have you decided if women and children really were rescued first?

Who was to blame for the *Titanic* disaster?

MISSION OBJECTIVES

- To be able to explain how several factors led to the sinking of the *Titanic* and the enormous loss of life.
- To decide who was most to blame for the tragedy.

The sinking of the *Titanic* caused a sensation on both sides of the Atlantic. Over 1500 people had lost their lives in the freezing waters and it wasn't just their grieving relatives who wanted to know who was to blame. Your task is to conduct an enquiry into the disaster and write a report for the US and British Governments. Your report should be entitled 'Why did the *Titanic* sink?' and you must come to a conclusion as to who was most to blame. Good luck!

EVIDENCE A:
Was it Captain Smith's fault?

Captain Smith was due to retire after the *Titanic*'s maiden voyage. Did he want to set a transatlantic speed record on his last ever trip? He ignored at least seven warnings from other ships nearby and the *Titanic* was travelling at 20 knots per hour – close to top speed – when it struck the iceberg. If the ship had been going slower, could it have turned out of the iceberg's way in time? Perhaps Captain Smith thought an iceberg couldn't sink a modern ship. He once said, 'I can't imagine anything causing a modern ship to sink. Ship building has gone beyond that.'

EVIDENCE B:
Was it Harland and Wolff's fault?

The *Titanic* was built at the Harland and Wolff shipyard in Belfast, Northern Ireland. About three million rivets were used to hold the ship together. When the wreck of the *Titanic* was finally discovered in 1985, some of the rivets were brought to the surface and analysed. The investigations showed that the rivets were made from poor-quality iron. When the ship struck the iceberg, the heads of rivets snapped off and sections of the ship were torn wide open. If the rivets had been made of more expensive, higher-quality iron, perhaps the hole in the *Titanic*'s side would have been smaller – and maybe the ship wouldn't have sunk at all. Further tests showed that the cheap rivets became **brittle** in extremely low temperatures – just like on the night of 14 April 1912.

EVIDENCE C:
Was it Thomas Andrews' fault?

Thomas Andrews was the naval architect who designed the *Titanic*. The ship was thought to be unsinkable by many because of the 16 watertight compartments that Thomas had designed in the hull. However, the compartments didn't reach as high as they should have done. Andrews had reduced their height to make more space for first-class cabins. If just two of the watertight compartments had reached all the way to the top, there is a chance that the *Titanic* wouldn't have sunk.

EVIDENCE D:
Was it Walter Lord's fault?

Walter Lord was the captain of a ship called the *Californian* which was only 19 miles away from the *Titanic* when it struck the iceberg. Despite being aware of icebergs in the area, Lord allowed his radio operator to go to bed at around 11:15pm. At around midnight, members of the *Californian*'s crew saw rockets being fired into the sky on the horizon. They woke up Captain Lord and told him, but he decided not to sail towards the fireworks – he decided it was just another ship having a cocktail party! Should Lord have made the *Californian* race towards the scene? Should he at least have insisted that the radio be turned on so they could have heard the *Titanic*'s **SOS** signals? How many more people would have survived if the *Californian* had been there to pull them from the icy waters?

EVIDENCE E:
Was it Bruce Ismay's fault?

Bruce Ismay was the man in charge of the White Star Line – the owners of the *Titanic*. He was also one of the first-class passengers on board the ship and managed to secure a place on one of the lifeboats before it went down. Ismay was eager to prove the *Titanic* was not only the biggest and most luxurious ocean liner, but also the fastest. Did he put pressure on Captain Smith to maintain top speed despite sailing through icebergs? Was he hoping that the *Titanic* would make a record crossing? One witness claimed she heard Ismay and Smith arguing on the evening of 13 April – was it over the speed?

Also, was Ismay responsible for more deaths than there should have been? The original design for the *Titanic* equipped it with 32 lifeboats – enough for everyone on board. The finished ship only had 20 – enough for just 1178 of the 2206 people on board. The White Star Line decided to remove some of the lifeboats to make room for more first-class cabins.

WISE-UP Words

brittle
SOS

Work

So who was to blame for the sinking of the *Titanic*? Start to work on your theory.

Step 1 Analyse the evidence.

Under the following headings, write a sentence or two outlining how each may have contributed to the sinking.

i) Captain Smith ii) The shipbuilders iii) Thomas Andrews iv) Captain Lord v) Bruce Ismay.

Step 2 Prioritise the evidence.

In your opinion, is one person more at fault than any other? Can you put your list in order of responsibility? Did one person's actions contribute more to the sinking than any other's? Write a paragraph or two explaining why you made your decision. Did some people have nothing at all to do with the sinking? If so, say who and how you arrived at this conclusion.

Step 3 Deliver your verdict.

Time to write up your report and present your findings:

- Start your report with a brief introduction to the disaster.

- Outline the role in the sinking of each person under investigation.

- Write a conclusion – is one person to blame or several, or a combination of all?

- Remember, if you don't blame one person, it doesn't mean your investigation has failed! There is often more than one factor to consider in most investigations.

—MISSION ACCOMPLISHED?—

- Can you tell someone about at least three of the things that led to the *Titanic* disaster?

- Have you decided who was most to blame for the loss of life?

BRITAIN AT WAR (1)

Despite all the developments and advancements that had been made over the years, the twentieth century was the bloodiest in human history. You may already know that it witnessed two world wars and that Britain was heavily involved in both of them. These wars were world-changing events that not only affected the lives of the soldiers fighting in them, but the lives of every man, woman and child in Britain. So what caused the world to erupt into war the first time? How was Britain involved? And what did it mean for the people who lived through it?

1: Why did the Great War start?

MISSION OBJECTIVES
- To understand how the Great War got its name.
- To be able to define the long-term causes of the Great War.

You can find evidence of the Great War in every town and village in Britain. The names of the dead soldiers, sailors and airmen are recorded on memorials just like the ones in Sources A and B. The Great War wasn't 'great' because men enjoyed themselves and had a great time; it was called the Great War because the world had never experienced such a big war before. Millions and millions of men, split into two sides (or **alliances**), spent over four years killing each other. To help them in their task, they used the deadliest weapons the world had ever seen. In total, around 9 million people were killed – that's over 5000 deaths every day, seven days a week, 365 days a year, for over four years. Such was the horror felt at this enormous **death toll** that many called it 'the war to end all wars'. So just how did the Great War start? What could so many countries fall out about? And why did so many young men volunteer to join the slaughter?

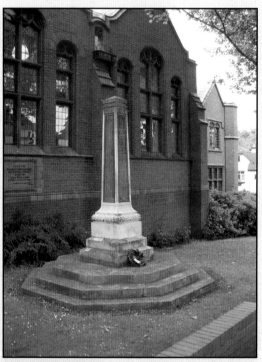

↵ **SOURCE A:** *This is a memorial to the 61 ex-students and one teacher of Castle High School, Dudley, who died during the Great War. Many schools, factories and sports clubs built memorials to record the names of their young men who fought and died for their country.*

SOURCE B: *The names of over 30,000 local men who died are recorded inside Birmingham's Hall of Memory. None of the bodies of the dead men were returned to Britain and memorials like these took the place of graves for grieving relatives.* ↱

➕ **Hungry for MORE**

Where is the nearest Great War memorial to you? Is it close enough for you to walk to it? Maybe your school has a memorial like Castle High School, Dudley. If so, why not go and visit it and read through the list of names? Are there any names that are the same as yours or your friends'? You can research some of the names and details of how they died on www.cwgc.org.

Long-term causes

World wars begin for a number of different reasons that build up over a number of years. Historians often like to divide the reasons why something happens into long-term and **short-term causes**. Look through the cartoons and maps that outline the **long-term causes** of the Great War.

Nationalism

We're simply the best!

At the beginning of the twentieth century, people started to take great pride in their countries. People of different nations, especially in Europe, were convinced that their people, country and way of doing things were best. Unfortunately, for many leaders of Europe, the best way to prove they were the best was to have a war with their rivals.

Militarism

People took great pride in their armies and navies. To make sure that theirs were the best, countries spent more and more money on bigger and bigger armies. Nobody wanted the smallest army, so countries got caught up in an **arms race**. To many, there was no point in having a big, expensive army if you weren't going to use it and whenever countries fell out, the temptation was always there to use their weapons.

Imperialism

It wasn't just Britain that had an empire; many other European countries did too. The race to gain control of other nations, particularly in Africa, led to tension and fierce rivalries among European countries. They began to see each other as a threat to their overseas possessions and saw war as the only way to remove this threat permanently.

Alliances

Key

Triple Entente

Triple Alliance

Work

1 a Write a sentence that defines the following terms: • arms race • allies.
  b Copy the terms from List A into your book and match them to the correct definitions from List B.
   List A
   militarism • alliances • imperialism • nationalism
   List B
   – Groups of nations that agree to back each other up in a war.
   – To love your country and think it is superior to others.
   – To take great pride in your country's armed forces.
   – To gain control of land and people around the world and build an empire.

2 Some historians have used the metaphor of comparing Europe in 1914 to two groups of mountain climbers, all tied together with one rope.
   – If one of the climbers slipped and fell, what's the best thing that could happen?
   – If one of the climbers slipped and fell, what's the worst thing that could happen?

SOURCE C: *As each country began to feel threatened, they looked for friends to back them up in a war – known as allies. Europe split into two alliances. Britain, France and Russia formed the Triple Entente, and Germany, Austria-Hungary and Italy formed the Triple Alliance. The idea was to put people off starting a war as it would mean fighting against three nations instead of one. Although this made them feel more secure, it meant it would only take one small disagreement between any two nations involved... and all of Europe would be dragged into a war.*

____ MISSION ACCOMPLISHED? ____

• Could you tell someone why the Great War got its name?

• Can you describe the long-term causes of the Great War?

Some historians have compared Europe in 1914 to a barrel of gunpowder in that it only needed a spark to make the whole thing explode. On 28 June 1914 the spark arrived. All it took was the murder of one man and his wife and all of the major nations of Europe plunged into war. So who was this man? How was he murdered and why? And how did his death lead to the Great War?

2: The short-term reason

MISSION OBJECTIVES

- To be able to describe the events that led to the death of Archduke Franz Ferdinand.
- To be able to explain how his assassination led to the outbreak of the Great War.

'Unhappy anniversary'

On 28 June 1914, the heir to the Austrian throne – Archduke Franz Ferdinand – arrived in the Bosnian city of Sarajevo. It was his wedding anniversary, so he was joined on the visit by his wife Sophie. Bosnia was part of the Austro-Hungarian Empire – but only since 1908 when it had been conquered by the Austrians. Many Bosnians were still deeply unhappy about this. They wanted to join with their neighbours, Serbia, and many Serbians wanted Bosnia to join with them. One gang of Serbians, known as the 'Black Hand', decided to take drastic action to highlight their cause – they planned to **assassinate** Archduke Franz Ferdinand. His visit to Sarajevo was the perfect opportunity.

1 Archduke Franz Ferdinand and his wife arrived at Sarajevo train station at 9:28am. They were driven towards the Town Hall to meet the Mayor. Crowds lined the streets and the car drove slowly so that the royal couple could wave to the people.

2 Six Black Hand assassins waited for the car by the Cumurja Bridge. As the open-topped car passed, one of the Serbians threw a bomb at the royal couple. The bomb ended up beneath the car behind and blew up, injuring several people. The Archduke's car sped off to the Town Hall with a terrified Ferdinand inside.

3 The Archduke cancelled the rest of his visit, but decided to visit those injured by the bomb before he went home. At 11:00am, he again got into the chauffeur-driven car – but it drove a lot faster this time! As they passed Schiller's cafe, the driver was informed that he'd taken a wrong turn. He stopped to turn around.

4 After the bomb attack, the assassins had split up and run into the crowds. By coincidence, one of the gang – 18-year-old Gavrilo Princip – was standing outside the cafe. He took out a pistol, walked towards the car and fired two shots. Ferdinand was hit in the throat; his wife Sophie was shot in the stomach. Both were killed.

↩ **SOURCE A:** *Princip is thought to have been terminally ill with tuberculosis when he murdered Franz Ferdinand. He survived another four years – long enough to see the terrible consequences of his actions.*

How did this murder lead to war?

28 July: Austria-Hungary blames Serbia for killing the Archduke. It attacks Serbia.

29 July: Russia, who has promised to protect Serbia against attack, gets its army ready to attack Austria-Hungary.

1 August: Germany, who supports Austria-Hungary, hears about Russian preparations for war. Germany declares war on Russia.

2 August: Britain prepares its warships.

3 August: Germany, whose plan is to defeat France BEFORE attacking Russia, declares war on France.

4 August: Germany asks Belgium to allow German soldiers to march through their country to attack France. Belgium says 'no'. Germany marches in anyway. Britain, who has a deal to protect Belgium from attack (dating back to 1839), declares war on Germany.

6 August: Austria-Hungary declares war on Russia.

12 August: Britain and France declare war on Austria-Hungary.

↳ **SOURCE B:** *Timeline of events.*

! **FACT** The final line-up

Italy didn't stick to the agreements it had made before the murder. Instead it joined Britain, France and Russia's side in 1915. In total, 28 countries joined the war and the major ones lined up like this:
ALLIES: Britain and her Empire • France • Belgium • Italy (after 1915) • Serbia • Romania (after 1916) • Portugal (after 1916) • Russia (until 1917) • USA (after 1917) • Japan
VERSUS CENTRAL POWERS: Germany • Austria-Hungary • Turkey • Bulgaria (after 1915)

Work 〜.

1 Imagine you were Franz Ferdinand's chauffeur on the day of the assassination. You have been called in as a witness by the police. Using the information from the cartoons, copy and complete this writing frame:

Crime:
Date:
Witness:

The Archduke, Franz Ferdinand, was dressed in

....

His wife was wearing

....

As I approached the Cumurja Bridge

....

The Archduke was furious so

....

Shortly after 11:00am I drove past Schiller's cafe, when I

....

It was just as I was reversing that

....

I did my best to help, but

....

2 Look at Source B. Why did:
  a Austria-Hungary attack Serbia?
  b Russia attack Austria-Hungary?
  c Germany support Austria-Hungary?
  d Germany invade Belgium?
  e Britain declare war on Germany?

3 Did Gavrilo Princip start the Great War? Explain your answer carefully – you may want to discuss it and/or plan your answer as a class first.

—— **MISSION ACCOMPLISHED?** ——

• Could you tell someone how and why Franz Ferdinand was murdered?

• Can you explain how this led to the major countries of Europe going to war?

When war was declared in August 1914, many people on both sides were convinced that the fighting would be over by Christmas. Indeed, many people rushed to join the army because they 'didn't want to miss the show'. They need not have worried – the war was to drag on for four years and three months. This was far longer than anybody had expected or feared. So why did the war last so long? Where did the fighting take place? And who finally won?

3: Over by Christmas?

MISSION OBJECTIVES

- To know where the fighting of the Great War took place.
- To be able to explain why the fighting wasn't over by Christmas.
- To be able to define the word 'stalemate'.

Germany's master plan!

The generals in charge of Germany's army had been expecting a major war for years. To get off to the best possible start, they came up with a number of plans that they could put into action when war was declared. Their worst nightmare was a war against France and Russia at the same time – known as a war on two fronts. A **front** is the name given to the area where two armies meet each other. A war against France and Russia would mean that the Germans would have to split their army in two – one going east to fight Russia and the other going west to fight France. The plan they came up with to deal with this problem was called the Schlieffen Plan (pronounced 'scleefen' and named after the man who thought it up). The idea was to quickly defeat France with a huge knock-out blow through Belgium before moving the soldiers east to face the enormous, but slow-moving, Russian army.

Germany's mistaken plan!

On 3 August 1914, the Germans put the Schlieffen Plan into action. Straightaway, things started to go wrong. For a start, the Belgian army – which the Germans expected to be a push-over – put up fierce resistance and slowed the charge to France right down. Then the British Expeditionary Force (BEF), a highly trained professional army of 125,000 men, held the Germans back at Mons. On 19 August, the Russians launched an attack on Germany. This was far quicker than the Germans had expected and before they had had a chance to capture Paris. They were forced to send troops east to face the Russians and, by September, the German army

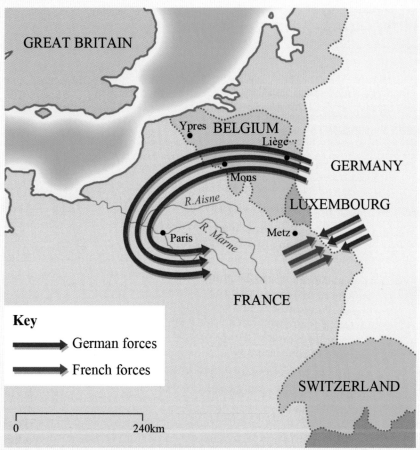

⌐ SOURCE A: *The Schlieffen Plan in theory.*

retreated 40 miles behind the River Aisne. There, they dug trenches and set up machine gun nests. The British and the French couldn't break through these defences and dug their own trenches directly opposite. By the end of 1914 the trenches stretched all the way from the English Channel to Switzerland. Neither side could find a way through. The war was stuck in a **stalemate**.

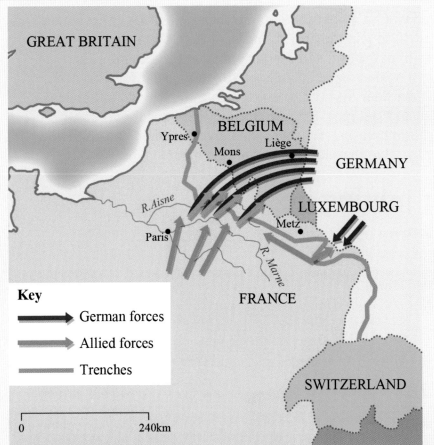

Key
- ➤ German forces
- ➤ Allied forces
- ▬ Trenches

0   240km

↱ **SOURCE B:** *The Schlieffen Plan – the reality.*

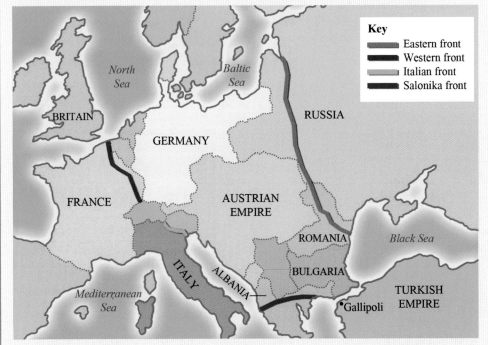

Key
- Eastern front
- Western front
- Italian front
- Salonika front

↱ **SOURCE C:** *Far from being a war of rapid movement, the fighting was bogged down on fronts that hardly moved throughout the war. Most fighting took place on the WESTERN FRONT (in France and Belgium), but there was an EASTERN FRONT too where Russians fought against Germans and Austrians. There was also fighting in Turkey (the SALONIKA FRONT) when they joined in on Germany's side and Italy (who joined in on Britain's side), as well as at sea and in the air!*

! FACT Past its sell-by date

The Schlieffen Plan was dreamt up in the nineteenth century. By the time it was put into action not only was Schlieffen dead, but the world had changed. Railways and lorries moved defending troops far quicker than they did in Schlieffen's time and steamships sped the BEF across the Channel. The French even hired over 600 taxi cabs to ferry extra troops into battle!

Work

1 Write a sentence defining the following words:

front • stalemate

2 Imagine you are the general in charge of the German army on 2 August 1914. Write a letter to the Kaiser (the German king) explaining your plans for winning the war for Germany.

3 Now imagine you are the same general at the end of September 1914. Write another letter to the Kaiser explaining what has gone wrong and why.

— MISSION ACCOMPLISHED? —

- Could you tell someone where the main fronts of the Great War were?
- Could you also tell them why the war wasn't over by Christmas?
- Do you know what the word 'stalemate' means?

When Britain declared war on 4 August 1914, the Government asked for volunteers aged between 19 and 30 to join the armed forces. At first, there was a great rush to 'join up' as a wave of patriotism and excitement swept the country. By Christmas 1914, over a million men had enlisted to 'do their bit for King and country'. It soon became clear that this wasn't going to be enough and the enthusiasm of 1914 didn't last long. So how did the Government encourage more men to join the war? What reasons did these men give for joining up? And how did the Government finally solve the shortage of fighting men?

4: Joining up

MISSION OBJECTIVES

- To understand the reasons why men chose to fight.
- To explain how the Government used propaganda to attract more volunteers.

The power of the propaganda poster

In 1914, people didn't have televisions or radios so the Government had to use different methods to get their message to the people. One of the main methods was to put posters up in every city, town and village in the country. These posters were designed to get very powerful messages across. White **propaganda** posters played on people's feelings to make them think that, if you were a young man, joining the army was the 'right thing to do'. Black propaganda posters tried to create hatred towards Germans. The Government hoped that if people hated Germany and its people, they were more likely to agree with the war and join the fight. Look through the following Great War posters and work out if they're black or white propaganda.

↵ SOURCE A: *One of the most famous recruitment posters of all time. It shows Earl Kitchener, the man in charge of getting enough men to fight, asking for volunteers to join the army. By a clever new technique, wherever you stand, Kitchener always seems to be staring and pointing directly at YOU.*

SOURCE B: *This poster shows a German nurse pouring water on the floor in front of a thirsty, injured British soldier. Two fat Germans laugh in the background. How do you think this made some British men feel?* ↱

SOURCE C: *What did the designer of this poster hope young women would go and do after they had read it?* ↱

TO THE YOUNG WOMEN OF LONDON

Is your "Best Boy" wearing Khaki? If not don't **YOU THINK** he should be?

If he does not think that you and your country are worth fighting for—do you think he is **WORTHY** of you?

Don't pity the girl who is alone—her young man is probably a soldier—fighting for her and her country—and for **YOU.**

If your young man neglects his duty to his King and Country, the time may come when he will **NEGLECT YOU.**

Think it over—then ask him to

JOIN THE ARMY TO-DAY

SOURCE D: *This poster attempts to show an example of life after the war. Why do you think the father looks so guilty?*

Daddy, what did YOU do in the Great War?

SOURCE E: *This poster claims that innocent British fishermen were captured and humiliated by the Germans. How would this make British people feel about Germans?*

HOW THE HUN HATES!

THE HUNS CAPTURED SOME OF OUR FISHERMEN IN THE NORTH SEA AND TOOK THEM TO SENNELAGER. THEY CHARGED THEM WITHOUT A SHRED OF EVIDENCE WITH BEING "MINE LAYERS". THEY ORDERED THEM TO BE PUNISHED WITHOUT A TRIAL. THAT PUNISHMENT CONSISTED IN SHAVING ALL THE HAIR OFF ONE SIDE OF THE HEAD AND FACE. THE HUNS THEN MARCHED THEIR VICTIMS THROUGH THE STREETS AND EXPOSED THEM TO THE JEERS OF THE GERMAN POPULACE.

BRITISH SAILORS! LOOK! READ! AND REMEMBER!

YOUR COUNTRY'S CALL

Isn't this worth fighting for?

ENLIST NOW

SOURCE F: *This poster showed a romantic version of Britain's countryside and asks people if it isn't worth fighting for. What kind of feelings would this create in young men?*

WISE-UP Words

patriotism
propaganda

Work

1 Write a sentence explaining the meaning of:

patriotism • propaganda

2 Copy this table into your book. Write the name of each source in the column in which you think it belongs. Write a sentence for each source explaining how it would make you feel.

White propaganda	Black propaganda

FACT Propaganda

Think of propaganda like advertising and adverts in newspapers and on TV. However, with advertising, *companies* try to make you think a certain way and believe different things about their product. With propaganda, *governments* and *politicians* try to get people to believe different things.

The push and pull of propaganda

The propaganda campaign had a remarkable effect. The message of the posters was backed up by the newspapers whose pages were filled with stories of victorious battles and acts of German savagery – with defeats hardly getting a mention. The result was that by January 1916, a total of 2.5 million men had agreed to fight. Some felt 'pushed' or pressured into joining up while others felt the 'pull' of the excitement of war and serving their King and country. Read through the reasons that these British servicemen gave for joining the Great War.

'I hate the thought of missing out. It's my chance to do something, you know, to contribute to the war effort. I might even get a gong if I'm lucky... and the girls; they love a man in uniform, don't they?'

SOURCE G: *Part of a letter written by a young soldier to his mum, Christmas 1914. A 'gong' is a nickname for a medal.*

'I was walking down Camden High Street when two young ladies said, "Why aren't you in the army with the boys?" I said, "I'm sorry, I'm only 17" and one of them said, "Oh we've heard that one before." Then she pulled out a feather and pushed it up my nose. Then a sergeant came out of one of the shops and said, "Did she just call you a coward? Come across the road to the Drill Hall and prove that you aren't a coward." I told him I was 17 and he said, "What did you say, 19?" To my amazement, I found I was soon being called Private S.C. Lang.'

SOURCE H: *S.C. Lang joined up in 1915. From* Forgotten voices of the Great War *by Max Arthur.*

Stay together, die together

The British Government thought that fighting alongside friends and neighbours rather than strangers would encourage people to join up – and they were right. Rival towns competed with each other to prove how patriotic they were and formed 'pals battalions'. Brothers, cousins, friends and workmates enlisted together. There was a footballer's battalion in London, alongside battalions of bankers, railway workers and even former public school boys. Although they were very successful, there were tragic consequences. Of the 720 Accrington Pals who fought, 584 were killed, wounded or missing in one attack. The Leeds Pals lost 750 of their 900 men and both the Grimsby Chums and the Sheffield City Battalion lost half of their men. This robbed entire communities of many of their young men and pals battalions were abandoned and broken up in 1916.

ACCRINGTON. BATT" E.L.R. B C° N° I PLATOON.

↵ **SOURCE I:** *A pals battalion of friends from Accrington, Lancashire, who all joined up together in 1914. One of the men, who is lying down on the right, survived the war, despite being wounded on three occasions. Sadly, there is no record of who else survived.*

'It was seeing the picture of Kitchener and his finger pointing at you – any position that you took up the finger was always pointing at you – it was a wonderful poster really. My mother was very hurt when I told her that I had to report to the army the next morning. I was 16 in the June.'

↳ **SOURCE J:** *Thomas McIndoe joined the Middlesex Regiment in 1914. From* Forgotten voices of the Great War *by Max Arthur.*

'A girl would come towards you with a delightful smile all over her face and you would think, "My word, she must know me." When she got about five paces away she would freeze up and walk past you with a look of utter contempt – as if she could have spat. It made you curl up and there was no replying as she had walked on. I was only 16 but went round the recruiting offices with extra zeal.'

↳ **SOURCE L:** *Norman Demuth of the London Rifle Brigade. From* Forgotten voices of the Great War *by Max Arthur.*

'I said to the boss, "I want to join the army, I want to be released from my job." He said, "Here in the steelworks, you're doing just as much for the country as if you're in the army." Well, I couldn't see myself going to work every day and going home every evening while my pals were suffering – and probably dying somewhere – they were serving their country. I said, "I've made up my mind – I must go."'

↳ **SOURCE K:** *F.B. Vaughn of the Yorks and Lancs Regiment. From* Forgotten voices of the Great War *by Max Arthur.*

! FACT Soldiers of the Empire
Around 1.4 million men from India, Pakistan and Bangladesh decided to help Britain in the struggle against Germany – convinced by posters that promised an 'easy life', 'good pay' and 'very little danger'. Fifty-three thousand of them died and another 64,000 were injured. Twelve were awarded the Victoria Cross – Britain's highest award for bravery.

Conscription and conscientious objectors

By the summer of 1916, the flood of volunteers had slowed down to a trickle. With thousands dead and many more returning home disabled, war didn't seem like such an exciting adventure. Unfortunately for the Government, they still needed more men to join the war. The solution they came up with was **conscription**. This meant that any man aged between 18 and 41 could be forced to join the army and an extra 2.5 million people were **called up** – but not without problems. Some men believed that war was wrong under any circumstances and they refused to join up – they became known as **conscientious objectors**.

There were around 16,000 conscientious objectors or 'conchies'. Some refused to fight because of their political beliefs – they saw the war as a way of Britain increasing its Empire. Others refused to fight because of their religious beliefs – many were Quakers or Jehovah's Witnesses who will not take life under any circumstances. Conchies had to appeal against being conscripted and most were willing to work in the war effort as long as they didn't have to fight. Some refused to do anything that would help Britain win the war – known as 'absolutists' – and around 1500 were sent to prison for the entire war. Some were even sentenced to death, but the executions never actually took place. Although very unpopular with the public at the time, many people now admire the conscientious objectors for taking a stand.

'There were, of course, different varieties of conscientious objectors – there were the political ones, the religious ones and those who just didn't want to bother. But it was not until I had contact with them that I could see that there was something at the back of this thing. Ever since, I've admired these men intensely. I would take my hat off to them anytime, because I realise what they did in defying British military might. They had far more guts than we did who were doing these things to them.'

↰ **SOURCE N:** *By C. Lippett, who was put in charge of guarding conchies.*

↰ **SOURCE O:** *A photograph of a group of 'conchies' who were being held in a camp as a result of their refusal to fight.*

WISE-UP Words

called up
conscientious objectors
conscription

↲ **SOURCE M:** *Soldiers from every part of the Empire fought in Britain's armed forces.*

Work

1 Read through sources G, H and J to L. Separate them into soldiers who felt pushed into joining the war and those who felt the pull of doing 'the right thing'.

Push	Pull

2 Write a couple of sentences explaining the problem with pals battalions.

3 a Read Source N. Explain two reasons why somebody might have become a conscientious objector.

b Was being a conchie an easy way out? Explain your answer carefully.

MISSION ACCOMPLISHED?

- Can you give someone at least three reasons why some men decided to volunteer?
- Do you know the difference between black and white propaganda?

5: Trench warfare

A soldier's basic training did nothing to prepare him for what he found on the front line. The deadly fire of the machine guns forced entire armies to live almost underground for months on end. As well as the mud, the cold and the wet, they lived with the knowledge that they could lose their lives at any moment. Look around these pages and see how the Great War soldiers fought, lived and died.

——— MISSION OBJECTIVES ———

- To be able to identify the main features of trench warfare.
- To be able to describe the typical experience of a soldier in the trenches.

1: **Duckboards:** These were placed on the ground to stop troops sinking in the mud.

2: **Fire step:** Soldiers stood on these to look and fire 'over the top'.

3: **Dugouts:** Rooms dug out of the back wall of trenches. Orders received by telephone.

4: **Periscope:** Enabled troops to see 'over the top' without risk of being shot.

5: Barbed wire: Slowed down attacking troops. Millions of miles of barbed wire was used.

6: Machine gun: Rapid-firing gun that mowed down attacking troops.

7: **Concrete bunker:** Reinforced subterranean bunker.

8: Artillery: Huge guns that fired enormous explosive or poisonous shells for miles.

9: Machine gun nest: Protected the machine-gunner from enemy fire.

10: Sandbags: Reinforced the walls, muffled explosions and soaked up moisture.

11: Aeroplanes: Helped spot targets for artillery, dropped bombs on the enemy and shot down enemy planes.

12: Communication trench: Linked the front line trench to the reserve trenches.

13: Reserve trenches: Soldiers went there to rest or to wait to go to the front line.

14: **Gas bell:** Would be rung to tell troops to put on gas masks.

Trench life

For the first time in a major war, many of the men who actually did the fighting and dying could read and write. As historians, this means we can learn a lot about what they went through in the trenches from the letters and diaries they left behind. Read through the following sources – adapted from genuine diaries and memoirs – and see the Great War through the eyes of ordinary soldiers.

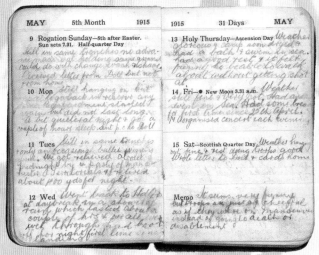

⮤ **SOURCE B:** *An actual Great War diary.*

1st: 'Expected rather a warm time but it did not occur and went back to reserve trenches.'

2nd: 'Still in the reserve trenches but C of [Commanding Officer] had a lot of us fatigued digging. Had orders that a big attack was coming off on Friday.'

3rd: 'The lads all still waiting to give the Turks a bit of bayonet. Received letter from Doll.'

4th: 'Artillery started at 11:00am and charge came off at 12:00 noon and everybody suffered very heavily and the Worcs kept up their reputation with the Bayonet. We took a trench, but had to vacate out owing to no flank support.'

5th: 'Had to take instruments back to headquarters and sniper caught me in the ankle and had to crawl about 90 yards with a hole in me and it was rather trying.'

Memo: 'What made me wild was after getting over the charge a sniper to get me next morning.'

⮤ **SOURCE A:** *Private Jack Folk served in the Royal Worcestershire Regiment and fought against Germany's ally, Turkey, in the Dardanelles campaign. This is his diary from the first week of May 1915.*

'The rain kept on and the water table was 2ft below. Our trenches were 7ft deep. We moved very slowly in a pug of yellow watery clay. When the evening came, it took about an hour to climb out. Some of our chaps slipped in and were drowned. They couldn't even be seen, but were trodden on later.'

⮤ **SOURCE C:** *Rifleman Henry Williamson served in the London Rifle Brigade and fought in Belgium on the Western Front.*

'On the night of 12 May we arrived in our trenches at about 4 o'clock in the morning. The first shell came across and landed not many yards from where I was standing, and the whole earth seemed to tremble at that moment. Sandbags, rifles and equipment went up into the air and a terrific shower of earth came down on top of us. After that the bombardment began in real earnest. The whole of the front line around the town of Ypres was a series of holes in which men crouched, waiting for the end.'

⮤ **SOURCE D:** *Trooper Stanley Down served in the North Somerset Yeomanry on the Western Front.*

'The water would be teeming with all little black things floating around, but we found that if we boiled it we killed all this stuff and brew it up for a drop of tea. If you smoked you had to be very careful; if Jerry saw any smoke he would send a grenade over because he knew there was someone there. Then there were the rats of course. I think they lived in corpses, because they were huge, they were as big as cats, I am not exaggerating, some of them were as big as ordinary cats, horrible great things.'

SOURCE E: *Fusilier Victor Packer served with the Royal Irish Fusiliers on the Western Front. 'Jerry' was a nickname for German soldiers. So was 'boche' and 'hun'.*

'When it was daylight you were set to clearing up the trenches of all things. That's the thing about the British Army – they never allowed you any time to yourself if they could find a job for you to do. We used to have to go along and pick up cigarette ends, matches and anything else lying about. It wasn't really necessary but I suppose it kept our minds off the terrible times we were having.'

SOURCE F: *Corporal Sidney Amatt served in the Essex Regiment.*

'Our trench was dug where a battle had taken place the year before. The ground was full of dead soldiers; they became part of the trench walls. I once fell and put my hand straight through the belly of a long-dead Frenchman. It felt like soft cheese and I remember wondering if I could die from infection. It was days before I got the smell out of my fingernails!'

SOURCE G: *Adapted from* A Victorian Son: An Autobiography 1897–1922 *by Stuart Cloete (1973).*

'Sitting in the front line on a firing step was very uncomfortable, with nothing to do and not much to talk about. It made one sit and think much more deeply than one would have done otherwise. I think it made you consider life much more seriously, whatever age you were. I was scared stiff of being maimed, but didn't mind dying because I knew something was going to happen afterwards.'

SOURCE H: *Private Norman Demuth served in the London Regiment.*

WISE-UP Words

concrete bunker
duckboards dugouts
fire step gas bell
periscope

Work

1 Write a week's worth of diary entries for an imaginary Great War diary. The main events of what took place on each day are listed below, but it's up to you to provide the details and colour of life in the trenches.

Monday – arrive at front line, repair trenches, receive letter.

Tuesday – terrible rainstorm, rumours of big attack coming.

Wednesday – close friend killed by German grenade.

Thursday – German artillery pounds your trench.

Friday – waiting and thinking about attack that is due the next day.

Saturday – go over the top at dawn to attack the German trench.

Sunday – this one is up to you!

MISSION ACCOMPLISHED?

- Could you tell someone about the main features and weapons used in trench warfare?
- Could you describe some of the experiences that soldiers of the Great War went through?

During the nineteenth century there had been enormous advances in technology and the use of machines. Most of Europe had gone through the industrial revolution and this meant that all sorts of jobs were now done in a quicker and more efficient way. Unfortunately for the soldiers going to fight in the Great War, the machines designed for killing people had got a lot more efficient too. The result of this was bloodshed and death on an unimaginable scale. So what were these advances in technology? How did they affect the way the war was fought? And which was the deadliest weapon of the Great War?

6: Weapons of WWI

MISSION OBJECTIVES

- To be able to explain why the new weapons used in the Great War were so deadly.
- To decide which weapons were the most effective.

Look carefully through the deadly weapons listed on these pages. Your task is to judge which you think was most deadly and why.

RIFLE

RANGE = 45%

KILLING POWER = 55%

DEFENSIVE ABILITY = 40%

The rifle was the standard weapon given to all soldiers in the Great War. It was lightweight so it could be carried easily and was deadly accurate up to 600 metres. Bullets were kept in a **magazine** underneath the rifle and the soldier had to pull back the **bolt** to reload it in between shots. Highly-trained soldiers could fire up to 15 aimed shots a minute.

POISON GAS

RANGE = 10%

KILLING POWER = 30%

DEFENSIVE ABILITY = 5%

In an attempt to get past the deadly machine guns, both sides tried using poison gas. The French first used tear gas at the beginning of the war, but it was the Germans who first made use of deadly chlorine gas. When it was inhaled, it quickly attacked the lungs and caused panic and coughing fits among the French soldiers who it was first used on. Britain and France quickly launched revenge gas attacks and new, deadlier poisons – such as phosgene and mustard gas – were soon developed. Unfortunately, if the wind changed direction, gas could do more harm than good. Later in the war, gas was put inside artillery shells which solved this problem, but by that time gas masks protected troops from the worst effects of the poison.

ARTILLERY

RANGE = 100%

KILLING POWER = 75%

DEFENSIVE ABILITY = 20%

Artillery is the name given to guns that fire large bullets – or **shells** – over long distances. They were heavily used in the Great War and the enemy's trenches were pounded for days to 'soften them up' before an attack was launched. It was the constant firing by the big guns that turned the landscape into featureless mud baths. Millions of shells were fired by both sides and the guns got bigger and more powerful, and their range got longer throughout the war. The Germans built a gun that could fire over 75 miles and even shelled Paris!

MACHINE GUN

RANGE = 45%

KILLING POWER = 85%

DEFENSIVE ABILITY = 90%

The machine gun dominated the battlefields of the Great War. A machine gun could fire up to 600 bullets a minute and attacking soldiers were mowed down in a hail of hot lead. Although they were heavy and needed a crew of five or six, one machine gun was worth around 100 rifles. Generals on both sides struggled with ways to get their soldiers past well-protected machine gun nests and they claimed millions of lives.

TANK

RANGE = 45%

KILLING POWER = 60%

DEFENSIVE ABILITY = 65%

This was another way of trying to get past the machine guns and this time it was a British invention. Tanks were bullet-proof vehicles that could travel over rough terrain, crush barbed wire and cross trenches. At first they were called 'landships', but were code-named tanks in an attempt to convince the Germans they were water tanks and so keep the invention a secret. The name stuck! Although they caused panic and terror on the battlefield, they were very slow (4mph) and unreliable. Although all sides saw the potential and built their own tanks, it wasn't until the next world war that tanks became battle-winning weapons.

FLAME-THROWER

RANGE = 10%

KILLING POWER = 60%

DEFENSIVE ABILITY = 2%

These were basically canisters of oil that were strapped to a soldier's back. The oil was forced through a nozzle (which the soldier held) and ignited. This sent a sheet of flame 15 metres towards enemy soldiers, which was especially deadly in tight spaces like dugouts and trenches. Any soldier seen carrying a flame-thrower became an instant target for enemy rifle and machine-gun fire. If the canister of oil was hit, the soldier would disappear in a ball of flame.

Work

1 Write a few sentences explaining why more lives were lost fighting in the Great War than in any war up to that point.

2 **a** Copy out and complete this chart in your book.

WEAPON: List the nine major weapons here.	RANGE: Is it a short (0–100 metres), medium (100m–1 mile) or long (1 mile+) range weapon?	KILLING POWER: Has it low (1 death at a time), medium (2–10 deaths) or high (10+) killing power?	Is the weapon used mainly for attack, defence or both?

b In your opinion, which was the Great War's most deadly weapon? Back up your opinion with facts and figures.

c In general, do the weapons used in the Great War make it easier for an army to attack or defend?

HAND GRENADE

RANGE = 15%

KILLING POWER = 55%

DEFENSIVE ABILITY = 25%

It was the Germans who first realised how useful small, hand-held bombs would be in trench warfare. Soon all sides were using them in large numbers to 'clear out' enemy trenches. Bombing parties would sneak across no-man's land with bags of grenades and hurl them into dugouts. Grenades exploded a few seconds after a pin was removed and the outer case would shatter into razor-sharp fragments. These fragments would cause horrific injuries to any soldier unlucky enough to be standing close by.

AEROPLANES

RANGE = 100%

KILLING POWER = 25%

DEFENSIVE ABILITY = 10%

When the Great War broke out in 1914, it had been less than ten years since the first man had taken to the air in a powered craft. When fighting began, the planes were very slow, clumsy and unreliable, and were used for keeping an eye on what the enemy was doing and spotting artillery. At first, pilots fired pistols and even threw bricks at each other, but soon 'fighter' planes armed with machine guns were developed. Not long after, 'bombers' were made to fly over enemy trenches and attack them from the air.

BAYONET

RANGE = 1%

KILLING POWER = 2%

DEFENSIVE ABILITY = 3%

Bayonets were long knives attached to the end of rifles. They were used to stab enemy soldiers in fierce hand-to-hand combat. Although very crude, they were a useful last resort when ammunition had run out.

___MISSION ACCOMPLISHED?___

• Could you tell somebody why the weapons used in the Great War caused such enormous bloodshed?

• Have you decided which weapon would have been the most deadly?

The sheer horror of trench warfare was too much for some soldiers to cope with. The constant danger of death, the relentless noise of shelling and witnessing close friends being killed in terrible ways all took their toll on the men at the front line. More and more men were diagnosed with a condition called shell shock. Some shook uncontrollably, others became paralysed despite suffering no physical injury. Many suffered panic attacks, cried constantly or were unable to speak. The British soldier in Source A would lie perfectly still for hours on end – not responding to any visitors or questions. However, whenever he heard the word 'bomb', he would fly into a panic and hide. So how did the British army cope with this problem? What would shell shock be called today? And what were the consequences for Private Harry Farr?

7: Shot at dawn

MISSION OBJECTIVES

- To be able to explain what 'shell shock' was and what it would be called today.
- To decide if Harry Farr was a coward or the victim of cruel injustice.

A shocking diagnosis

Shell shock was first diagnosed as an illness in 1915, but doctors struggled to find a way to cure it. They tried rest, hypnosis, counselling and even electric shocks through the brain. Many men just needed time away from the front line to recover. Unfortunately, when they did get better, they were often sent straight back to fight. Obviously, their symptoms soon returned and they often ran away – unable to handle the situation any longer. Commanding officers were keen to maintain discipline and when these men were caught, they were charged with **desertion** or **cowardice**. In total, Britain shot 306 of its soldiers for these 'crimes' during the Great War. The French shot 600, but the Americans and Australians shot none of their own men. Official figures show that the Germans shot fewer than 50.

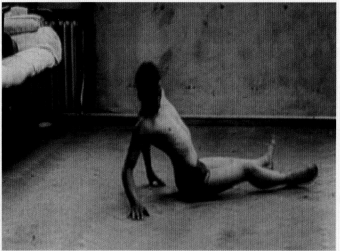

↵ **SOURCE A:** *A shell-shock victim.*

A step too Farr?

Your task over these four pages is to consider the case of Private Harry Farr (see Source B). He was put on trial (known as a **court martial** in the army) charged with cowardice, found guilty and shot dead at 6:00am on 18 October 1916. Was this verdict correct? Was he suffering from shell shock? Should he have been in hospital rather than looking down the barrels of a firing squad?

Farr's background

Private Harry Farr, who lived in London with his wife and baby daughter, had been a professional soldier in the army since 1908. He had been fighting in France for nearly two years and, in that time, he had reported sick with his 'nerves' three times. Each time he had been sent to hospital – once for five months – and he shook so violently that a nurse had to write his letters home to his wife. But, as he wasn't physically injured, he was returned to the front line each time he recovered. These adapted notes from his court martial tell the story of what happened on his final return to the trenches.

Court Martial at Ville-Sur-Ancre, 2 October 1916

Alleged Offender: No. 8871 Private Harry T FARR 1st Battalion – West Yorkshire Regiment.

Offence Charged: Section 4. (7) Army Act: Misbehaving before the enemy in such a manner as to show cowardice.

Plea: Not Guilty.

↵ SOURCE B: *Private Harry Farr.*

THE PROSECUTION

1st Witness: Sergeant Major H HAKING

'On 17 September, at about 9:00am, FARR reported to me well behind the lines. He said he was sick but had left his position without permission. He said he couldn't find his commanding officer. I told him to go to the dressing station [a trench hospital]. They sent him back saying he wasn't wounded. I sent him back to the front lines.

At about 8:00pm, his commanding officer (Captain BOOTH) told me FARR was missing again. Later on I saw FARR back where I'd first seen him well behind the line. I asked him why he was there. He said, "I cannot stand it". I asked him what he meant and he repeated, "I cannot stand it". I told him to get back to the front line and he said, "I cannot go". I then told BOOTH and two other men to take him back by force. After going 500 metres, FARR began to scream and struggle. I told him that if he didn't go back he would be on trial for cowardice. He said, "I'm not fit to go to the trenches". I then said I'd take him to a doctor but he refused to go saying, "I will not go any further". I ordered the men to carry on but FARR again started struggling and screaming. I told the men to leave him alone and FARR jumped up and ran back to where I'd first seen him early in the day. He was then arrested.'

2nd Witness: Captain J W BOOTH

'On 17 September 1916 at 3:00pm I told FARR to get back up to his trench. Later that evening, I could see he was missing without having received permission. At about 9:00pm, I saw him well away from where he should have been. Sergeant Major HAKING ordered me to take him back to his trench under escort. After about 500 metres, FARR became violent and threatened the three of us. FARR was later arrested.'

3rd Witness: Private D FARREL (one of the soldiers ordered to take FARR back to his trench)

'On 17 September 1916, at about 11:30pm, I was ordered by Captain BOOTH to take FARR back to the trenches. After going 500 metres, he started struggling and saying he wanted to see a doctor. The Sergeant Major said he could see one later. FARR refused to go any further. I tried to pull him along. The Sergeant Major told me to let go and FARR ran off.'

4th Witness: Corporal W FORM

Corporate FORM said exactly the same as Private FARREL, the third witness.

Work ⌒.

1 a Write a sentence or two to explain these terms:

shell shock • desertion • cowardice • court martial

 b How many people did the British shoot for cowardice and desertion during the Great War?

2 Up to this point, what is your impression of i) Sergeant Major Haking and ii) Private Harry Farr?

THE DEFENCE

Harry Farr was not given an opportunity to ask someone to help him with his defence. Instead, he defended himself.

1st Witness: The accused, Private H FARR

'On 16 September 1916, I started to feel sick. I tried to get permission to leave the trenches but couldn't because people were asleep or unavailable. Eventually, I found Sergeant Major HAKING on 17 September at 9:00am and he told me to go to the dressing station. They said I wasn't physically wounded and sent me back to my trench. I started to go but felt sick again so I told an ordinary officer where I was going and went back well behind the front line again.'

'When I saw Sergeant Major HAKING, I told him I was sick again and couldn't stand it. He said, "You're a f****** coward and you'll go back to your trench. I give f*** all for my life and I'd give f*** all for yours so I'll get you f****** well shot". I was then escorted back to my trench. On the way, we met up with another group of soldiers and one asked where I'd been. Sergeant Major HAKING replied, "Ran away, same as he did last night". I said to HAKING that he'd got it in for me.'

'I was then taken towards my trench but the men were shoving me. I told them I was sick enough already. Then Sergeant Major HAKING grabbed my rifle and said, "I'll blow your f****** brains out if you don't go". I called out for help but there was none. I was then tripped up so I started to struggle. Soon after, I was arrested. If no one had shoved me I'd have gone back to the trenches.'

Court Question: Why haven't you been sick since you were arrested?

Answer by FARR: Because I feel much better when I'm away from the shell fire.

2nd Witness: Sergeant J ANDREWS

'FARR has been sick with his nerves several times.'

Character Witness: Lieutenant L P MARSHALL

'I have known FARR for six weeks. Three times he has asked for leave because he couldn't stand the noise of the guns. He was trembling and didn't appear in a fit state.'

Character Witness: Captain A WILSON

'I cannot say what has destroyed this man's nerves, but on many occasions he has been unable to keep his nerves in action. He causes others to panic. Apart from his behaviour when fighting, his conduct and character are very good.'

The entire court martial took about 20 minutes. Soon after, the judging panel gave its verdict... GUILTY. They said 'The charge of cowardice is clearly proved and the opinion of Sergeant Major HAKING is that FARR is bad. Even soldiers who know him say that FARR is no good'.

On 14 October 1916, Harry Farr's death sentence was confirmed by Sir Douglas Haig, the man in charge of the British army. He was shot at dawn on 18 October 1916. He refused to be blindfolded. According to his death certificate, 'death was instantaneous'. He has no known grave and doesn't appear on any war memorials. At first, his widow was told he had been killed in action, but was later told the truth when her war pension was stopped. Widows were not entitled to a pension if their husband had been shot for cowardice.

Why might Sir Douglas Haig, the man in charge of the British army, think it was important to execute soldiers like Harry Farr? What do you think he was worried would happen if Farr had been allowed to go home unpunished? Why was it important to make an example out of 'deserters' and 'cowards'?

The Shot at Dawn Campaign

In the years following the war, many relatives of the executed men campaigned to have their names and reputations cleared. They believed it was the army's lack of understanding about shell shock – not cowardice – that had led to many of the men's deaths. In June 2001, a memorial to the 306 British soldiers killed by their own side was unveiled by Mrs Gertrude Harris – the daughter of Private Harry Farr. In 2006, the British Government looked into the cases once more and decided to **pardon** all the men who had been 'shot at dawn'. Harry Farr's 93-year-old daughter said, 'I am so relieved that this ordeal is now over and I can be content knowing that my father's memory is intact. I have always argued that my father's refusal to rejoin the front line, described in the court martial as resulting from cowardice, was in fact the result of shell shock, and I believe that many other soldiers suffered from this; not just my father'.

⌐ SOURCE C: *This memorial at Alrewas, Lichfield is based on a young soldier named Herbert Burden. He lied about his age to join and, when he ran away after seeing all his friends killed in a battle, he was executed. At the time of his death he was 17 years and 10 months old – still officially too young to have been in the army in the first place.*

★ WISE-UP Words

court martial
cowardice
desertion
pardon

! FACT Shocking stuff

In 1922, the British War Office Committee announced that shell shock didn't exist and that it was a collection of already known illnesses. Today, it is recognised as a genuine condition and is called post-traumatic stress disorder.

Work

1 a Write a definition of the word 'contradict'.

b In what ways does Harry Farr's version of events on 17 September 1916 contradict Sergeant Major Haking's?

c In what ways are the two versions similar?

d Why do you think it is difficult for two versions of the same event to agree with each other all the time?

2 a In your opinion, was Harry Farr a coward or was he suffering from shell shock? You should include details from some of the witnesses in your answer.

b Write two letters.

The first should be from Sergeant Major Haking, one of the commanding officers of Harry Farr. It was common practice for commanding officers to write home to the family of any dead soldiers in their 'care'. Imagine you are Haking and write a letter to Harry's widow informing her of the situation surrounding his death.

The second letter to Harry's widow should be from one of Harry Farr's friends, perhaps Captain Wilson.

c In what ways are the letters similar and/or different? Give reasons for your answer.

——— MISSION ACCOMPLISHED? ———

- Can you explain what caused the condition called shell shock?
- Do you know what we would call it today?
- Have you decided whether Farr deserved his fate or not?

The Great War was the first **total war**. This meant it wasn't just the armies that were dedicated to winning the war, but the country, including the people back at home. As a result, whole countries became targets, and women and children were dragged into a war like never before. So just how was British society changed? What did this mean for the lives of civilians? And how did the Germans attack them?

8: Home front

———— MISSION OBJECTIVES ————

- To be able to explain how the Great War affected everyday life in Britain.
- To know how and why British **civilians** were at risk between 1914 and 1918.

Loss of freedom

The Government passed the Defence of the Realm Act in order to arrest anybody accused of helping the enemy. However, it was soon being used to stop anyone criticising either the war or the Government. People became worried that traditional British freedoms were being taken away as one man was fined £100 for saying that Germans would soon invade Britain and capture London. Other people were taken to court for urging soldiers not to fight. Newspapers were **censored** so they only said the things that the Government agreed with. Wasn't Britain meant to be the country of free speech?

> 'At first the Censorship Office let us mention that the dead of both sides were noticeable after a battle. Later, it allowed only German dead on the battleground. Later still, no dead were permitted.'

↳ **SOURCE A:** *From* I was there! *by Sir John Hammerton who worked as a journalist during the Great War.*

The economy

Many people were actually better off during the war. Families of soldiers were paid an allowance and wages rose because of the shortage of workers. There was no unemployment and many families had two wages coming in for the first time. It wasn't all good news though. Inflation doubled throughout the war, making something that cost £5 in 1914 cost £10 in 1918. The cost of the war put enormous strains on the Government and it was forced to borrow huge amounts from the USA. As a result, income tax was raised in order to pay for the debt.

Working women

With so many men away fighting for their country, the factories and farms found it difficult to find a workforce. But it was more important than ever that they kept producing goods. In fact, the war demanded that the factories were busier than ever, making **munitions**, uniforms and weapons. Also, a drop in food imports meant British farms had to produce more and more food. There was no option but to turn to women and soon they were doing all sorts of jobs that people had previously believed only men could do. The contribution of women in factories and in the Land Army (groups of women who worked on farms) was essential in allowing Britain to carry on fighting. They proved beyond all doubt that women were the equal of men and, in 1918, all women over 30 were given the vote.

↳ **SOURCE B:** *Women were pressed into all sorts of essential jobs they would never have dreamt of doing before the war.*

SOURCE C: *The amount of women employed making munitions.* ↱

Year	Women employed making munitions
1914	200,000
1915	250,000
1916	500,000
1917	800,000
1918	950,000

Because the home front was so important for Britain's ability to win the war, the Germans decided to attack British cities. The idea was to disrupt the production of factories and to scare people into wanting the war to end. They also tried to cut off all food imports so Britain would be starved into surrender.

The threat from above

The first ever air raid on Britain took place in January 1915. German Zeppelins (enormous propeller-driven airships filled with hydrogen gas) dropped bombs on Great Yarmouth. London was later bombed in response to French attacks on German cities and, in total, there were over a hundred raids on Britain. The Zeppelin attacks did disrupt factory production and around 1500 civilians were killed – with many more terrified.

↰ **SOURCE D:** *Schoolchildren being taught about the dangers of Zeppelins. The word 'pluck' means bravery.*

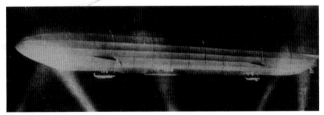

↰ **SOURCE E:** *The enormous German airships were called Zeppelins.*

REMEMBER SCARBOROUGH!

The Germans who brag of their "CULTURE" have shown what it is made of by murdering defenceless women and children at SCARBOROUGH.

But this only strengthens

GREAT BRITAIN'S
resolve to crush the

GERMAN BARBARIANS

ENLIST NOW!

↰ **SOURCE F:** *'Remember Scarborough' propaganda poster.*

The threat from the sea

At ten past eight on the morning of 16 December 1914, the German First High Seas Fleet unleashed a huge bombardment of the English towns of Hartlepool, Whitby and Scarborough. The attack lasted for over an hour and over 1100 shells were fired by the Germans – killing 137 people and wounding around 600.

The threat from under the sea

German submarines (or U-boats as the Germans called them) were a great threat to Britain. By cutting off supplies of food and ammunition – especially from the USA – they caused **rationing** to be introduced in 1917. This ensured everyone got a fair share of what was available. The first thing to be rationed was sugar, but coal, electricity, gas, butter, margarine and meat were rationed by early 1918. Submarine warfare backfired on the Germans when they sank the RMS Lusitania in 1915. Of the 1198 people that were killed, 128 were Americans. This turned many people in the USA against Germany and in favour of joining the war.

SOURCE G: *One of the many German U-boats.* ↱

Work

1 In what way did the Great War affect the freedom of speech in Britain?

2 Define the following words: civilian • censorship • rationing • U-boat • Zeppelin

3 Create a histogram (bar chart) based on the information in Source C.

4 Write a few sentences explaining how the Great War may have helped to get women the vote.

5 a In what way were people better off financially during the Great War?

  b In what ways were people worse off financially during the Great War?

6 Look at Sources F and G. How do you think the raids by the navy and Zeppelins made people feel about Germany and the war in general?

___ MISSION ACCOMPLISHED? ___

- Can you name at least three ways in which everyday life was affected in Britain during the Great War?
- Could you tell somebody how some British civilians were killed between 1914 and 1918?

The Great War ended in 1918 – but it was not won or lost on the battlefield. The stalemate at the front line was never broken and the fighting only came to an end when countries were unable to supply their enormous armies with soldiers and their populations back home with food. 1917 was a key year in the history of the war. Britain had lost an ally when Russia pulled out of the war when ordinary workers seized control of their country and killed the entire Russian Royal Family. But Britain had also gained an ally when the USA declared war on the Triple Alliance after German U-boats sank American ships. With the USA's enormous army and limitless resources, it was just a question of time before the war ended. So when exactly did the shooting end? How many people had died? And how did people try to come to terms with such an enormous tragedy?

9: How did 'Poppy Day' start?

MISSION OBJECTIVES

- To be able to explain how the Great War ended.
- To understand the origins of Remembrance Sunday.

The Armistice

The Germans launched an all-out attack in a last-ditch attempt to defeat Britain and France before the American army could reach Europe. It failed and, back in Germany, the civilians were forced to eat cats and dogs to survive. There were soon riots on the streets and the German King was forced to **abdicate** (run away) to Holland. The Government that replaced him knew that all hope was lost and called for an **armistice** (ceasefire). Finally, at 11:00am on the eleventh day of the eleventh month of 1918, the guns fell silent.

'The trees by the roadside were riven and splintered, the cracked stumps stuck up uselessly into the air, flanking the road like a byway to hell. Every five square yards held a crater. The earth had no longer its smooth familiar face. It was diseased, pocked, rancid, stinking of death in the morning sun. Yet (oh, the catch at the heart!), among the devastated cottages, the twisted trees and the desecrated cemeteries, opening up to the blue heaven, the poppies were growing! Clumps of crimson poppies thrust out from the lips of craters, undaunted by the desolation, heedless of human fury and stupidity.'

↰ SOURCE A: *From* Sagittarius Rising *by Cecil Lewis, a British pilot who fought on the Western Front.*

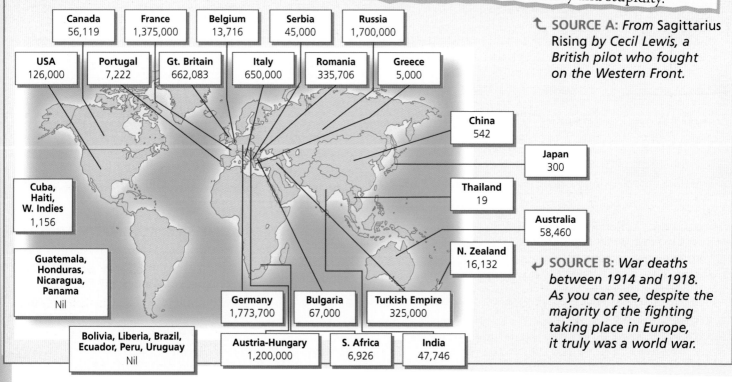

Canada 56,119	**France** 1,375,000	**Belgium** 13,716	**Serbia** 45,000	**Russia** 1,700,000
USA 126,000	**Portugal** 7,222	**Gt. Britain** 662,083	**Italy** 650,000	**Romania** 335,706	**Greece** 5,000

China 542

Japan 300

Cuba, Haiti, W. Indies 1,156

Thailand 19

Australia 58,460

Guatemala, Honduras, Nicaragua, Panama Nil

N. Zealand 16,132

Germany 1,773,700

Bulgaria 67,000

Turkish Empire 325,000

Bolivia, Liberia, Brazil, Ecuador, Peru, Uruguay Nil

Austria-Hungary 1,200,000

S. Africa 6,926

India 47,746

↵ SOURCE B: *War deaths between 1914 and 1918. As you can see, despite the majority of the fighting taking place in Europe, it truly was a world war.*

Lest we forget

When the war came to an end, there were only 12 towns or villages in the entire country that hadn't lost a young man in the fighting. The remains of thousands were never found and even bodies that were identified were never returned home. This robbed grieving relatives of a funeral for their loved ones, so many turned to the war memorials that sprung up all over the country. People were determined to keep the memories of those young men – and the terrible events that killed them – alive so that future generations wouldn't repeat the same mistakes. Nobody was sure as to the best way to commemorate the dead, but in 1919, the Government agreed to hold a two-minute silence on the Sunday closest to 11 November. It is called 'Remembrance Sunday', but people sometimes call it 'Poppy Day' for short.

WISE-UP Words

abdicate
armistice

↰ SOURCE C:
The national war memorial, known as the Cenotaph, being unveiled in 1919 and being commemorated on Remembrance Sunday today.

↵

SOURCE D: *In 1919, people began to donate money for poppies to wear on their lapels. This not only raised money for injured soldiers and war widows, it also allowed people to show their respect for the dead. The idea was a huge success and soon artificial poppies were being distributed all over the country. Today, around 36 million poppies are distributed in the UK.* ↱

Work ～～～～.

1 Name two important events that shaped the war in 1917.

2 Write down the exact date the Great War ended.

3 Look at Source B.

   a Turn these figures into either a bar chart or a pie chart.

   b In total, how many people were killed in the Great War?

4 Read Source A. Why do you think the poppy was chosen as a symbol of the Great War? Explain your answer carefully.

5 Write a few sentences explaining why people should wear a poppy today.

—— MISSION ACCOMPLISHED? ——

• Can you tell someone why and when the Great War ended?

• Do you know why people began to commemorate the end of the war every November and why they chose the poppy as their symbol?

When the Great War ended in November 1918, the British Prime Minister, David Lloyd George, made the following announcement to Parliament: 'At eleven o'clock this morning came to an end the cruellest and most terrible war that has ever scourged mankind. I hope we may say that thus, this fateful morning came to an end all wars.' He wasn't alone in wanting to see an end to all wars and, in January 1919, he met with the leaders of France and the USA to reshape the world. It soon became clear that they had very different ideas about how to avoid more wars. So just what were these ideas? Who won the argument? And did their ideas work?

10: How did countries try to avoid more wars?

MISSION OBJECTIVES

- To be able to explain how the world was reorganised after the Great War and who was most responsible.
- To decide whether the League of Nations was a success or failure.

The 'Big Three'

In January 1919, politicians from the winning countries met at the Palace of Versailles, near Paris, to decide what was to happen to the beaten enemy.

The three most important politicians at the Paris Peace Conference were the leaders of France, Great Britain and the USA. They were nicknamed the 'Big Three' because they represented the three most powerful winning countries. The Germans – who were top of the people's 'hit list' – were not allowed to send any politicians to put their viewpoint across; nor were the Austro-Hungarians, the Turks or Bulgarians.

David Lloyd George – Prime Minister of Great Britain

Aims:
Was elected by the British public to 'hang the Kaiser' and 'make Germany pay'. He wanted to keep Germany weak; however, he also wanted to avoid humiliating them. Wanted to end the German threat to the British Empire and Navy.

Woodrow Wilson – President of the United States of America

Aims:
The USA joined the war in 1917 and didn't suffer as much as Britain and France. He wanted to prevent Germany becoming aggressive but didn't think they should be punished. Wanted different national groups to have the right to rule themselves – known as self-determination.

George Clemenceau – Prime Minister of France

Aims:
Around 1.4 million Frenchmen had been killed in the Great War and huge areas of the country had been destroyed. He wanted to have revenge on Germany for all of this suffering. Wanted Germany to pay for all of the damage that the war had caused. Wanted to weaken Germany's armed forces so they would never be able to attack France again.

In June 1919, the politicians announced their decision to the world. Germany's punishments, set out in a huge document called the Treaty of Versailles, were the first to be published. German politicians, sent over for the day, were told to sign the peace agreement… or face invasion! They signed.

Germany must pay for the war in money and goods. The figure was set at £6 600 million. They must sign to agree that they had started the war too.

Germany to have no air force or submarines. Only tiny army and navy. No tanks or submarines allowed. No German soldiers allowed anywhere near France.

Germany to hand over colonies to Britain and France.

Parts of countries cut off to make new countries.

League of Nations set up. All countries should join this so they can talk about their problems rather than fight.

The League of Nations

After the losers were punished, the winners turned their attentions to trying to stop wars forever. They decided to set up a League of Nations, a kind of international club for settling problems peacefully. Its headquarters would be in Geneva, Switzerland. About 40 countries joined up straightaway, hoping to solve any disputes by discussion rather than war. If one nation did end up declaring war on another, all the other member nations would stop trading with the invading country until a lack of supplies would bring the fighting to an end.

The League would aim to help in other ways too. Countries would work together to fight diseases, stop drug smuggling and slavery, and improve working conditions. However, fewer than half the countries in the world joined – Germany wasn't allowed and politicians in the USA voted against it – and it didn't have its own army to go in and stop trouble. Yet, for a few years, it seemed to work well.

Successes of the League:	Failures of the League:
• Freed 200,000 slaves.	• The League never had its own armed forces.
• Helped 400,000 prisoners of war return home.	• The USA never became a member. Japan, Germany and the Soviet Union all left.
• Worked hard to defeat diseases such as leprosy, cholera and smallpox.	• It couldn't stop Japan invading China in 1931.
• Sorted out a dispute between Finland and Sweden.	• It couldn't stop Italy invading Abyssinia (Ethiopia) in 1935.
• Sorted out a dispute between Greece and Bulgaria.	• It couldn't stop Germany expanding its territory in Europe between 1936 and 1939.

WISE-UP Words

treaty

↵ **SOURCE A:** *The 'Big Three' argued for many months but, eventually, in June 1919, the Germans were summoned to the Palace of Versailles to sign a new* **treaty** *(a contract between countries). If they had refused the war would have started again. The treaty of Versailles (Germany's punishment) is the best known, but the other losing countries (Austria-Hungary, Turkey and Bulgaria) lost land and weapons, and were fined too.*

Work

1 a Who were the 'Big Three'?

b Why do you think these men made most of the important decisions after the war had finished?

2 a Make a copy of Source A.

b Overall, which of the 'Big Three' do you think would have been most happy with the Treaty of Versailles? Explain your answer very carefully.

c Give three reasons why the Germans may have been unhappy with the Treaty of Versailles.

3 a How did the League of Nations try to stop wars?

b What were its two main weaknesses?

c In its early years, was the League of Nations a success or not? Give examples to go with your answer.

—MISSION ACCOMPLISHED?—

• Do you know which countries the 'Big Three' came from?

• Can you explain why the Germans were not happy with the Treaty of Versailles?

• Have you decided if the League of Nations was a success or not?

The rise of the USA

MISSION OBJECTIVES

- To understand how the USA became one of the richest and most influential countries of the twentieth century.

If you look in magazines and newspapers, or on television, you will find the USA is often in the news. This is partly because since the beginning of the twentieth century, the USA has become one of the richest and most powerful countries in the world – and it's certainly one of the most influential.

But the USA has not always been in this position. In the 1500s, for example, Spain was the world's leading power – and in the 1800s it was Great Britain and the British Empire. So how did the USA come to dominate the twentieth century? Why did the USA overtake other countries as the world's leading economic nation? And just how influential has the USA been in some of the key areas of twentieth-century life?

The USA and the Great War

The USA's rise is strongly linked to the Great War of 1914–18. Before the war the USA was a strongly developed nation with a large population, many raw materials and lots of factories producing top-quality goods. But the USA didn't join in the war when it started. Instead it sold food, weapons and other goods to Britain and its allies. This created many more jobs in the USA and made lots of business people very rich. The USA eventually joined the war in 1917, on Britain's side, and although 100,000 American soldiers died by the time the war finished a year later, the impact of the fighting was much greater in France, Germany, Russia and Britain. These nations were exhausted by the war – millions of men had been killed or injured and they had lost valuable farmland, railway lines, factories, cattle, and so on. Now the USA, untouched by any of the fighting, moved in to provide the world with all the goods they needed. Indeed, by the early 1920s the USA was producing 70% of the world's petrol, 55% of the world's cotton and 80% of the world's corn. And American workers were earning on average nearly twice as much as workers in other countries.

The Henry Ford factor

An American businessman, Henry Ford, even revolutionised the way that goods were produced. Using an 'assembly line' in his car factory, he was able to produce cars cheaper and quicker than ever before. Ford's assembly line was copied across the world and used to produce all sorts of products like radios, telephones, clothes and watches (see Source A). Amazingly, most of the goods we buy today are made in the same way – on an assembly line.

SOURCE A: *A cartoon showing how Ford's assembly line worked. Before this cars were hand-made by specialists who worked at their own pace. The cars stayed in one place while workers wasted time and energy walking about getting tools and carrying pieces of equipment to the cars. One car could take nearly two days to build.* ↴

1 An electric conveyor belt carried the partly assembled car past the workers who stood in the same spot and did the same job, for example, fitting a wheel or a door over and over again.

SOURCE B: *An advert for a Ford motor car. America led the world in advertising. Colourful billboards appeared by the roadside and imaginative advertising campaigns could be seen in newspapers, magazines and at the cinema. Americans even pioneered new ways to buy things: 'buy now, pay later' schemes meant customers could purchase goods 'on credit' and pay them off in small instalments – a system still very much in use today!* ↱

2 The tools and equipment the workers needed were brought to them so they didn't waste time fetching things. One man would only be responsible for one or two small jobs. Ford himself said, 'The key is to keep everything moving. Take the work to the man and not the man to the work.'

Her habit of measuring time in terms of dollars gives the woman in business keen insight into the true value of a Ford closed car for her personal use.

This car enables her to conserve minutes, to expedite her affairs, to widen the scope of her activities. Its low first cost, long life and inexpensive operation and upkeep convince her that it is a sound investment value.

And it is such a pleasant car to drive that it transforms the business call which might be an interruption into an enjoyable episode of her busy day.

3 For many years, Ford made just one type of car – The Model T or 'Tin Lizzie' as it was nicknamed. It was mass-produced. Costs were kept low because there was just one engine size, one colour available (black – Ford didn't want workers wasting time changing the paint in spray guns!), no side windows, no speedometer and no windscreen wipers.

4 As Ford's factory got quicker, the price of the car got lower. Costing nearly $800 in 1911, the price in 1928 was only $295. As a result, 15 million people bought Model Ts between 1911 and 1929! By the time production stopped and Ford changed to different models, there were six Tin Lizzies driving out of his Detroit factory every minute!

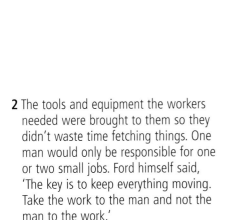

The roaring twenties

The USA in the 1920s was a period in American history when people had lots of fun, enjoyed loud music, wild parties and new forms of entertainment. Although life was still hard for some Americans, historians tend to call this time the USA's 'golden age' of the 'roaring twenties'. The sources on the next few pages show a snapshot of the USA at this time.

Wild women

The USA enjoyed a new-found freedom in the 1920s. The most fashionable young ladies were known as **flappers** and were recognised by their short bobbed hair and even shorter skirts. They wore lots of makeup, smoked cigarettes, drank alcohol in public and spent all night at nightclubs. Above all though, flappers wanted to dance and a new style of music – jazz – swept the USA. Along with the music came new dances like the One Step, the Black Bottom and the Charleston. And the 'flapper phenomenon' was copied by women all over the world!

↵ **SOURCE C:**
The flapper phenomenon. Flappers were certainly the first generation of females to embrace 'girl power'.

Box office boom

One of the USA's biggest success stories of the 1920s was the movie industry. By 1930 over 100 million Americans a week were 'going to the picture shows' and film actors such as Charlie Chaplin, Rudolf Valentino, Laurel and Hardy, and Clara Bow became celebrity superstars and film goers would copy their hair, clothes and lifestyles. What we would now call celebrity magazines first appeared at this time too. In 1927 the world's first 'talking film' – *The Jazz Singer* – was released and was a worldwide success. The 1920s also saw the birth of Mickey Mouse… and within ten years 'animated films' had begun to take the film world by storm. In fact, animated films or 'cartoons' remain incredibly popular today and account for a large proportion of box office takings.

SOURCE D: *This poster is of A Dog's Life. By the time this movie was made, English-born Chaplin was earning about $1500 a week – that's over £100,000 in today's money. It is fair to say that Chaplin was possibly the world's first worldwide movie star!* ↱

"The One and Only"

Charlie Chaplin
His Signature
In his First Million Dollar Picture
"A DOG'S LIFE"
A "First National" Attraction

SOURCE E: *A photograph of Al Capone on the front cover of one of the USA's biggest-selling magazines.*

WISE-UP Words

flappers

Gangster's paradise

Alphonse Capone was a notorious gangster who supplied alcohol all over Chicago, one of the USA's largest cities. Alcohol was banned all over the USA from 1920 to 1933, but Capone smuggled in booze from abroad. He owned hundreds of illegal bars too and controlled it all using a violent gang of fellow crooks. Capone achieved celebrity 'bad boy' status in the USA and was cheered when he was seen out in public. Everyone knew of his activities, but it was impossible to convict him for many of his crimes because of his control of the police. He was eventually jailed in 1931 for not paying his taxes.

SOURCE F: *A photograph of Walt Disney and his most famous creation, Mickey Mouse. Born in Chicago in 1901, Walt Disney began making short cartoons in the 1920s. Mickey Mouse appeared in 1928, followed by Pluto (1930), Goofy (1932) and Donald Duck (1934). He made his first full-length cartoon (Snow White) in 1937 and his first theme park opened in 1955 (Disneyland in California).*

A consumer society

The USA was one of the world's first countries to have electricity in the majority of people's homes – nearly 70% of US houses had it by 1927. This meant that workers could spend their hard-earned cash on any number of ultra-modern, electric-powered 'gadgets' that had recently been invented: vacuum cleaners, gramophones (ask your teacher!), toasters, washing machines, radios, telephones, refrigerators, irons, ovens and much more. Huge demand for these goods (let's face it, we all love new, state-of-the-art technology!) created jobs in the factories that made them. And all the time, the assembly line meant that companies could make goods quicker and cheaper than ever before.

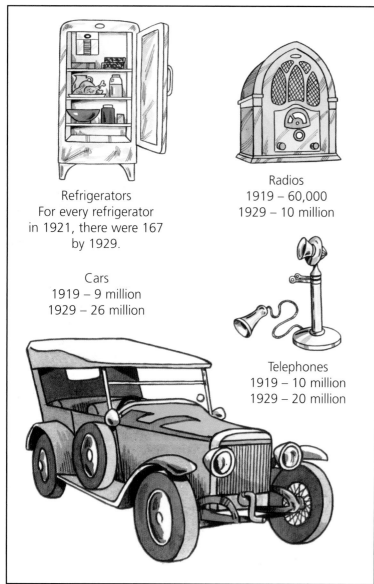

Refrigerators
For every refrigerator
in 1921, there were 167
by 1929.

Radios
1919 – 60,000
1929 – 10 million

Cars
1919 – 9 million
1929 – 26 million

Telephones
1919 – 10 million
1929 – 20 million

↰ **SOURCE G:** *The growth in sales of consumer goods during the 1920s. Amazingly, by 1929, the USA made nearly 50% of all manufactured goods purchased in the world.*

! FACT Buy, buy, buy
A selection of consumer goods available to buy in 1925.

The jazz age

Jazz was the new music of the 1920s – and it swept the world. For the first time, white people were exposed to black music – and millions loved it! This new sound, originating in the black neighbourhood of Harlem, New York, provided great opportunities for black musicians such as Louis Armstrong, Duke Ellington, Bessie Smith, Fats Waller and Benny Goodman. They made big money from nightclub performances, radio appearances and record sales.

↵ **SOURCE H:** *A photograph of Louis Armstrong. A South African trumpet legend, Hugh Masekela, said that 'Louis Armstrong loosened the world, he helped people say 'yeah' and to walk with a little dip in their hip. Before Louis Armstrong, the world was definitely square, just as Christopher Columbus thought! And what was the greatest band of the twentieth century? Forget the Beatles – it was Louis Armstrong and his Hot Five Jazz Band – this band altered the course of pop music!'.*

Work

1 In your own words, explain how the Great War helped American industry.

2 a In no more than 50 words, describe how Ford's assembly line worked. You could draw a diagram to go with your explanation if you wish.

   b In which ways was the assembly line an improvement on previous methods of making cars?

3 Draw a diagram or create a poster or leaflet that summarises the main features of entertainment, industry and popular culture in the USA in the 1920s. Make sure you mention the assembly line, the flappers, jazz music, sport, film and cartoons, gangsters and consumer goods.

   Top tip: Why not imagine you were creating a diagram or poster for a Year 6 pupil who had never heard of any of the things you have just learnt about when studying 1920s USA?

4 In your own words can you describe at least three ways in which 1920s USA influences – or has made an impact on – our lives today?

Sporting superstars

The USA in the 1920s saw the birth of sport as 'big business'. For the first time, sportspeople became sports stars with celebrity status. People were no longer just interested in how their favourite stars performed on the track or sports field; instead they wanted to know all about their private lives too – what they wore, where they ate and who they dated!

Babe Ruth of baseball's New York Yankees was probably America's greatest sports hero after setting a home run record – 60 in the 1927 season – which lasted over 30 years. By 1930, he was earning $80,000 a year – the equivalent of nearly £7 million a year today. Bobby Jones took the golfing world by storm too, winning the British Open in 1926, 1927 and 1930, and the US Open in 1923, 1926, 1929 and 1930.

Radio broadcasts, newspapers and magazines helped bring major sporting events to a mass audience. Around 60 million radio listeners (the equivalent of EVERYONE in Britain!) heard the 1927 World Heavyweight boxing title fight between Jack Dempsey and Gene Tunney.

↵ **SOURCE I:** *Baseball superstar Babe Ruth playing for the New York Yankees. Note the huge crowd and the photographers taking pictures of his every move!*

— **MISSION ACCOMPLISHED?** —

• Can you describe three ways in which 1920s USA still influences our lives today?

TASK 1 The poor in 1900

In 1901, Seebohm Rowntree looked at the lives of poor people in York. In his report, he said that many people lived below the 'poverty line' (the minimum amount of money a person needed to buy proper food, clothing and shelter). Rowntree said that no matter how hard a person worked, there were certain times when they couldn't help falling below the 'poverty line'.

Study the graph below carefully. It appeared in Rowntree's report, *Poverty: A Study of Town Life*, published in 1901.

a Draw and label a neat copy of this chart in your book.

b Write down the three times in a lifetime when a person fell below the line. For each time, explain why it happened.

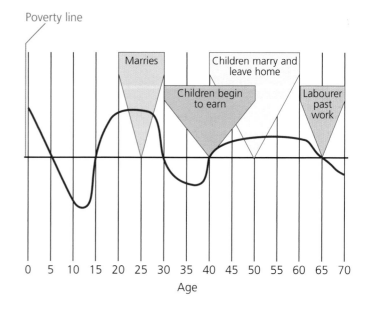

TASK 2 A Titanic wordsearch

This wordsearch includes 12 words associated with *Titanic*. Search carefully for each word, writing it down every time you find one. Next to each word, write a sentence or fact that demonstrates your understanding of the topic.

As an example, one has been done for you.

ISMAY: Bruce Ismay was in charge of the White Star Line, the owners of *Titanic*.

R	M	A	V	B	E	L	F	A	S	T	T	N	O	K
I	W	I	M	I	O	A	I	M	A	I	D	E	N	F
G	N	I	C	S	I	C	B	F	O	G	C	C	E	W
K	A	O	L	E	I	S	T	E	E	R	A	G	E	B
O	S	G	T	G	B	C	M	H	G	B	A	C	E	T
E	X	B	R	P	N	E	I	A	Y	E	O	E	S	E
L	P	H	T	I	M	S	R	T	Y	G	S	A	S	L
K	J	R	R	I	D	A	E	G	N	T	E	R	T	F
A	U	E	M	G	F	B	H	R	C	A	A	A	B	S
N	W	S	S	T	E	P	H	T	N	S	L	A	R	R
A	R	T	S	E	H	C	R	O	U	T	E	T	G	D
X	G	Y	M	N	A	S	I	U	M	O	N	E	A	I
I	B	A	I	H	T	A	P	R	A	C	S	U	T	Y

TASK 3 Murder in Sarajevo, 28 June 1914

Look at the following eight statements about the events in Sarajevo on 28 June 1914. You may notice that the order of events is all mixed up *and* each statement contains two spelling mistakes.

- The Archduke is unhurt and his car speeds of to his meeting with the mayor at the town haul. He is furious.
- Franz Ferdinand and his wive arrive at Sarajevo raleway station at 9:28am.
- Immediately, Austria-Hungary blames Serba four killing the Archduke and plans an attack.
- The driver takes a rong turn and has to reverse back. At this moment, a Serbian terorist called Gavrilo Princip shoots and kills the Archduke and his wife.
- On there way to the town hall, a bomb is throne at the Archduke's car and the explosion injures several people.
- Princip is arressted and beeten up in jail.
- The Archduck and his wife get into a dark-grean, open-topped car.
- After his meating, the Archduke desides to visit the injured people in hospital.

a With a partner, work out the correct chronological order of events.

b In your book, copy out each statement (in the correct chronological order) and correct each spelling mistake as you write.

c The events of 28 June 1914 started a chain reaction that drew most of Europe into a terrible war. Design a flow diagram that charts how each country was dragged into war in the few weeks after 28 June.

TASK 4 Odd one out

Here are six groups of words or phrases. In each group there is an odd one out. What do the three words have in common that the fourth does not have? When you think you have found it, write a sentence or two about why you think it doesn't fit in with the others.

a France • Germany • Russia • Great Britain

b parapet • sandbag • duckboard • France

c Great Britain • Germany • Austria-Hungary • Turkey

d volunteer • conscription • recruitment • conscientious objector

e shell • hand grenade • bayonet • bullet

f mud • tank • machine gun • rifle

TASK 5 Great War anagrams

In the anagram list you will find:

- a new invention in 1916
- something that burns the skin
- another name for foot soldiers
- a specialist soldier who shoots at his enemy one at a time
- a small hand-held bomb
- big guns
- a device used to look over the parapet
- the name of the muddy wasteland between two lines of trenches
- something that can fire hundreds of bullets per minute
- an itchy problem
- the blade attached to the end of a rifle
- missiles fired by big guns
- the planks of wood used to cover up a muddy trench floor
- a painful disease
- a small trench-loving rodent

All the answers are given below, but the words and letters have been mixed up. Can you unravel them?

ENTCHR TFOO • PEIRSN • NHDA ARNDEEG

• LRATYRILE • ON AMN'S ADNL • OBDDCKSARU

• ISORPECEP • RTA • KTASN • TMDSAUR AGS

• AIMCHNE NUG • CELI • YNBTOAE • LHLSES

• IYAFNRNT

WHO RULES?

By the start of the twentieth century, power had moved from kings and queens and into the hands of politicians. But it was only a tiny percentage of the population who decided exactly who those politicians were. Over the course of the century, this gradually changed so that, in Britain, every person over the age of 18 had a say in the way it was ruled. Power moved from politicians... to the people!

1: When did Britain become a democracy?

MISSION OBJECTIVES

- To be able to explain what the words 'democracy' and 'reform' mean.
- To decide when Britain became truly democratic.

In 1900, Britain was considered to be a **democracy**. The word democracy comes from two Greek words: *'demos'*, which means 'people', and *'kratos'*, which means 'rule' or 'power'. In 1900, Britain was ruled by Parliament, which was chosen by the people in an election, and was therefore a democracy. Or was it? Less than 30% of the population was allowed to vote in these elections – and no women. This led people to question whether Britain really was a democracy and demand changes. So what were these **reforms**? When did they take place? And when did Britain truly become a democracy?

Who had the right to vote?

1900:
In order to vote you must:

Be male.
Be over 21 years old.
Have been living at the same address for at least 12 months.
Be a homeowner or renting accommodation for more than £10 per year (about £600 in today's money).

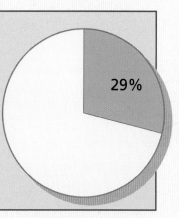

29%

1918:
In order to vote you must:

If male: Be over 21.
If female: Be over 30 and married to a homeowner or be over 30 and a homeowner.

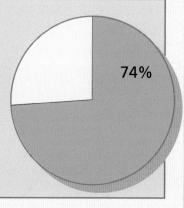

74%

1928:
In order to vote you must:

Be over 21.

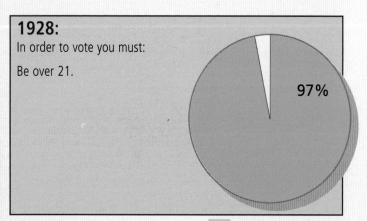

97%

1969:
In order to vote you must:

Be over 18.

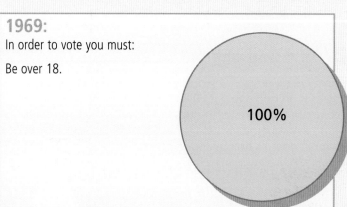

100%

Key: percentage of population over 18 that could vote.

Name: Dr J.G. Cash
Age: 45
Occupation: Family doctor
Place of residence: Bingham, Nottinghamshire, home owner
Time at this address: Ten months

Name: Miss Karen O'Rourke
Age: 32
Occupation: Fashion designer
Place of residence: Birmingham, lodger paying £20 per year rent (around £1200 in today's money)
Time at this address: Two years

Name: Mr Matthew Hill
Age: 18
Occupation: Telephone engineer
Place of residence: Bristol, lodger paying £8 per year rent (around £480 in today's money)
Time at this address: Three months

Name: Mrs Jessica Cash
Age: 41
Occupation: Baker
Place of residence: Bingham, Nottinghamshire, married to home owner
Time at this address: Ten months

Name: Mr Michael Steven
Age: 71
Occupation: Retired farmer
Place of residence: Highlands of Scotland
Time at this address: 71 years

Name: Miss Victoria Ball
Age: 26
Occupation: Lawyer
Place of residence: Greater Manchester
Time at this address: Three years

WISE-UP Words

democracy   reform

! FACT Workers of the world unite!
When working-class people were given the right to vote, it caused enormous changes to British politics. Their voting power meant that the Labour Party ('labour' is another word for 'work') quickly grew in size and popularity and, in 1924, the first Labour government was formed.

Work

1 Write out the following years as subtitles in your book:

   1900 • 1918 • 1928 • 1969

   Then study carefully the pie charts on page 48 and the character profiles on page 49. Under each year, write out the names of the people who were able to vote. Then write out the names of those who couldn't and explain why they didn't qualify for the vote.

2 Define the following terms:

   democracy • election • reform.

3 In what year, if any, do you think Britain became a proper democracy? Explain your answer carefully.

! FACT Votes for all! Well, nearly.
Not everybody is allowed to vote in a General Election. Members of the House of Lords, involuntary mental patients, prisoners and non-citizens (foreign workers) are banned from taking part.

___ MISSION ACCOMPLISHED? ___

• Could you tell someone what the words 'democracy' and 'reform' mean?

• Have you decided when Britain became a democracy?

In 1900, no woman in Britain – more than half of the population – had the right to vote. The nation was completely ruled by men from Parliament and women were expected to know their place. It was widely believed (by men of course – and some women, including Queen Victoria) that a woman's place was in the home, looking after her children and husband. If a woman had a job, they were always paid less than men and they were only allowed to work in positions deemed suitable by men. Some women obviously thought this was terribly unfair and decided to do something about it. So how did these women try and win the vote? What tactics did they use? And what finally won the vote for women?

2: How did women win the vote?

————————— MISSION OBJECTIVES —————————
- To explain who the suffragettes and suffragists were.
- To decide what finally won the vote for women.

Mothers for justice

By 1900, over 50,000 women were members of the National Union of Women's Suffrage Societies (suffrage is another word for vote). Known as **suffragists**, they collected petitions, wrote to Parliament and went on marches to highlight their cause. By 1905, they had got nowhere – and some of their members decided to change tactics. Known as the **suffragettes** and led by Emmeline Pankhurst and her daughters Christabel and Sylvia, their motto was 'deeds not words'.

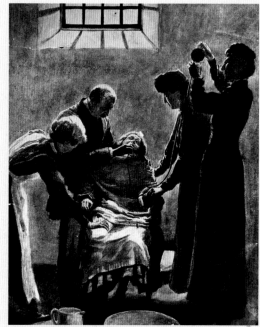

↳ **SOURCE B:** *Hunger strikers were force-fed meat and lime juice. The suffragettes tried to use this harsh treatment to gain sympathy for their cause.*

Spectacular suffragettes!

The Pankhursts decided that the best way to highlight their cause was to commit spectacular stunts that would guarantee an appearance in the newspapers. They disrupted political meetings, chained themselves to railings in Downing Street, pelted politicians with eggs and flour and smashed Parliament's windows with stones. They set fire to churches and railway stations, some poured acid on golf courses and others attacked MPs on the way to work. When they were arrested and fined, they refused to pay and were sent to prison – knowing this would make the papers. Soon, they were refusing all food in prison (hunger strike). This gave the Government a terrible choice – free the suffragettes or let them starve to death! At first, they released all hunger strikers, but soon decided to force-feed them instead. All this guaranteed that the suffragettes were front page news!

A WOMAN'S MIND MAGNIFIED

↳ **SOURCE A:** *This poster from 1900 shows what many men thought of women's mental abilities.*

'The activities of the suffragettes had reached a stage at which nothing was safe from their attacks. Churches were burnt, buildings and houses were destroyed, bombs were exploded, the police assaulted and meetings broken up. The feeling in the House [of Commons] caused by the actions of the suffragettes hardened opposition to their demands. The result was a defeat of their Bill by 47 votes, which the Government had previously promised to support.'

↳ SOURCE C: *The Speaker of the House of Commons writing about the events of 1913. Many MPs sympathised with the cause of votes for women, but didn't want to look as if they had given in to the suffragettes' demands.*

'What good did all this violent campaigning do us? For one thing our campaign made women's suffrage a matter of news – it had never been that before. Now the newspapers are full of us.'

↳ SOURCE D: *Written by Emmeline Pankhurst in My Own Story (1912).*

SOURCE F: *From a Government enquiry into the quality and output of women's war work.* ↱

↳ SOURCE E: *Here the Pankhursts are being prevented from approaching Buckingham Palace by the police.*

WISE-UP Words

munitions   suffragists suffragettes

War brings a truce

By 1914, women had still not won the right to vote. When the war broke out, the Pankhursts called off their campaign and asked supporters to help with the war effort. With more men leaving to become soldiers, women got the chance to do jobs they'd never done before. They became bus drivers, milk deliverers, police officers and car mechanics. Thousands of women worked in **munitions** factories too (see Source F). By the end of the war, many people felt women had earned the right to vote. In 1918 Parliament changed the voting laws to allow women over the age of 30 to vote.

Quality:
Metal – women's work better than men's • Aircraft woodwork – women equal to men • Bullet making – women equal to men • Shell making – women's work poorer than men's
Quantity:
Metal – women's production equal to men's • Aircraft woodwork – women's production equal to men's • Bullet making – women's production equal to men's; in some cases, women produce 20% more than men • Shell making – women's production behind men

Work

1 Define these words: sexist • suffragist • suffragette

2 Write a sentence explaining the suffragette motto – 'deeds not words'.

3 Read Source D. How did the suffragettes intend to win women's right to vote?

4 Read source C. How may the actions of the suffragettes have damaged support for their cause?

5 Which factor do you think was the most important for winning women's right to vote?
   • Women proved they were equal with war work.
   • The suffragettes' campaign highlighted the injustice.

Now write a few sentences explaining your choice.

! FACT No votes for women!

Not all women agreed with the Pankhursts. There was even a Women's Anti-Suffrage League that campaigned to stop women getting the vote. They were doomed to fail and by 1928, all women over the age of 21 had the right to vote. Women had finally got the same political rights as men.

___ MISSION ACCOMPLISHED? ___

• Could you tell someone what the difference was between a suffragist and a suffragette?

• Have you decided why women were finally granted the vote?

The Derby is one of the most famous horse races in the world. Every year, thousands of people – including the Royal Family – flock to Epsom Downs to watch the best horses and riders in the land battle it out for the prestigious trophy. It always gets plenty of coverage in the newspapers, which is why a suffragette named Emily Davison thought it would make the ideal opportunity for their next publicity stunt. Historians cannot agree over what happened next. What we do know is that Davison was knocked down and killed by the King's horse, Anmer, and that over 20,000 people attended her funeral. But did Davison deliberately kill herself to become a suffragette **martyr**? Did she misjudge the speed of the horses and die in a tragic accident? And what does the evidence say?

3: The Emily Davison mystery

MISSION OBJECTIVES
- To be able to describe the tragic and unusual event that took place at the 1913 Derby.
- To decide whether Emily Davison committed suicide or was killed in a tragic accident.

Read through the following pieces of evidence before finalising your conclusions in the Work section.

EVIDENCE A

Emily Davison's prison record. She was a very militant suffragette who believed in 'deeds not words'.

March 1909 One month in prison for obstruction (blocking a road)

September 1909 Two months for stone throwing

November 1909 One month for stone throwing

November 1910 One month for breaking windows

January 1912 Six months for setting fire to post boxes

November 1912 Ten days for assaulting a vicar who she mistook for a Member of Parliament

EVIDENCE B

From a book by G Colmore, *The Life of Emily Davison*, 1913. The Suffragette Summer Festival was a week-long meeting of hundreds of suffragettes.

'She was able to go to the [Suffragette Summer] Festival on the opening day, Tuesday 3 June. Emily was never brighter than on that day. She stayed long at the fair and said she should come every day, "except tomorrow. I'm going to the Derby tomorrow".

"What are you going to do?"

"Ah ha!"

It was her usual answer… when she had planned something. "Look in the evening paper," she added, "and you will see something." '

EVIDENCE C

From an eyewitness, John Ervine, who stood near to Emily Davison on the day.

'The King's horse, Anmer, came up and Ms Davison went towards it. She put up her hand, but whether it was to catch hold of the reins or protect herself, I don't know. It was all over in a few seconds. The horse knocked her over with great force and then stumbled and fell, throwing the jockey violently onto the ground. Both he and Ms Davison were bleeding a lot. I feel sure that Ms Davison meant to stop the horse and that she didn't go onto the course thinking the race was over.'

EVIDENCE D

From Sylvia Pankhurst's *The Suffrage Movement: An Intimate Account of Persons and Ideals*, published in 1931.

'Her friend declared that she would not have died without writing a farewell message to her mother. Yet she sewed the [suffragette] flags inside her coat as though to make sure that no mistake could be made as to her motive when her body was examined.'

DAILY SKETCH.

No. 1,333—THURSDAY, JUNE 5, 1913. Liverpool: 46-47, Shoe-lane, E.C. Manchester: Withy-grove, Telephone:—Editorial and Publishing: 6676 Holborn. Advertisements: 10,723 Central. (Registered as a Newspaper.) ONE HALFPENNY.

HISTORY'S MOST WONDERFUL DERBY: FIRST HORSE DISQUALIFIED: A 100 TO 1 CHANCE WINS: SUFFRAGETTE NEARLY KILLED BY THE KING'S COLT.

WISE-UP Words

martyr

EVIDENCE E

The front page of a newspaper published the day after the Derby and before Davison had died of her injuries. Look closely at the photograph. Why do you think there were so few reliable witnesses despite the thousands of people who attended the race?

EVIDENCE F

Part of the official report surrounding Davison's death. She had asked for the flags a few days before the race meeting.

FOUND ON THE BODY OF EMILY DAVISON

OFFICIAL POLICE REPORT

2 large suffragette flags (green, white and purple stripes) pinned inside the back of her coat; 1 purse (containing three shillings, eight pence and three farthings); 8 postage stamps; 1 key; 1 helper pass for the Suffragette Summer Festival, Kensington, London; 1 notebook; 1 handkerchief; some envelopes and writing paper; 1 race card; 1 return railway ticket.

EVIDENCE G

Adapted from the writings of Emily Davison herself. These events occurred in Holloway Prison, two weeks before her release after a six-month sentence for arson.

'As soon as I got the chance I threw myself over the prison railings. The idea in my mind was that one big tragedy would save many others; but the netting prevented any injury. Then I threw myself down on an iron staircase, a distance of 10 to 13 metres, but the netting caught me again. I felt I had only one chance left, so I hurled myself head first down the staircase, a distance of three metres. I landed on my head with a mighty thud and was knocked out. When I recovered I was in agony.'

Work

1 Copy this table into your book:

Tragic accident	Political martyr

Write a brief description of each piece of evidence in the column in which you think it belongs.

2 Now imagine you are part of a Government enquiry team that has been given the job of deciding how and why Emily Davison died. You must explain your answer clearly and outline the evidence that has led you to your conclusion. Good luck!

——MISSION ACCOMPLISHED?——

- Could you describe the shocking tragedy that took place during the 1913 Derby?
- Have you decided if Emily Davison was a political martyr or the victim of a tragic accident?

Different ways to run a country

MISSION OBJECTIVES

- To be able to explain the differences between a democracy and a dictatorship.
- To be able to list the main features of both.

No two countries in the world are run in exactly the same way. Britain has different laws and ways of doing things from France, which in turn is run differently from the USA. It's not just the laws that are different; there are also different punishments (some countries have the death penalty, for example), currencies, systems of education and healthcare – even the side of the road you must drive on! But despite these differences that have evolved over the centuries, it is possible to place most countries into one of two categories. So what are these categories? What are the main differences between the two? And which would you prefer to live in?

Post-war problems

In the 1920s and 1930s, countries argued about which was the best way to organise their countries. These disagreements built up and eventually spilled over into another war. In order to fully understand the build up to the Second World War, it is important that you know the main features of, and differences between, a **democracy** and a **dictatorship**.

This Government is a joke!

I completely disagree with you – but I'd fight to the death to defend your right to say it!

Type of Government

DEMOCRACY

Origins Started in Ancient Greece. Developed gradually over hundreds of years, mainly in Europe and the USA.

Beliefs Ordinary people have a say in how their country is governed. They vote in regular elections in which there are several political parties to choose from. The people are represented by the organisations they elect – for example, Parliament or councils.

Comments The people have a number of 'freedoms' or rights:

- freedom of speech (the right to say what you think)
- freedom of information (the right to read, listen to and watch what you want)
- freedom of belief (the right to worship any religion)
- freedom in law (the right to a fair trial – if arrested, 'you have the right to remain silent' too!)
- freedom of association (the right to join or form a political party, join a trade union or any other organisation – even the Boy Scouts!).

Democracies in the 1920s and 1930s: Britain, France and the USA

Democracies to dominate?

As the Great War was won by democratic countries, it was hoped that democracy would spread to most countries in the world. Unfortunately, many countries were in such a mess and their people so desperate, that they had no patience for politicians to argue about how to sort it out.

More and more people began to think that what they needed was a strong leader to take control and make all of the decisions – a dictator! Incredibly, between 1919 and 1939 over 30 countries became dictatorships. It was the rule of some of these dictators that brought about the Second World War.

Type of Government
DICTATORSHIP

Origins For thousands of years, some people have tried to totally control others. The controllers are usually backed up by large numbers of supporters and lots of weapons.

Beliefs Ordinary people have no say in how their country is run. There are no regular elections because the country is run by one political party or one man – the dictator (usually helped by his 'friends' and his army)

Comments People have very few 'freedoms' or rights:

- there is no free speech (if they criticise their leaders, they are likely to be arrested)
- there is no freedom of information (the dictator controls the newspapers, books, magazines, films and so on)
- not all religions are allowed – if any!
- there is no legal freedom (the police can arrest whom they want, when they want and keep them in jail without trial)
- people can only join groups or associations allowed by the dictatorship.

Dictatorships from the 1920s and 1930s:
Italy, Spain, USSR (Russia) and Nazi Germany

NO ELECTIONS
(this year or any other)
Signed: *The Dictator*

This Government is a joke!

WISE-UP Words

democracy
dictatorship

Work

1 **a** In your own words, explain what a democracy is. You must use no more than 50 words.

 b In your own words, explain what a dictatorship is. Again, use no more than 50 words.

 c Do you live in a democracy or a dictatorship? Explain how you made your decision.

2 Work with a partner. One of you must choose to describe a dictatorship, the other a democracy. Using only ten words each, explain to your partner the political system you have chosen. They must fully understand what a dictatorship or a democracy is by the end of your presentation.

- Use drawings to help you.
- Perhaps you could mime some of the features of your system.
- Which words will you use? Remember, you're only allowed to use ten words to describe your choice of democracy or dictatorship.
- Set aside an amount of time to prepare!

3 What kind of country would you prefer to live in? Explain your answer very carefully, making sure you use capital letters and full stops.

──MISSION ACCOMPLISHED?──

- Could you explain the differences between a dictatorship and a democracy to someone?

55

Two types of dictatorship

MISSION OBJECTIVES

- To be able to explain what fascism and communism are.
- To be aware of the countries in which these political theories took hold.

Britain, France and the USA were the major victorious nations in the Great War. It was hoped that other countries around the world would become democracies too. But many countries rejected democracy and decided to rule their countries by dictatorship instead. You might assume that all the dictatorships would gang up together against the democracies, but not all dictatorships are the same. So just which countries became dictatorships? What were the two types of dictatorship called? And what are the differences between the two?

A communist dictatorship

Communism is a theory about how to organise society that was dreamt up by a German man called Karl Marx. He believed that, like human beings themselves, society was evolving.

Marx believed that when the workers took control of society, everybody would be equal (men and women) and everything would be shared. There would be no different classes, no very rich people and no very poor people. There would be no private property and the Government would run farms, factories and stores for the benefit of all people. There would be no need for money as the Government would provide everybody with everything they needed and all people would lead the same simple lives. Marx believed that the whole world would eventually live under the **communist** system.

Communists, like Karl Marx, believed societies were evolving and that workers would soon seize power. This, they believed, would lead to a better and fairer society.

↵ **SOURCE A:** *Marx died in London in 1883. An inscription on his grave reads: 'Workers of all lands unite'. In the years following his death, Marx's ideas became more and more popular around the world – especially with poor people!*

↳ **SOURCE B:** *The flag of the USSR. In 1922, Russia, together with the smaller countries it controlled, was renamed the Union of Soviet Socialist Republics (USSR). 'Soviet' is the Russian word for council and 'Socialist' is another word for communist. The flag itself tells a story: the red background represents the revolution and the golden star represents power. This power is now controlled by the factory workers (who are represented by the hammer) and the farm workers (who are represented by the sickle). In reality, the power was controlled by one man – the leader of the Communist Party.*

CASE STUDY 1: THE USSR

The first country in the world to adopt the communist system was Russia. During the Great War, nearly two million Russian soldiers were killed and there were massive food shortages in the cities. In 1917 ordinary Russians who believed in the communist way of life rebelled against their King, Tsar Nicholas II. After a bitter civil war, the entire Russian Royal Family was killed and Russia officially became a communist country.

However, although Marx had written a great deal about how a communist society would work, he didn't write exactly how one would be set up. Not everyone in Russia was keen on the changes that were taking place so the communists forced people to be equal and to share. They ran the country as a dictatorship.

- No other political parties were allowed to exist, only the Communist Party.

- Newspapers, books, films and radio broadcasts were all controlled by the communists. Any person who spoke out against this was an 'enemy of the state' and sent to prison (or executed). Millions of people 'disappeared' in communist Russia.

- Nobody was allowed to have any open religious beliefs. Only the communist way of life was to be worshipped.

- All work, housing, healthcare and education was controlled by the communists. Jobs, houses, hospitals and schools were provided for all Russians. The state owned everything... and provided for everyone.

For many Russians, this was a much better way of life than they were used to. Everything was provided for them so long as they were prepared to work and didn't complain! However, communism terrified people in other countries – especially the rich and members of royal families. Their worst nightmare was that communism would spread to their country. As a result, the USSR had few friends around the world and became more and more isolated.

A fascist dictatorship

CASE STUDY 2: ITALY

Italy had fought on the winning side in the Great War. Over 600,000 Italians had been killed and the Government hoped that this sacrifice would be rewarded with land from the losing countries. They were wrong and Italy gained hardly any new land at all.

By 1919, Italy had seemed to have lost its way and the people were suffering from high unemployment and rising food prices. Bands of armed ex-soldiers roamed the countryside stealing and murdering. Those Italians that weren't suffering were terrified that communists might take over and take their money and belongings off them.

Increasingly, Italians began to turn to a young politician called Benito Mussolini – a former soldier and schoolteacher. He promised to bring discipline, glory and pride back to Italy, but at a price. He had a theory called **fascism** – from the Italian word 'fascio', meaning bundle – and formed the Fascist Party in 1919. The idea behind fascism was that the country would be much stronger if everybody worked together rather than for themselves or the class they belonged to.

↰ **SOURCE C:** *Italy's fascist flag. The eagle is a traditional symbol of power and alertness, whilst the bundle the eagle is clutching is called a 'fasces'. The bundle of sticks represents strength in number, unity and law – the axe symbolises power.*

SOURCE D: *Mussolini, Italy's fascist leader, mounted huge displays, with uniforms and special salutes. Mussolini once said, 'A minute on the battlefield is worth a lifetime of peace... better to live one day like a lion than a hundred years like a sheep'.* ↴

CREDERE OBBEDIRE

In reality, a **fascist** government controlled every aspect of someone's life (that's right; another type of dictatorship!). Education, newspapers, films, radio and even sport all carried the same message: the needs of one person are not important; it's what Italy needs that counts. People were still free to run their own businesses and make money, but there were tight controls on the workers and strikes were banned. In return, the Fascist Party would 'look after' Italy and build roads and railways, which gave people jobs. Those still unemployed could join the army, which would be greatly increased in size. Unlike communists, fascists didn't believe in equality. They believed that men were superior to women and that some races and nations were superior to others. Mussolini argued that Italians were superior and used the ancient Romans as evidence to support this. People seemed to like being told they were the best and the Fascist Party got more and more popular.

In 1922, Mussolini (who wanted to be called Il Duce – the Leader) announced he was marching to Rome to take over the country. His supporters – known as blackshirts because of their uniforms – marched with him and made a strong impression on the King. He gave in and made Mussolini Italy's new Prime Minister. Soon, all opposition was banned and communists were beaten up or murdered.

Mussolini's tactics didn't go unnoticed by a 34-year-old up-and-coming politician living in Germany. His name was Adolf Hitler. Perhaps fascism could make Germany great too?

WISE-UP Words

communism
communist
fascism fascist

⤷ SOURCE E: *Mussolini held enormous rallies like this one to make fascism and Italy appear strong.*

Work

1 Match up the names on the left with the correct description on the right.

Fascism	The fascist leader of Italy who took control in 1922.
Communism	A German, living in London, who first thought up the theory of communism.
Mussolini	From 1922, this was the new name for Russia and the areas it controlled.
USSR	One of the symbols of Italy's Fascist Party.
Karl Marx	A political system where all people are equal and all property and business is owned by the state and run for the benefit of all.
Fasces	A political system where the government controls all aspects of people's lives in an attempt to make the nation stronger than others.

2 a Find two similarities and two differences between the dictatorships of the USSR and Italy.

b Why were richer people across Europe worried about the spread of communism?

c Why did Mussolini become popular in Italy after the end of the Great War?

3 a Draw a neat copy of the communist flag in your book.

b Underneath, write a sentence or two about it.

c Draw a copy of the fascist flag in your book.

d Underneath, write a sentence or two about it.

___MISSION ACCOMPLISHED?___

- Could you tell somebody the main features of a communist dictatorship?
- Could you tell somebody the main features of a fascist dictatorship?
- Do you know which countries became communist and fascist dictatorships?

Adolf Hitler: choirboy, artist, tramp, soldier, politician

—————————— MISSION OBJECTIVES ——————————
• To be able to remember at least five facts and dates about Adolf Hitler's life up to 1933.

Adolf Hitler is one of the most infamous men ever to have lived. He is known mainly for his association with World War Two and his hatred of the Jews. But his time as leader of Germany only covers the last 12 years of his life! What about his early life? What was he like as a young man? How and why did he get involved in politics? And why was this Austrian (yes, he wasn't German at all) chosen to be Germany's leader in 1933?

CHOIRBOY

Adolf Hitler was born in 1889 in Braunau, a small town in Austria. His dad was a hard-drinking bully who worked as a postman. He died when Hitler was 14. His mum spoiled Hitler and insisted he went to a respectable school in order to get good grades and a well-paid job. But he failed his examinations and left school at 16. For the next two years he read books, listened to music and painted pictures. His mum died when he was 17. After her death, he left his home town and travelled to Vienna, the capital city of Austria, looking for work.

↲ SOURCE A: *Hitler (circled) at school in 1899, aged ten. He was in the local church choir for five years.*

'He always wanted his own way. He was boastful, bad-tempered and lazy... He ignored advice and got angry if he was told off.'

↳ SOURCE B: *One of Hitler's teachers said this about him after he left school (from* The Twentieth Century, *by J D Clare, 1993).*

SOURCE C: *A photograph of Hitler's mother, Klara. Her death due to breast cancer affected Hitler deeply. It is claimed he carried a photograph of her wherever he went and held it in his hand when he committed suicide in 1945. Klara had five children in total, but only Adolf and his younger sister, Paula, lived beyond childhood. When Hitler became leader of Germany, Paula changed her surname to Wolff (Adolf's nickname) to avoid any unwanted attention. She had no children and died in 1960.* ↱

ARTIST AND TRAMP

In 1907, Hitler arrived in Vienna hoping to 'make it big' as an artist. He tried to get into the Vienna Art Academy, one of Europe's best art colleges, but failed to pass the entrance exam. Without any qualifications, he ended up living in a hostel for tramps.

For the next five years, Hitler earned money any way he could – cleaning windows, painting houses, drawing and selling postcards in the street. He grew to hate people of foreign races, particularly rich Jewish people. He felt that foreigners were ruining Austria by taking over all the jobs and introducing their way of life.

'On the very first day there sat next to the bed that had been given to me a man who had nothing on except an old torn pair of trousers – Hitler. His clothes were being cleaned of lice, since for days he had been wandering about without a roof over his head.'

↳ **SOURCE D:** *Another tramp in the hostel remembers Hitler's arrival (from* Weimar Germany, *by Josh Brooman, 1985).*

↳ **SOURCE E:** *One of Hitler's early paintings. He could draw buildings well but didn't draw people very well at all – he certainly wasn't talented enough to get into art college.*

Report on Lance Corporal Hitler, Third Company (volunteers)

Hitler has been with the regiment since 1914 and has fought splendidly in all the battles in which he has taken part.

As a messenger, he was always ready to carry messages in the most difficult positions at great risk to his own life.

He received the Iron Cross (Second Class) on 2 December 1914 and I now feel he is worthy of receiving the Iron Cross (First Class).

↥ SOURCE F: *Hitler as a soldier in the Great War. Hitler said that war was the greatest of all experiences.*

SOLDIER

Hitler left Austria in 1913 to avoid being called into the army. He went to live in Munich, Germany. When the Great War started in 1914, he decided to be a soldier after all, and volunteered to join the German army.

Hitler worked all through the war as a messenger in the trenches. It was a dangerous job and he was wounded several times, once when a piece of metal sliced through his cheek. He nearly died. He won six medals for bravery, in total, including the 'Iron Cross, First Class', one of the highest awards a German soldier could win.

Hitler was in hospital when the war ended, having been temporarily blinded in a gas attack. He wrote that he buried his head in his pillow and cried when he heard the news. He blamed Germany's surrender on weak politicians… and, of course, the Jews.

↵ SOURCE G: *A report of Hitler by his commanding officer during the Great War. The Iron Cross was the highest medal awarded in the German army.*

FROM POLITICIAN TO PRISONER

Hitler stayed in the army after the war, working as a V-man, spying on new political groups to see if they were dangerous. One group he investigated wasn't dangerous at all – they had few members and funds of only 7.5 marks – about £4. They were called the German Workers' Party.

After a few months, Hitler decided to join this new political party. He liked many of its ideas and became member number 555. Before long, he was making speeches and writing articles to local newspapers about the party's beliefs and ideas for a better Germany. Hitler spoke passionately about the need for Germany to get itself a stronger leader who would get revenge for the defeat in the Great War. He also claimed that the Jews were 'germs' that must be 'destroyed'. By 1921, Hitler was running the party – and he changed its name to the National Socialist German Workers' Party – or Nazi Party for short!

Soon Hitler made the **swastika** the symbol of the Nazis and used brown-shirted 'storm troopers' to beat up the people who disagreed with him when he made speeches (see Sources H and I).

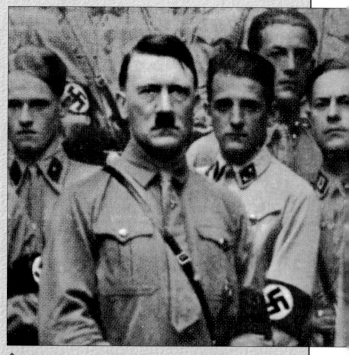

↥ SOURCE H: *The Nazi flag. The symbol in the centre is known as the 'crooked cross' or the swastika. It became Germany's official symbol in 1935.*

↥ SOURCE I: *Hitler pictured with his storm troopers. The 'brownshirts', as they were nicknamed, were Hitler's own private army of thugs that beat up people who criticised him.*

Hitler's views made him popular and in 1923 he felt confident enough to try to take over Germany. He tried to start a revolution in Munich – one of Germany's largest cities – hoping it would spread to other places. It failed and Hitler was put in prison for treason. While in prison, he wrote a book about his life and his ideas called *Mein Kampf* (German for 'my struggle'). When Hitler was released in 1924 (for good behaviour), his book started to get him a reputation as a man whose ideas might be able to put Germany 'on the right track' again. And, while many ordinary Germans didn't quite understand (or agree) with all his views, many certainly liked his ideas for making Germany great again.

↵ **SOURCE J:** *The front cover of an English translation of* Mein Kampf, *Hitler's manifesto written while he was in prison, which was published in 18 weekly parts.*

FROM POLITICIAN TO LEADER

When Hitler was let out of prison he went back to running the Nazi party. By 1928, Hitler and the Nazis were very well known but they were still only the eighth largest political party in Germany. Then, in 1929, world trade began to slow down and a 'Great Depression' started. This means that countries stopped buying and selling to each other. German factories closed and millions lost their jobs. Lots of people lost their homes and in big cities the streets were full of starving people looking for work. Soon people, including Hitler, started to promise solutions to all Germany's problems. 'Vote for me' was Hitler's message, 'and I'll provide you with work and bread'. As more and more people lost their jobs, the Nazis got more and more votes. By 1932, the Nazis were the largest political party and Hitler became Germany's Chancellor (or Prime Minister) in January 1933.

'He is... one of the greatest speakers of the century. Adolf Hitler enters a hall. He sniffs the air. For a minute he gropes, feels his way, senses the atmosphere. Suddenly he bursts forward. His words go like an arrow to his target, he touches each private wound on the raw... telling it what it most wants to hear.'

↰ **SOURCE K:** *A Nazi election poster of 1932. The writing means 'Our last hope: HITLER'. Who do you think this poster was aimed at?*

↵ **SOURCE L:** *Otto Strasser, a German, wrote this after hearing Hitler speak. Strasser hated Hitler but recognised his excellent speaking skills.*

WISE-UP Words

swastika

Work ⌇.

1 a Make a timeline of 12 important events in Hitler's life up to 1933. The first event in his life has been started for you:

1889: Born in Braunau, a small town in Austria. His father…

b Choose two events in Hitler's life that you would regard as important turning points. Explain why each event you have chosen was so important.

2 Answer the following questions in full sentences.

a Why did Hitler fail to get a place in the Vienna Art Academy?

b Whilst living in Vienna, why did Hitler begin to hate foreigners, especially Jews?

c In your opinion, was Hitler a good soldier? Give reasons for your answer.

d What was a V-man?

e Hitler always said he was the seventh member of the German Workers' Party, even though he wasn't. Even his membership card showed he wasn't one of the earliest members! So why do you think Hitler always claimed he was such an early member?

f What was the swastika?

g Who were the 'brownshirts' and how did they help Hitler?

h Write down three facts about *Mein Kampf*.

i In your own words, explain how Hitler's Nazi Party went from the eighth most popular political party in Germany in 1928 to Germany's most popular political group in 1932.

——MISSION ACCOMPLISHED?——

- Can you recall five key dates in Adolf Hitler's life and say exactly what happened on each of these?

What was life like in Hitler's Germany?

MISSION OBJECTIVES

• To understand how life under the Nazi dictatorship differs from the democratic system we live in today.

Adolf Hitler was asked to become Chancellor by the President of Germany, Paul von Hindenburg. At this time, the President was the most powerful man in Germany and the Chancellor was his chief minister. When President Hindenburg died one year later, Hitler made himself both Chancellor AND President. He started to call himself **Führer** (supreme leader) and immediately got all members of the army to swear an oath (promise) of loyalty to him.

'I swear by God that by this sacred oath I will give complete obedience to the Führer Adolf Hitler... and am ready as a brave soldier to risk my life at any time for him.'

↳ **SOURCE A:** *The Oath of Loyalty, 1934. Note that the promise is made to Hitler, not Germany. Why do you think Hitler felt this oath was one of his first priorities?*

Hitler quickly started to change things. Having worked so hard to get into power, he was determined to stay there. His secret police force, the dreaded **Gestapo**, hunted out anyone who might be against Hitler. They had the power to arrest and imprison people without trial and set up a web of informers who would report any 'moaners' to them. Children were encouraged to report their parents or teachers if they spoke out against the Führer and, by 1935, every block of flats or housing estate had a 'local ruler' who listened for negative comments. By 1939, there were well over 100,000 people in prison for 'anti-Hitler crimes'... they were known as Enemies of the State.

'The Nazi Government must have total control over every aspect of life. Government will be in the hands of one person, a genius, a hero, with total responsibility for culling on behalf of a pure race in the national interest.'

↳ **SOURCE B:** *Part of a Nazi press release from 1934. 'Culling' means to kill or remove any unwanted people.*

SOURCE C: *Based on an interview with a former inmate of one of Hitler's prisons. They were known as* **concentration camps.** ↱

Who was on Hitler's hate list?

Hitler was determined to crush anyone who didn't fully support him. He once declared that any opponents would 'have their skulls bashed in'. However, most of Hitler's hatred was based on race. He believed that humans were divided into races and some races were better or superior to others. Hitler said the best races were the 'pure' ones that haven't interbred and 'mixed' with others. He added that the master race of pure Germans – or Aryans – were the rightful rulers of Europe. He felt that superior races (like the Germans) had the right to dominate 'inferior' races, such as Jews, gypsies, Slavs (such as Russians) and black people.

People who were disabled in any way or mentally impaired were also targets for Hitler because they damaged the purity of the German race. Hitler thought these people should be eliminated so their illnesses and disabilities could not pass on to their children. 300,000 men and women were compulsorily **sterilised** in families with **hereditary** illnesses; 720,000 mentally ill people were gassed and 5000 mentally impaired babies killed.

'The prisons were full. Tramps, prostitutes and beggars were a common sight, but there were other prisoners too. Anyone who refused to join the army was sent to prison and so were people who'd been a member of any other political party except the Nazis. Trade union leaders were also inside and I once met a woman who had been reported for telling a joke at the Führer's expense. Another favourite tactic of the Gestapo was to accuse a man or woman of being homosexual – there were many in prison accused of this "crime".'

Hitler reserved his greatest hatred for the Jews. He saw them as an inferior race that cared more about themselves than the greatness of Germany. He thought they were involved in a great conspiracy to take over the world and blamed them for Germany's loss in the Great War. Jews, Hitler said, must therefore be destroyed. Sources D, E and F show how Jews were persecuted in Nazi Germany in the 1930s.

↰ **SOURCE D:** *A photograph of a park bench in Berlin. The sign on the bench reads: 'Not for Jews'. Sometimes whole villages and towns displayed signs which read: 'Jews enter this place at their own risk'!*

LAWS AGAINST JEWS, 1933–1939

March 1933 All Jewish lawyers and judges sacked.

April 1933 All Jews banned from any sports clubs. All Jewish teachers sacked.

September 1933 'Race studies' introduced in German schools.

January 1934 All Jewish shops marked with a yellow star of David – a symbol of the Jewish religion – or the word *Juden* (German for 'Jew'). Soldiers to stand outside shops turning people away.

September 1935 Jews not allowed to vote. Marriages between Jews and non-Jews banned.

January 1936 No Jew allowed to own any electrical equipment (including cameras), bicycles, typewriters or music records.

July 1938 Jewish doctors sacked.

August 1938 Male Jews must add the name 'Israel' and female Jews must add the name 'Sara' to their first names.

November 1938 Jewish children banned from German schools.

December 1938 Jewish and non-Jewish children forbidden to play together. Jews banned from using swimming pools.

April 1939 Jews can be evicted from their homes for no reason.

September 1939 Jews no longer allowed out of their homes between 8:00pm and 6:00am.

Work

1 Write a sentence or two to explain the following words:

Führer • Gestapo • concentration camp • sterilisation

2 Look at Source E.

a Write down five laws or policies that made life uncomfortable or difficult for German Jews.

b Next to each of your choices, explain why you think it was introduced by the Nazis. One has been done for you:

January 1934: Soldiers stood outside Jewish shops and told people not to shop there. I think this was introduced to ruin Jewish businesses – if they had to close their shops, they might leave Germany altogether.

↲ **SOURCE E:** *Each of these laws was designed to make life more and more uncomfortable for German Jews. Hitler saw them as an inferior race that cared more about themselves than the greatness of Germany. There were approximately 500,000 Jews in Germany in 1934 (about 1% of the population). By the time Hitler stopped Jews from leaving the country (1941), nearly 80% had already left for new lives in other places.*

↰ **SOURCE F:** *This humiliating photograph of a married couple was taken in 1933. It shows an Aryan woman and a Jewish man being bullied by the Nazis. The woman's sign reads 'I live with a pig and only go with Jews'. Her husband's sign reads 'Instead of Jews, I only take young German girls to my room'.*

	Lesson 1	Lesson 2	Lesson 3	Dinner	Lesson 4	Lesson 5	Lesson 6
BOYS	German	History/Geography	Eugenics/Nazi theory	**Sport and music clubs**	Physics and Chemistry	PE: boxing, football and marching	Maths
GIRLS	German	History/Geography	Eugenics/Nazi theory		Biology/health and sex education	Cookery	Maths

⤴ **SOURCE G:** *A typical timetable for a day's education at a mixed school in Berlin, 1936.* **Eugenics** *is the scientific study of how to improve races. What major differences do you notice about the education process for the different sexes?*

Question 46:

The Jews are aliens in Germany. In 1933, there were 66,060,000 people living in Germany. Of this total, 499,862 were Jews. What is the percentage of aliens in Germany?

Question 52:

A bomber aircraft on take off carries 144 bombs, each weighing ten kilos. The aircraft bombs a town full of Jews. On take off with all bombs on board and a fuel tank containing 1000 kilos of fuel, the aircraft weighs about eight tons. When it returns from its victorious mission, there are still 230 kilos of fuel left. What is the weight of the aircraft when empty?

Question 67:

It costs, on average, four RM (reichmarks) a day to keep a cripple or a mentally ill person in hospital. There are currently 300,000 mentally ill, lunatics and so on in Germany's hospitals. How much would the German Government save if they got rid of all these people?

⤴ **SOURCE H:** *Youngsters were* **indoctrinated** *(brainwashed) to think like Nazis. Textbooks were rewritten to get across the Nazi message. Even teachers had to belong to the German Nazi Teachers' League and were made to put across Nazi ideas in their lessons – or face the sack. These questions are adapted and translated from a German textbook during the Nazi period.*

Why were the young so important to Hitler?

Hitler took great trouble to make sure that young people were loyal to him and the Nazi Party.

He realised that in future he may have to call on these people to put up with hardships, to fight and perhaps die for him. It was important therefore that young people thought that Hitler and the Nazis were the best thing that ever happened to Germany. He needed young men who were 'as fast as a greyhound, as tough as leather and as hard as steel'. He wanted tough, strong, practical girls too... but for an entirely different reason – they were to be the wives and mothers of a future generation of soldiers.

⤴ **SOURCE I:** *A picture from a German school textbook in 1935. Children were taught to recognise Jews at a glance. Look for: i) the way the Jewish children and adult (on the left) are drawn. Why have they been drawn this way? ii) the reaction of the other children to the Jews' departure; iii) the Jewish boy on the right pulling another child's hair – why has this been included?*

Outside school, young people had to belong to the Hitler Youth Organisation. From the ages of six to eighteen, boys and girls spent a few evenings a week and several weekends a year learning new skills and being taught how to show their loyalty to Hitler. Boys tended to learn military skills (model making, shooting practice and hiking) whilst girls learnt about cookery, housework and motherhood.

↩ **SOURCE J:** *A photograph of a smiling Hitler and a six-year-old member of the Hitler Youth Organisation.*

SOURCE K: *An extract from the guidebook of the Hitler Youth Organisation. It describes what a ten to fourteen year-old boy had to do to get an 'Achievement Award'. Would you be tough enough?* ↴

Work ‿‿‿‿‿.

1 Why do you think Hitler and the Nazis put so much effort into organising the lives of young people?

2 Look at Source G.

  a In what ways is this timetable different to school timetables today?

  b Why do you think boys and girls were taught different things?

  c What is 'eugenics' and why do you think the Nazis put this on every school's timetable?

3 Look at Source H.

  a In what ways are these questions different to ones that appear in your maths books today?

  b Why do you think questions like these appeared in German textbooks?

4 a Draw up two posters, both showing how the Nazis were trying to organise the lives of young people. One poster should be aimed at the young people themselves. The other should be for their parents.

  b In what ways are the posters different?

1) Complete the following lessons:
  i) Life of Hitler
  ii) Germans abroad
  iii) Germany's rightful place in the world
  iv) National holidays of the German people
  v) Five flag oaths
  vi) Six Hitler Youth songs

2) Complete the following athletic tests:
  i) Run 60 metres in 10 seconds
  ii) Long jump 3.25 metres
  iii) Throw a small leather ball 35 metres
  iv) Pull up on a bar twice
  v) Somersault backwards twice
  vi) Swim 100 metres

3) Hiking and camping tests:
  i) A day's hike of 15 kilometres
  ii) Camp in a tent for three days
  iii) Put up a two-man tent and take part in putting up a twelve-man tent
  iv) Make a cooking pit and find water for cooking
  v) Know the names of the most important trees
  vi) Use the stars to find your place on a map

4) Target practice:
Hit a bull's eye on a target at a distance of eight metres with an air gun

Was it a sexist society?

In Hitler's eyes, a woman's most important job was to have children – lots of them, especially boys.

Women were encouraged to stay at home and be good wives and mothers. Going out and getting qualifications and a professional job was frowned upon as it might get in the way of producing lots of babies. Loans were given to newly married couples – the equivalent of a year's wages – to encourage them to have children. On the birth of a first child, they could keep a quarter of the money. On the birth of another they could keep the second quarter. They could keep the third quarter on the birth of a third child and keep the lot on the birth of a fourth. Every year, on 12 August, the birthday of Hitler's mother, the Motherhood Medal was awarded to women who had the most children.

'All single and married women up to the age of 35 who do not already have four children should produce four children by racially pure German men. Whether or not these men are married is not important. Every family that already has four children must set the husband free for this action.'

⌐ **SOURCE L:** *A Nazi law written in 1943. It never came into effect.*

How did Hitler please ordinary Germans?

The vast majority of ordinary Germans did well out of Hitler's rule between 1933 and 1939. Right from the start, he said he would provide work, bread and restore national pride. He said he would make sure that Germany regained its rightful place in the world.

In 1933, there were six million people out of work, but this figure had reduced to 200,000 by 1938. The Nazis provided work by building roads, schools, hospitals, railways... and by making the army bigger and building tanks, fighter planes and battleships. Hitler started to get back land Germany had lost after its defeat in the Great War and many Germans felt a sense of pride in this. If the German people were prepared to ignore some of the crueller things happening to a minority of people, and not complain too loudly, it seemed that life was better under Hitler's leadership.

⌐ **SOURCE M:** *A Nazi poster of 1937 showing what Nazis thought a woman's role in life should be. Look for: i) the plain, simple image of a woman breastfeeding her baby. Makeup and wearing trousers were frowned upon by the Nazis. Permed or dyed hair was banned and slimming was discouraged because it was not thought to be good for childbearing; ii) her husband working on the land, providing for Germany whilst his wife takes care of things at home; iii) the church in the background. Hitler thought the ideal woman should stick to the 'three Ks' – Kinder, Kirche and Kuche (children, church and cooking).*

❚❚ PAUSE for Thought
Why do you think Hitler wanted so many boys?

SOURCE N: *Hitler introduced a savings scheme to help millions of ordinary Germans save up for an affordable car. The 'people's car' or 'Volkswagen' was launched in 1938. Built by Ferdinand Porsche (who went on to design sports cars), it was based on a sketch by Hitler himself. It was purposely designed to look like a beetle because Hitler was a big admirer of the insect's fighting nature. In this photograph, Hitler is inspecting the first ever model. But the whole savings scheme was a big swindle. Not one ordinary German citizen received their car; the money was used to buy weapons!*

'I don't know how to describe the emotions that swept over me as I heard Adolf Hitler... when he spoke of the disgrace of Germany I was ready to spring on any enemy... I forgot everything but Hitler. Then, glancing around, I saw that the thousands around me were drawn to him like a magnet as well.'

SOURCE O: *The feelings of a man who attended a Nazi rally in 1937.*

How did Hitler get his message across?

Hitler was determined to control the way people thought. The Nazis controlled all newspapers, films, radio, plays, cinema and books – and made sure they put across Nazi ideas. One of Hitler's most trusted friends, Doctor Joseph Goebbels, was put in charge of propaganda and **censorship**. He became a master of mind control. He had loud speakers placed on all city streets so that people could hear Hitler's speeches when they were doing their shopping and ordered all books written by Jews or communists to be destroyed. He banned jazz music because it was played mainly by black American musicians and even had a war film destroyed because it showed a drunk German sailor. He even introduced the death penalty for telling an anti-Hitler joke!

'[The Nazis] drew up massive leisure programmes for working people. The biggest programme provided workers with cheap holidays... a cruise to the Canary Islands, for example, cost 62 marks, the equivalent of two weeks' wages. Although most workers could afford this, it was only loyal and hardworking members of the Nazi Party who were given places on the cruise liners. For those who could not get a place on a cruise ship, there were walking holidays... skiing holidays... two weeks in Switzerland... or a tour of Italy. [The Nazis arranged] sports matches... outings to the theatre and the opera. It had its own symphony orchestra, which toured the country playing music in areas not usually visited by orchestras. It laid on evening classes for adults.'

SOURCE P: *Adapted from Hitler's Germany, by Josh Brooman, 1991.*

Work

1 Read Source L. In your own words, explain how this law tried to encourage Germans to have more children.

2 a How did Hitler create jobs?

  b What effect do you think the creation of lots of jobs had on his popularity?

3 a In 1937, a leading Nazi said: 'The only people who have a private life in Germany today are those who are asleep.' Use the information and sources on pages 64 to 69 to give examples of how people's private lives were affected by the Nazis.

  b Why do you think Hitler put someone in charge of propaganda and censorship?

  c Why do you think he gave the job to one of his most trusted friends?

MISSION ACCOMPLISHED?

• In no more than 150 words, answer the question 'What was life like in Nazi Germany?'

TASK 1 Votes for women

Read the following 1910 newspaper report very carefully. It appeared the day after a 'Votes for Women' march in London had turned to violence.

---

120 ARRESTED

Suffragettes attack House of Commons

D I S G R A C E F U L   S C E N E S

Reckless women charge at police

True to their word, about 300 Suffragettes marched on the House of Commons yesterday and the scenes of violence were worse than any other of which they had been guilty. It was a picture of shameful recklessness. Never before have otherwise sensible women gone so far in forgetting their womanhood. One woman campaigner fell in the mud, to the disgust of decent men but to the delight of others. One obese Suffragette threw her untidy self against smiling policemen until she ran out of breath. A few more of the desperate pushed at the heroic police in rugby style until they were swung back by a powerful neck or waist grip. Arrests were only made in extreme cases and many women were sadly disappointed not to be taken into custody. Even so, 120 people were arrested, including some men.

---

a Who were the suffragettes?

b Is this newspaper report biased for or against the suffragettes? Quote any words or phrases that support your view.

c Rewrite the news article in an unbiased way, using the facts in the article.

d In what ways is your news report different from the original?

TASK 2 Note making

Note making is an important skill. To do it successfully, you must pick out the key words in each sentence. The key words are the ones that are vital to the meaning. Without these words, the sentence makes no sense.

For example: The first day of the Battle of the Somme was a terrible day in British history – 20,000 British soldiers were killed and 35,000 were wounded.

The key words are: first day; Battle of the Somme; 20,000 British soldiers killed; 35,000 wounded.

a Now write down the key words in the following sentences about Hitler's early life. The key words are your notes.

- Adolf Hitler was born in 1889 in Braunau, a small town in Austria.

- His bullying father died when Hitler was 14 and his mother died when he was 17. He left school when he was 16 and dreamt of being a famous artist.

- Hitler failed to get into the Vienna Art Academy and ended up living in a hostel for tramps. He earned money by cleaning windows, painting houses and selling postcards on the streets. He began to hate the rich Jews of Vienna.

- He joined the army when the Great War started in 1914 and won medals for bravery as a trench messenger. By the time the war ended, he had managed to win the highest medal in the German army – the Iron Cross (First Class).

- Hitler was temporarily blinded in a gas attack and was in hospital when the war ended. He blamed Germany's defeat on weak German politics and Jews! He hated the way Germany was punished after the war and decided to go into politics.

- After the war ended, Hitler was given the job of spying on some of the many new German political parties. He went to a meeting of one called 'The German Workers' Party' and liked their ideas. He joined the party and was soon its leader.

- Hitler changed the party's name to 'The National Socialist German Workers' Party' or 'Nazi Party' for short. They used the swastika as their emblem.

b Why not make notes on other topics you have studied?

TASK 3 The Jews in Nazi Germany 1933–1939

Once in power, the Nazis quickly began to make life difficult for Germany's Jews. One of the first things they did was to organise a boycott of Jewish shops. This photograph of two Nazis pinning up a notice on a Jewish clothes shop was taken on 1 April 1933 – study it carefully and then answer the questions in full sentences.

a What is a 'boycott'?

b Why do you think the Nazis organised boycotts of Jewish shops?

c What do you think the poster might say?

d What effect do you think the poster might have had on the shoppers?

e What does the word 'persecute' mean?

f In what other ways did the Nazis persecute Jews up to 1939?

TASK 4 What's missing?

a Using the clues, copy out the following names, labels or words from your studies so far. Some have missing vowels; others have missing consonants.

b Write a sentence or two explaining each name, label or word.

i) S _ f f r _ g _
(another word for vote)

ii) _ m _ l y D _ v _ s _ n
(Derby, 1913)

iii) _ a _ i _ _ _ o _ _ _ e o _ _ e
(British PM at the end of the Great War)

iv) T r _ _ t y _ f V _ r s _ _ l l _ s
(punished Germany)

v) _ e a _ u e o _ _ a _ i o _ _
(to prevent future wars)

vi) d _ m _ c r _ c y
(voting for leaders)

vii) _ i _ _ a _ o _ _ _ i _
(one leader, no right to vote)

viii) M _ s s _ l _ n _
(Italy's fascist leader)

ix) _ o _ _ u _ i _ _
(USSR after 1922)

x) _ e i _ _ a _ _ _
(Hitler's book)

xi) _ _ a _ _ i _ a
(crooked cross)

xii) F _ h r _ r
(supreme leader)

xiii) G _ s t _ p _
(secret police)

xiv) _ i _ _ e _ _ o u _ _
(tough Nazi kids)

xv) Eu _ e _ i _ _
(race science)

BRITAIN AT WAR (2)

Unfortunately, the Great War was not the war to end all wars. In fact, many historians have argued that the seeds of the Second World War were sown at the end of the Great War. Advances in technology and tactics meant that World War II was very different from World War I – and even more deadly. Bombs were bigger, tanks were faster and planes could fly further. All this meant that civilians – ordinary men, women and children – were caught up in the fighting more than ever before. It is estimated that around 72 million people lost their lives due to the Second World War – making it the deadliest war in human history. It also saw Britain facing the prospect of being invaded and conquered for the first time since 1066.

1: Why was there another world war?

_____ MISSION OBJECTIVES _____

- To describe how World War II began.
- To decide whether appeasement was a good way of dealing with Hitler.

Unlike the Great War that began in 1914, the reasons why the Second World War began are quite straightforward. Germany, under the leadership of Adolf Hitler, invaded other countries until Britain and France declared war to try and stop him. But why did Hitler invade these countries? How did Britain and France react? And could the war have been avoided?

At the end of the Great War, Germany was forced to sign the Treaty of Versailles (Source A). This was very unpopular with many Germans and, by promising to ignore the treaty, Hitler persuaded many people to vote for him. Hitler had three main aims in his dealings with other countries. Firstly, he wanted to get all the land back that Germany lost after the Great War. To do this, he believed he would have to build up his army, navy and air force – despite being banned from doing this by the Treaty of Versailles. Secondly, he wanted to join all of the German-speaking people in Europe together in one big country. Finally, he wanted to make Germany bigger by taking land from weaker, neighbouring countries. He believed that true Germans were the greatest and most powerful race and needed extra living space (he called it 'Lebensraum') to reach their full potential.

Treaty of Versailles

- The Great War is Germany's fault.

- The Germans must pay for the war... until 1988. The money will go to the British and French.

- Germany can only have a small army (100,000 men), a small navy (six battleships) and no submarines, air force or tanks.

- Germany must hand over huge areas of its land to the winners. Some of the land will be used to make new countries like Poland and Czechoslovakia.

- Germany must never unite with Austria ever again.

- No German soldiers can go into an area known as the Rhineland, a German region close to France.

Signed Britain, France, Italy, the USA and all other winners.

↳ **SOURCE A:** _The agreement or treaty reached at the end of the Great War. Not surprisingly, most Germans hated it. Hitler swore revenge!_

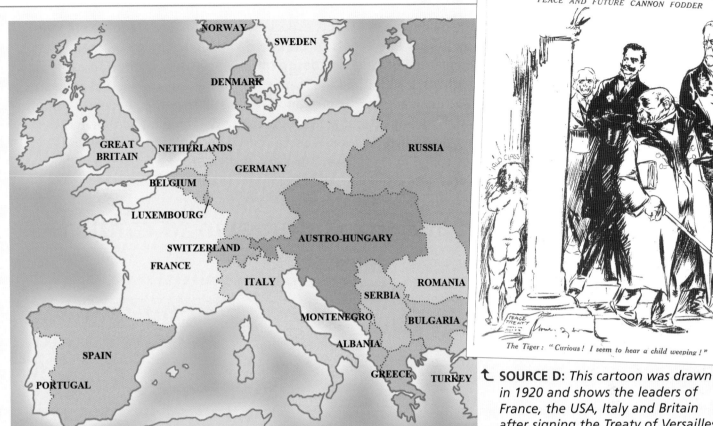

SOURCE B: *Europe before the Great War.*

SOURCE C: *Europe after the Treaty of Versailles.*

PEACE AND FUTURE CANNON FODDER

The Tiger: "Curious! I seem to hear a child weeping!"

SOURCE D: *This cartoon was drawn in 1920 and shows the leaders of France, the USA, Italy and Britain after signing the Treaty of Versailles.*

Work

1 Explain why Hitler (and millions of other Germans) hated the Treaty of Versailles.

2 a Look at Sources B and C. List the countries you think Hitler might invade.

 b Explain why you chose the countries you have.

3 a Look at Source D. If that child was born when the Treaty of Versailles was signed in 1919, how old would they be in 1939?

 b Why do you think the artist has drawn the child crying about the Treaty being signed?

In the 1930s many people in Europe, especially in Britain and France, were still traumatised by the terrible events of the Great War. Unlike many Germans, they did not feel humiliated or have any desire for revenge. They wanted to avoid more wars at all costs. Hitler had made no secret of his aims to increase the size of Germany, but the leaders of France and Britain still hoped a peaceful solution could be found. They hoped that if they showed understanding and gave Hitler everything he asked for there would be no reason for fighting to break out. This policy was called **appeasement** and the British Prime Minister, Neville Chamberlain, was convinced it would guarantee peace in Europe.

2: Appeasement and the countdown to conflict

1933
Three days after Hitler came to power, he began to increase Germany's armed forces. This is known as **rearmament**. Britain and France did nothing to stop him.

1936
Hitler sent his troops into the area of Germany known as the **Rhineland** – despite what the Treaty of Versailles said! His soldiers were under strict orders to retreat if they were attacked. Britain and France did nothing to stop him.

1938
Hitler's troops marched into **Austria** – the country of his birth. Again he broke the Treaty of Versailles. Again Britain and France did nothing.

1938
Hitler announced that he wanted control of an area that contained many German speakers. Chamberlain and the French leader visited Hitler and agreed to let Germany have **Sudetenland** as long as he promised not to ask for anything else! The Czech leaders were not even involved in the talks.

1939
Hitler invaded all of **Czechoslovakia** and exposed his promises as lies. Chamberlain realised he had been tricked and made a pact to help Poland if Hitler attacked them.

1939
On 1 September German troops invaded **Poland**. Two days later Britain and France declared war on Germany.

MISSION OBJECTIVES
• To know why the Second World War started.

LITHUANIA
GREAT BRITAIN
HOLLAND
BELGIUM
GERMANY (EAST PRUSSIA)
1939 POLAND
GERMANY
—1936 RHINELAND
—1938 SUDETENLAND
1939 CZECHOSLOVAKIA
FRANCE
1938 AUSTRIA
SWITZERLAND
ITALY

! FACT Who was next on Hitler's hit list?

Poland was quickly defeated. Hitler's troops then invaded Norway, Holland, Belgium and France. Hitler then turned his attention to the USSR and launched a massive surprise invasion in June 1941. His troops got within 60 miles of the Russian capital before being forced back by the severe winter and the enormous Soviet army. Neville Chamberlain was replaced as British Prime Minister by Winston Churchill in May 1940.

Chamberlain: Champion of peace or coward?

Neville Chamberlain's policy of appeasement has been controversial with historians. Some have seen him as a peace-loving man who had little option other than to act the way he did. Others have seen him as a coward who failed to stand up to Hitler's bullying when he had the chance. Read through the following arguments and make up your own mind.

Argument 1

Many British people, including Chamberlain, agreed with Hitler that Versailles was unfair. Hitler was only getting back what rightfully belonged to Germany.

Argument 2

Appeasement gave Hitler the advantage. When war came it was against a strong Germany that had built up its armies and had the raw materials, industry and people of Austria and Czechoslovakia.

Argument 3

Stalin's USSR was seen as a greater threat than Hitler by many people at this point. It was hoped that a strong Germany would stop the spread of communism.

Argument 4

Appeasement was morally wrong and was another word for weakness or cowardice. It allowed Hitler to break international law and gave away parts of countries against their will.

Argument 5

Chamberlain misjudged Hitler. He was not like a normal leader who would listen to reason and stick to promises.

Argument 6

Britain was too weak to stop Hitler. In 1938, the British military told Chamberlain they weren't ready to fight Hitler. Appeasement gave Britain time to rearm and survive Hitler's attacks when they came.

Argument 7

Hitler would have been defeated if Chamberlain had stood up to him when he occupied the Rhineland. He missed the perfect opportunity to stop Hitler at the beginning.

Argument 8

In 1936, 100,000 British people joined the British Peace Pledge Union and promised: 'Never again will I support a war.' The British people were not in favour of a war to help the Austrians or the Czechs.

WISE-UP Words

appeasement
rearmament

Work

1 The following statements are fictional explanations for Chamberlain's actions (or lack of them!). Match each statement to its year and the name of the crisis.

'Hitler is Austrian – and many Austrians want to be part of Germany anyway!'

'He's only moving soldiers around his own country.'

'This is the final straw – it can only mean war.'

'Versailles was too harsh. Germany should be allowed a bigger army, navy and an air force.'

'Hitler has promised me this is his final demand. If it means giving away part of Czechoslovakia to avoid war, I'll do it!'

'Hitler has made me look a fool! We must now make a stand with Poland.'

Years: 1933 • 1936 • 1938 • 1938 • 1939 • 1939

Crises: the Sudetenland crisis • the invasion of Poland • the invasion of Austria • the invasion of Czechoslovakia • rearmament • the occupation of the Rhineland

2 Read through the arguments for and against appeasement. Copy out the table and write a brief description of each argument in the correct column:

Arguments for appeasement	Arguments against appeasement

3 Was appeasement the correct policy to use when dealing with Hitler? Explain your answer carefully.

___ MISSION ACCOMPLISHED? ___

• Do you know why the Second World War started? Have you decided whether appeasement was the right tactic to use against Hitler?

Towards the end of 1940, posters like the one in Source A began to appear all over Britain. They featured five smiling fighter pilots and a famous quotation from Britain's Prime Minister, Winston Churchill. So why was this poster published? Why were the pilots smiling? And why did 'so many' people have to be thankful to 'so few'?

3: Who were the 'Few'?

———— MISSION OBJECTIVES ————
- To be able to explain what 'Operation Sealion' was.
- To decide why Hitler wasn't able to invade Britain in September 1940.

Key

🔱 German occupied land

■ German allies

□ Neutral countries

SOURCE B: Hitler's conquests up to 1940.

SOURCE A: 'Never was so much owed by so many to so few' poster.

By July 1940, Hitler was 'Master of Europe'. He was friendly with, or his armies had successfully invaded, most European countries (see Source B). Britain and the USSR could stop him... and Britain was to be first on his hit list.

On 1 August 1940, Hitler signed top secret plans to begin the invasion of Britain. Code-named 'Operation Sealion', the aim was to get German soldiers onto British soil by 15 September (see Source C). After that, German troops would move towards London and other major British cities with the goal of controlling the whole country by Christmas.

GERMAN GOVERNMENT
TOP SECRET DIRECTIVE NO. 17, 1 AUGUST 1940

TOP SECRET

FROM: ADOLF HITLER

In order to establish the conditions necessary for the final conquest of Britain, I intend to step up the air and naval war more intensively.

i) From 6 August, German bombers should attack British airfields and destroy all the RAF's aircraft. These bombers should be protected by fighter aircraft.

ii) If Britain does not surrender after all her aircraft are destroyed, the German army, escorted by the German navy, will land on beaches between Folkestone and Brighton on 15 September.

The success of Operation Sealion hinged on the complete defeat of Britain's air force. Hitler believed that if the Luftwaffe (German air force) could win control of the skies, it would be far easier for German ships to transport soldiers over the English Channel to begin the land invasion of Britain. If the RAF was destroyed, British planes could not attack the ships bringing across his troops.

Throughout the summer of 1940, German and British pilots fought each other in the 'Battle of Britain' high above southern England. From the start, the odds were stacked against the British:

- The Germans had 824 fighter planes and 1017 bombers in service. Britain only had about 600 fighter planes.

- It took five minutes for German planes to cross the Channel from France. However, it took 15 minutes for British planes to take off and reach the invading planes after they were spotted.

- Many of the British pilots were part-timers and had not received the same level of training or experience as the Germans who trained 800 new pilots a month. The British trained just 200.

↵ **SOURCE C:** *A summary of Operation Sealion. The RAF was the Royal Air Force, the official title of Britain's air force.*

Work

1 By July 1940, why were some people calling Hitler the 'Master of Europe'?

2 a What was 'Operation Sealion'? Try to give a really detailed answer.

  b Do you think Hitler had good reason to believe that an invasion of Britain was possible by 15 September? Give reasons for your answer.

SOURCE D: *A photograph of RAF pilots 'scrambling' to get to their planes to intercept approaching enemy aircraft. In total, over 3000 pilots fought against the Germans in the Battle of Britain. Over 2000 were from Britain but they were joined by New Zealanders (102), Poles (141), Canadians (90), Czechs (86), South Africans (21), Americans (7) and many more.* ↴

Throughout the summer of 1940, the fate of the entire British nation rested on the shoulders of a handful of young men. The outcome of the Battle of Britain not only depended on the bravery and skill of the pilots, but on the performance of the machines they flew. Look at the planes below from both sides that fought to the death in the skies in England.

The planes of the RAF!

THE HAWKER HURRICANE

MAX SPEED: 328 mph

WEAPONS: Eight machine guns mounted in wings.

CREW: Pilot only

RECOGNITION: A short, sturdy plane with a wooden body (fuselage), that could turn sharply and take a lot of damage before the pilot had to 'bail out'. The **Hurricane** was the most common RAF **fighter** and shot down more German aircraft than the **Spitfire**.

THE SUPERMARINE SPITFIRE

MAX SPEED: 362 mph

WEAPONS: Eight machine guns mounted in wings.

CREW: Pilot only

RECOGNITION: Sleek and beautiful, the Spitfire is one of the most famous planes in the world. It was fast, handled extremely well, and was more than a match for the German fighters.

The planes of the Luftwaffe

MESSERSCHMITT ME109

MAX SPEED: 357 mph

WEAPONS: Two machine guns mounted on the engine and two cannon in wings.

CREW: Pilot only

RECOGNITION: This fast, shark-like plane had square-tipped wings and bright yellow noses. They were the most deadly and feared of all the German aircraft.

MESSERSCHMITT ME110

MAX SPEED: 349 mph

WEAPONS: Four machine guns and two cannon in nose, one rear-firing machine gun in cockpit.

CREW: Pilot and gunner

RECOGNITION: Heavily armed and able to fly long distances, this twin-engined plane was slow and clumsy to turn and was easy meat for the RAF fighters.

HEINKEL HE 111

MAX SPEED: 247 mph

WEAPONS: Three machine guns in nose, top and belly and 2000kg of bombs.

CREW: Pilot, gunner and bomb-aimer

RECOGNITION: The most common German **bomber**, the Heinkel was slow, lightly armed and had large sections of glass over the cockpit. This allowed the pilot to see clearly – but offered no protection from a hail of bullets. When they did get past the RAF, they inflicted heavy damage on British airfields, towns and cities.

Hungry for MORE

Other aircraft were used by both sides during the Battle of Britain. See if you can find out more and work out why they are not as well known as the ones on this page.

By the end of August, the RAF was only days away from defeat. Its airfields were badly damaged and it didn't have enough pilots. However, the Germans were encountering big problems too. Brand-new radar technology meant that the British could detect enemy planes before they reached Britain. A system of 51 radar stations directed British fighters to the Germans in a matter of minutes, leaving them enough fuel to attack the German planes time and time again. In fact, it soon became clear that the Germans were losing more planes than the British. More importantly, the Germans were only making about 150 new planes a month whilst the British were producing over 550!

At 2:00pm on 15 September, Prime Minister Winston Churchill asked his air force commander what British fighter planes were available other than the ones in the air. 'There are none,' came the reply. However, 15 September saw the final major engagement of the Battle of Britain. On that very day, Germany lost 60 aircraft to Britain's 25! The next day, Hitler postponed Operation Sealion 'until further notice'. He had failed to defeat the RAF by his 15 September deadline and was forced to cancel his invasion plans. Instead, he started to target London in huge night-time bombing raids in an attempt to bomb the British into surrender. This was known as 'the Blitz'.

The RAF pilots who fought in the Battle of Britain became known as the 'Few', after Winston Churchill honoured their victory with this speech: 'Never in the field of human conflict was so much owed by so many to so few'.

WISE-UP Words

bomber   fighter
Hurricane   Luftwaffe
RAF   Spitfire

Work

1 a Draw a simple bar chart displaying the top speeds of the planes involved in the Battle of Britain.

b Which plane would you choose to fly into combat? Give reasons for your answer.

c Why do you think the Spitfire is better known than the Hurricane? Remember, the Hurricane shot down more German planes.

2 Look at this list of reasons why Germany lost the Battle of Britain. Explain, in your own words, how each reason made a difference to the outcome of the battle:
- The British had radar.
- Hitler lost patience and started bombing London.

Can you add any reasons of your own to explain why Germany lost the Battle of Britain?

3 a In your own words, explain what Churchill meant when he said, 'Never in the field of human conflict was so much owed by so many to so few'.

b Using Source A (page 76) to inspire you, design your own poster to thank the 'Few' and let the British public know how much they owe them.

Date	Official British figures	Official German figures	Figures agreed after the war
8–23 Aug	755	213	403
24 Aug–6 Sept	643	243	378
7–30 Sept	846	243	435
TOTAL	**2244**	**699**	**1216**

SOURCE E: *Fighters and bombers lost by the Luftwaffe in the Battle of Britain. Which set of figures do you think is most accurate and why?*

MISSION ACCOMPLISHED?

- Could you tell someone what Operation Sealion was?
- Have you decided what the most important factor was in Hitler's failure to conquer Britain?

During the Great War, some of Britain's cities had been bombed by the German air force and over 1000 people had been killed. During the years between the First and Second World Wars, great advances had been made in aircraft technology. It was clear that Britain's towns were once more going to be targeted – and this time on a much bigger scale. The Government was determined to be ready and, as well as digging lots of air-raid shelters, they decided to move over one million people away from the danger areas. This was known as **evacuation** and it changed the lives of many people for ever. So where were people evacuated from? Where were they moved to? And what did this mean for the people of Britain?

4: 'Mr and Mrs Jones would like a nice little boy'

―――――――――――――――――― MISSION OBJECTIVES ――――――――――――――――――

- To be able to define the word 'evacuation' and explain why it took place.
- To describe the typical experiences of an evacuee.

City slickers and country bumpkins

For four days in September 1939, the Government took over Britain's entire transport system. All of the buses and trains were used to move the most vulnerable people in society from the towns that were certain to be bombed to the countryside (which was much safer from attack).

Armed with suitcases full of clothes, a gas mask packed into a cardboard box and a name tag tied to their coats, thousands of children left the familiar surroundings of city life for a completely new experience in the countryside. Some would love their new life... but many others would hate every second of it!

None of the children knew where they were going and nothing prepared them for the ordeal they would go through when they reached their countryside reception areas. There were two main methods of finding a new home or 'foster family'.

↵ SOURCE A: *Numbers of people evacuated by the British Government in September 1939.*

827,000	School-children
524,000	Mothers and children under five
13,000	Pregnant women
7000	Blind and disabled people
103,000	Teachers

⌐ SOURCE B: *An evacuated child, photographed in September 1939.*

METHOD NO. 1

GRAB A CHILD – the children were lined up and local people would choose the ones they wanted. Obviously, the smarter, cleaner girls would go first... and the dirtier, scruffy little boys would be left until last.

METHOD NO. 2

HUNT THE HOME – evacuated children, or evacuees as they were called, were led around the town or village and taken door-to-door. Homeowners were asked if they would foster a child for a while.

'Villagers stood around watching us as we got out of the bus and went into the school. What followed was like an auction. Villagers came in to choose children. "Mr and Mrs Jones would like a nice little boy." Nobody wanted the awkward combination of a girl of 11 and such a small boy, from whom I had promised my mother never to be separated. We were left until the very last. The room was almost empty. I sat on my rucksack and cried.'

↳ **SOURCE C:** *The thoughts of one young girl remembering what happened to her and her brother when she was evacuated (from* SHP Peace & War, *by Shephard, Reid and Shephard, 1993).*

'They unloaded us on the corner of the street; we thought it was all arranged, but it wasn't. The billeting officer [the man in charge of housing the children] walked along knocking on doors and asking if they'd take a family. We were the last to be picked. You couldn't blame them; they didn't have any coloured people there in those days.'

↳ **SOURCE D:** *An example of a family who had to hunt for a home (from* Keep Smiling Through, *by Caroline Long, 1989).*

★ WISE-UP Words
evacuation

Work

1 Look at Source A.

  a What is meant by the word 'evacuation'?

  b Make a copy of the bar chart, making sure you label it correctly.

  c Look at the different groups of people evacuated in September 1939. Do you think the Government got it right? Which groups of people would you have moved first? Give reasons for each of your choices.

2 Look at Source B. By looking at the photograph, write down all you can find out about this boy and what is happening to him.

- Why do you think he has a label tied to his coat?
- What is his suitcase for? What do you think it contains?
- Who do you think the woman is?
- Why is there a line of children behind him? And why is the boy out of line?
- How do you think the boy feels? Describe his emotions.

Compare your answers to the rest of the class.

3 Look at Sources C and D.

  a Describe the two different methods used to find these two young families a new home.

  b Write down the reasons why they each had problems finding a new home.

  c Do either of the reasons surprise you? Give reasons for your answer.

⏸ PAUSE for Thought

Suppose you were evacuated now. You can take just ten of your things with you. Write a list of what you would take, giving reasons for each.

Evacuation wasn't easy for anyone – evacuees or hosts. Some children settled down happily and loved their new lives in their new homes and schools – others hated country life and were homesick. The country people had to put up with a lot too. Some of the children arrived badly clothed, very thin and covered in lice and nits. Some of the 'rougher' evacuees shocked their foster families by swearing and being naughty. One young evacuee in Northallerton, Yorkshire, spent a whole day blocking up the local stream – later that night it was found that he'd flooded six houses and the local church!

> 'Rosie whispered. She whispered for days. Everything was so clean. We were given face cloths and toothbrushes. We'd never cleaned our teeth up till then. And hot water came from the tap and there was an indoor toilet. And carpets. And clean sheets. This was all very odd and rather scary.'

↱ **SOURCE E:** *A 13-year-old boy remembers his evacuation to Buckinghamshire with his sister Rosie.*

> 'My foster mum thought she was onto a good thing with me and the other 11-year-old girl I was put with. We did her shopping for her, cleaned her house, cooked, washed up and even looked after her whining three-year-old when she went out.'

↱ **SOURCE F:** *Unhappy times for an 11-year-old girl evacuated to Cambridgeshire.*

> 'One evacuated child from the South of England... on arrival at the billet [his new home], was asked by the hostess, "Would you like some biscuits, dear?" "Biscuits?" the boy replied. "I want some beer and some bloody chips. That's what I get at home!"'

↱ **SOURCE G:** *An extract from the* Newcastle Evening Chronicle *in 1940. Some boys found country life hard to get used to!*

> 'I love my six lads from London as if they were my own. They've made this dreary, lonely war quite enjoyable for me.'

↱ **SOURCE H:** *One rich woman from Devon, commenting on the evacuees in her house.*

↳ **SOURCE I:** *Children had to carry gas masks everywhere in case poison gas was dropped.*

↱ **SOURCE J:** *The countryside was a whole new world to many inner-city kids. Here they are nervously looking at a tame fox.*

! FACT Picture this

Many city children had never seen a farm animal before. They were shocked to see what cows, chickens and sheep looked like. In October 1939, BBC News broadcast this description of a farm animal written by a young evacuee. Can you guess what animal he's describing?

'It has six sides... at the back it has a tail on which hangs a brush. With this it sends flies away so they don't fall into the milk. The head is for growing horns and so that the mouth can be somewhere... the mouth is to moo with. Under the animal hangs the milk... when people milk, the milk comes and there is never an end to the supply. How the animal does it I have not realised... one can smell it far away. This is the reason for fresh air in the country...'

In case you weren't sure, the boy is describing a cow!

After a few months of life in the British countryside, most children returned to their lives in the city. The enemy bombers hadn't arrived as expected and by March 1940, nearly one million children had gone home. However, later that year the mass bombing of British cities – 'the Blitz' as it was known – began and many children, but not all, returned to the country.

! FACT Unwanted or forgotten?

When some of the evacuated children finally returned home after the war, they found their homes had been bombed and their parents were missing. Some parents had even abandoned their children on purpose. About 40,000 children remained 'unclaimed' after the war!

Work ——————.

1 Look at Source E. It tells you a lot about the kind of life Rosie led before she was evacuated.

   a Write down at least five things it tells you.

   b How had her life changed?

2 a Who do you think enjoyed evacuation more – the evacuated children or their new families? Try to give reasons for your answer.

   b Did everyone enjoy evacuation? What evidence is there on these pages that some children AND their families did not like evacuation at all?

3 Look at Source K.

   a Who is standing next to the tree?

   b What is he doing – and why?

   c Why was this poster produced?

   d What is the message of the poster?

4 Imagine you are one of the children in one of the sources you have been reading. Write a short letter home about your new life. Use your imagination (sensibly) to build up a picture of your new surroundings for your family back home. Compare your letter with other people's letters in your class.

↖ SOURCE K: *A Government poster issued in 1940.*

_____ **MISSION ACCOMPLISHED?** _____

- Can you tell someone what the word 'evacuation' means?
- Do you know why it took place in Britain in 1939?
- Have you described the kind of things evacuees went through?

83

In 1992, a statue of Sir Arthur 'Bomber' Harris – the Head of RAF Bomber Command during the Second World War – was unveiled in London. Immediately protesters threw paint at the statue and demanded it was taken down! So why did people have such hatred for a man who took the fight to the evil of Nazi Germany? Why did other people want to put up a statue of him? And on which side of the argument do you belong?

5: 'Bomber' Harris

MISSION OBJECTIVES

- To be able to explain why the German city of Dresden was bombed.
- To decide if Sir Arthur Harris should be praised or paint-bombed.

The death of Dresden

On 13 February 1945, 805 British planes dropped 2690 tons of bombs on the German city of Dresden. Before long, an area of 11 square miles was burning so ferociously that temperatures reached 1000 degrees Celsius – ten times hotter than a boiling kettle. The inferno sucked in all the oxygen, creating **firestorms** and suffocating those who didn't burn to death. It is estimated that 150,000 people died in this single raid.

Your task over the next two pages is to formulate an opinion. You must establish:

- Why the attack took place in the first place.
- Why the raid caused so many deaths.
- What the bombing of Dresden achieved.

Your ideas and opinions will then be used to complete a final piece of work.

New targets

Bomber planes changed the face of war between 1939 and 1945. American and British planes dropped nearly three million tons of bombs on 131 German cities. This killed nearly one million men, women and children, and made eight million people homeless. German planes dropped bombs on British cities too – 40,000 people died in air raids on London, Coventry, Glasgow, Hull and other cities.

When the war began, both sides had tried to use **precision bombing** to hit key targets, such as factories, ports, bridges, major roads and railway stations. The idea was to destroy the enemy's ability to fight by making it impossible to make weapons, build ships or move soldiers around. However, precision bombing didn't work – bombs rarely hit their intended targets.

So **area bombing** was introduced instead. This devastating new type of attack meant that whole towns and cities were bombed in order to make sure that everything was destroyed... including the enemies' will to fight!

↰ SOURCE A: *A statue of Sir Arthur Harris put up in London in 1992. Interestingly, he was the only war commander not to have a statue made immediately after the war!*

Why bomb Dresden?

In October 1944, a detailed report by the British on Dresden concluded that the city was an 'unattractive target'. In other words, there was no point in bombing the place! However, in January 1945, British spies reported that thousands of German soldiers were collecting in Dresden before being sent off to fight. All of a sudden, Dresden had turned into a key bombing target – and this may have influenced the decision to attack.

Firestorm

The planes dropped a mixture of **incendiary** and high explosive bombs. Incendiary bombs are specifically designed to start fires. Dresden, being an ancient city with many wooden-framed buildings, started to burn very quickly. The fact that the city was packed with people running away from the Russian army meant that any large fire was sure to kill many thousands.

The bombs soon created a firestorm. In a firestorm, the hot air that rises from burning buildings is replaced by cooler air rushing in from outside. Soon, hurricane-force winds of up to 120mph were 'superheating' the fire.

What did the attack achieve?

Historians have argued for years about the bombing of Dresden – did the attack help Britain win the war? Some are sure it helped whilst others questioned whether it was necessary at all. Perhaps the following sources will help you form your opinion.

'Every day that the war went on cost the lives of countless more... so the numbers killed at Dresden, dreadful as they were, were nothing like so dreadful as the numbers of people Hitler was killing... A decisive blow was needed to end the war quickly.'

⌐ SOURCE B: *From an article written by historian Dr Noble Frankland, in 1985.*

'Many German towns were severely devastated by bombing, but the effect on the amount of weapons, tanks and fighter planes the Germans produced was small... the bombings didn't make the German people lose the will to fight either. The German people proved calmer and more determined than anticipated.'

⌐ SOURCE C: *Adapted from the report of the British Bombing Survey Unit, set up at the end of the war to study the effects of area bombing on Germany.*

⭐ WISE-UP Words

area bombing
firestorm
incendiary
precision bombing

Work

1 You might wish to work in pairs, threes or fours for this task.

A TV company has decided to stage a debate on whether the statue of Sir Arthur Harris should be removed or not. Use the information from these two pages (and anything else you can find out) to produce a report that can be used in the televised debate. Your report must either be in support or against the actions of Harris. Whether your reporting team is for or against Harris, you should try to consider:

- Whether Dresden was an acceptable target or not. Does the use of incendiary rather than explosive bombs tell us anything about the attack?

- Was Harris acting in Britain's best interests to try to win the war – or was he a war criminal guilty of killing innocent people?

- What do you think people felt about the bombing of German cities at the time? Was Harris doing something that most British people supported?

- In a war, is everyone who helps build weapons – including workers and their families – a fair target? Can Harris be criticised for killing any Germans – after all, weren't they all part of Hitler's evil empire?

- Did the bombings actually achieve anything? Did they help Britain win the war?

You can write down your conclusions as a report or why don't you hold the debate in your classroom and present your report as part of the show?

____ MISSION ACCOMPLISHED? ____

- Can you tell someone why the RAF bombed Dresden?

- Have you decided whether 'Bomber' Harris deserved his statue?

At 7:55am on Sunday 7 December 1941, 183 Japanese bomber planes launched a surprise attack on Pearl Harbor, a huge American Navy base in Hawaii. In less than two hours, 21 US warships were sunk or damaged and over 2000 Americans were killed. The next day, the USA and Britain declared war on Japan. Three days later, Germany and Italy showed their support for Japan by declaring war on the USA. World War II had gone truly global. The fighting in the Pacific was brutal and was only brought to an end when the most terrible weapon in the history of the world was used. But why did Japan attack an American base? In what ways was the fighting different from that in Europe? And were the Americans right to drop nuclear bombs on Japanese cities?

6: The end of World War II: why were nuclear bombs used?

MISSION OBJECTIVES

- To explain how and why the USA joined the Second World War.
- To decide whether it was right to drop nuclear bombs on Japan in 1945.

Japan's eastern empire

Japan was the first country in the **Far East** to industrialise, but Japan has no natural resources of its own. In order to get supplies of coal, oil, timber, rubber, gas, copper, and so on, the Japanese Government had been invading neighbouring countries throughout the 1930s. By attacking **Pearl Harbor**, they were hoping to destroy the massive American Pacific fleet – the only thing that could stop them taking all the land they wanted. The plan seemed to have worked – for a while at least. Japanese forces swept through the Far East, conquering Hong Kong, Malaya, Singapore, the Dutch East Indies and New Guinea by May 1942.

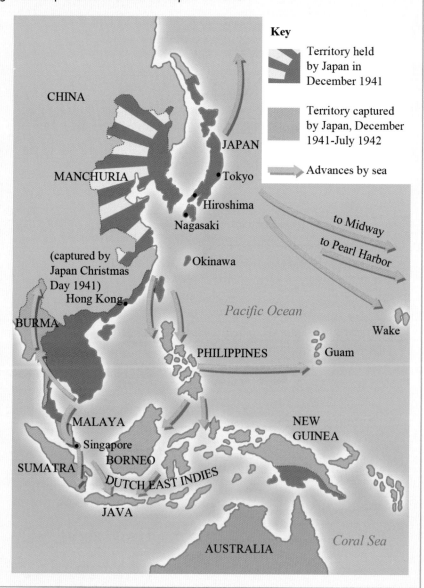

SOURCE A: *The Japanese advance seemed unstoppable. Their committed army, navy and air force quickly defeated British forces – taking 80,000 British soldiers prisoner in Singapore.* ↱

The Empire falls back

By the end of 1942, the USA – with the help of thousands of British Empire troops – was winning battles and taking back land in the Far East. By 1944, American troops had 'island hopped' right up to the Japanese mainland. The Japanese fought fanatically, believing it was a great honour to die for their country and a disgrace on their families if they were taken prisoner. Thousands of suicide bombers called **kamikaze** flew planes packed with explosives into American ships. Despite the desperate defence, by July 1945 the Japanese were fighting a lost cause. The war in Europe was over and the USA, Britain and Russia could now concentrate all their efforts on defeating Japan.

'Their faces were burned, their eye sockets hollow, the fluid from their melted eyes had run down their cheeks. Their mouths were mere swollen, pus-covered wounds, which they couldn't open wide enough to take a drink from a teapot.'

↳ SOURCE B: *A description of some men found hiding in bushes after the bombings (from J Hershey's account of the effects of the bomb, 1946, in* SHP Peace & War, *by Shephard, Reid and Shephard, 1993).*

'In Hiroshima, 30 days later, people who were not injured in the bombing are still dying mysteriously and horribly from an unknown something which I can only describe as the atomic plague.'

↳ SOURCE C: *The account of one of the first British journalists to visit Hiroshima. He is describing the effects of radiation sickness, which caused death and illness decades after the bomb was dropped.*

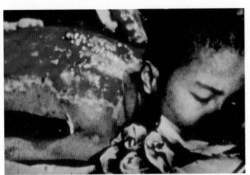

↳ SOURCE D: *One of the thousands of civilians who suffered terrible burns from the bomb blast.*

SOURCE E:
An aerial photograph of the bomb that destroyed a whole city. ↱

Final victory

The American President, Harry S Truman, had to decide how to end the war. The choice he made changed the world for ever. On 6 August 1945, a B29 bomber dropped a single bomb on the Japanese town of Hiroshima. The bomb exploded 570 metres above the ground in an enormous blast many times brighter than the sun. Those closest to the explosion were evaporated in the 300,000 centigrade heat, leaving nothing but burnt shadows on the ground. Anyone within half a mile of the bomb when it went off was turned into smoking black ash within seconds. The Americans estimated that 79,000 people had been killed. The Japanese claim 240,000 had lost their lives. On 9 August a second bomb was dropped on the port of Nagasaki. The Americans claim 20,000 died in this blast – the Japanese claim it was 50,000. Japan surrendered and the Second World War was over.

Work

1 In no more than 50 words, explain why Japan launched a massive attack on Pearl Harbor.

2 Define the word 'kamikaze'.

3 Why do you think so many people were willing to become kamikaze pilots?

4 Why do you think Japan finally surrendered?

So why did the USA drop the bomb?

Over the years, people have claimed that there were a number of reasons why President Truman ordered the nuclear bombs to be dropped:

- Some Americans believed that Japan would never surrender. Experts calculated that over half a million American soldiers would die if they had to invade Japan.

- The bombs cost a lot of money to develop (over $2000 million) so the Americans wanted to test them properly.

- The Japanese had been very cruel to any soldiers they had captured. Some Americans felt they needed to be taught a lesson.

- The USA wanted to show the world, in particular the USSR, how powerful and advanced it was.

'Even killing one American soldier will do. Use your awls [woodwork tools] for self defence. Aim for the enemy's belly. Understand? The belly? If you don't kill at least one, you don't deserve to live.'

↰ **SOURCE H:** *This is what Kasai Yukiko, a high school pupil, was told to do by her teacher if the Americans invaded in 1945.*

'There is no doubt in my mind that these bombs saved many more lives than the tens of thousands they killed. They saved prisoners of war... allied servicemen and millions of Japanese – for, let there be no mistake, if the [Japanese] Emperor and his cabinet had decided to fight on, the Japanese would, literally, have fought to the last man.'

↰ **SOURCE F:** *A British prisoner of war, 1945.*

'We were talking about the people who hadn't hesitated at Pearl Harbor to make a sneak attack, destroying not only ships but the lives of many American sailors.'

↰ **SOURCE G:** *From a 1965 interview with James Byrnes, US Secretary of State.*

'This barbarous weapon was of no real use in our war against Japan. They were already defeated and were ready to surrender... the scientists and others wanted to make this test because of the vast sums that had been spent.'

↰ **SOURCE I:** *Admiral William Leahy, one of President Truman's advisors in 1945. He wrote this in 1950.*

↵ **SOURCE J:** *Not a single bomb had been dropped on Hiroshima before 6 August 1945. The Americans could be sure that all this damage was the result of the nuclear bomb. This meant the Americans could accurately test how powerful the bomb was. Out of Hiroshima's 78,000 buildings, 70,000 were destroyed.*

JAPAN WAS SEEKING PEACE **BEFORE** THE FIRST ATOM BOMB WAS DROPPED ON HIROSHIMA, ACCORDING TO DOCUMENTS JUST LEAKED TO THE U.S. PRESS.

"DON'T YOU SEE, THEY HAD TO FIND OUT IF IT WORKED..."

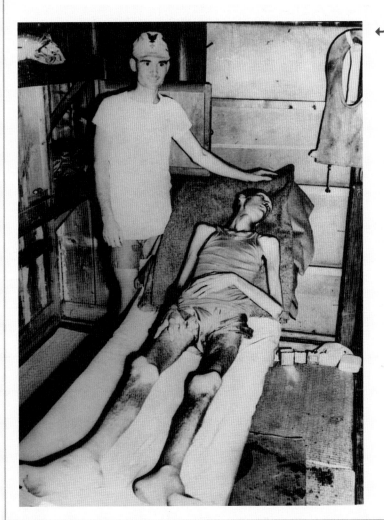

↵ **SOURCE K:** *A British cartoon from 1945. Many believed the bomb was dropped to show the USSR just how powerful the USA was.*

↵ **SOURCE L:** *This American soldier was nearly starved to death while being held prisoner by the Japanese. Thousands of Allied (including British and Australian) soldiers were treated brutally as the Japanese had no respect for those who surrendered.*

WISE-UP Words

Far East
kamikaze
Pearl Harbor

Work

1 Write out the following reasons for dropping the bomb as sub-titles in your exercise book. Make sure to leave five lines between each subtitle.

To save Allied soldiers from dying

To justify spending so much money

To get revenge on Japan

To show the USSR who was boss

Now read through sources F to L. Each source supports one of the arguments for dropping the bomb. Write a brief description of each source under the sub-heading that you think it belongs to.

2 **a** Do you think the USA was right to use the bomb? Please note this is a difficult question as there are good arguments on both sides.

b Do you think they needed to drop two bombs?

— MISSION ACCOMPLISHED? —

• Can you tell someone why the USA entered the war?

• Have you decided whether the attacks on Hiroshima and Nagasaki were justified?

Between 1942 and 1945, millions of people were sent by force to one of six specially built camps in Eastern Europe. The camps were surrounded by electrified razor wire fences and tall watchtowers packed with machine gun carrying guards. Once inside the 'prisoners' were either shot or gassed to death! Not surprisingly, the camps soon picked up a terrifying nickname – they were known as 'death camps'. But who committed these appalling crimes? And why? What sort of people were sent to these so-called 'death camps'? And what exactly happened once inside them?

7: What was a death camp like?

MISSION OBJECTIVES

• To understand how – and why – the Nazis managed to organise the mass murder of millions of Jews.

The six death camps were built by the Nazis during the Second World War when they controlled most of Europe. Hitler saw this as an opportunity to get rid of all the people he hated – tramps, the mentally impaired, the chronically sick, disabled people, gypsies, homosexuals, political opponents… and especially Jews. In total, approximately six million Jews were killed in Hitler's death camps.

The persecution begins

Jews had been treated badly in Germany for many years. As soon as Hitler became leader of Germany in 1933 he introduced laws and rules that made their lives more and more difficult. Jews were sacked from their jobs, banned from voting and forbidden to marry non-Jews. Soldiers stood outside their businesses and turned shoppers away, and they could even be evicted from their homes for no reason. In November 1938 a mass attack on Jews all over Germany (known as the 'Night of Broken Glass') led to the destruction of thousands of Jewish shops, homes and synagogues. Dozens of Jews were killed and thousands arrested. Lots of Jews left Germany to live in nearby countries, but found themselves back under Nazi rule when Germany invaded during World War II. And as the war went on, more Jews became trapped under Hitler's rule all over Europe – three million Jews in Poland, 2.7 million in western Russia and over one million in France, Holland, Belgium, Denmark, Norway and the Balkans.

▌ **FACT**

Historians still disagree about the origins of Hitler's hatred of the Jews. He was brought up at a time when **anti-Semitism** (prejudice against Jews) was common in Germany and Austria. Millions saw them as a selfish race who were only interested in making money rather than improving the nation. Some say the failure of a Jewish doctor to cure Hitler's beloved mother of breast cancer when he was young hit him particularly hard. By the time Hitler was an adult, he felt the Jews were part of an evil conspiracy to take over the world and should be destroyed.

SOURCE A: *A Nazi storm trooper standing outside a shop owned by a Jew, preventing shoppers from going inside. The sign reads 'Germans, defend yourselves. Do not buy from the Jews'.* ↱

Ghettoes and the execution squads

Hitler's method of dealing with the Jews under his control was brutal. In some countries they were bricked into separate areas outside the cities (called **ghettos**) or sent to work in labour camps where they worked to death. Execution squads (called '*Einsatzgruppen*') went out into the countryside in mobile vans and shot, or gassed, as many Jews as they could find. In Kiev (in the Ukraine) 33,771 Jews were marched out into a ravine and shot over two days in September 1941. But to many fanatical Nazis, the destruction of Europe's Jews was not happening quickly enough – and by the end of 1941 leading Nazis had begun working on plans for what they called 'a final solution to the Jewish question'.

The final solution

On 20 January 1942, Nazi leaders met to finalise their plans for the mass murder of every Jew in Europe, either by working them to death or killing them in poison gas chambers. This amounted to an estimated eleven million people – and six death or extermination camps were to be specially built for this purpose.

⤴ **SOURCE B:** *A photograph of local workers under Nazi order in Warsaw, Poland building a brick wall round the Warsaw Ghetto in 1940. At this time, the population of the Ghetto was estimated at 440,000 people, nearly 40% of the whole Warsaw population. However, the ghetto itself was only about 5% of the size of Warsaw!*

SOURCE C: *The main entrance to Auschwitz, one of the largest and probably the most infamous death camp. The photograph shows the railway lines upon which the cattle trucks would arrive with their 'cargo' of Jews.*

Work _____.

1 a What was the 'final solution'?

b In what way was the final solution different from the way the Nazis treated Jews in the first few years of the war?

2 Write a sentence or two about the following terms:
- anti-Semitism • ghetto
- *Einsatzgruppen*.

Inside a death camp

The death camps – Auschwitz, Belzec, Chelmno, Majdanek, Sobibor and Treblinka – were supplied with Jews from the countries that the Nazis had taken over... and the killing was on a vast scale.

When they arrived at a death camp, the prisoners were immediately sorted into two groups: those who looked over 15 years old and were strong and healthy were sent to the left; the old, the sick, pregnant women and women with young children were sent to the right. Those on the left (usually about 10%) were put to work helping to murder the ones on the right. Any refusals would result in an immediate death sentence.

'I was suddenly summoned, Himmler [the man in charge of the "final solution"] said:
The Führer has ordered the Jewish question to be solved once and for all... I have therefore earmarked [chosen] Auschwitz for this purpose. You will treat this order as absolutely secret, even from your superiors. The Jews are the sworn enemies of the German people and must be eradicated. Every Jew we can lay our hands on is to be destroyed now... without exception.'

↳ SOURCE D: *From the memoirs of Rudolf Hoss, first commandant of Auschwitz.*

Number of Jews killed		%
Poland	3,000,000	90
Germany	210,000	90
Czech	155,000	86
Holland	105,000	75
Hungary	450,000	70
Ukraine	900,000	60
Romania	300,000	50
Russia	107,000	11

Key

⬛ Extermination camps

🔺 Concentration camps

━━ Transport routes (rail)

↳ SOURCE E: *A map of Europe showing the main concentration and extermination camps. Concentration camps tended to be more like prisons where inmates were put to work in terrible conditions. They were often worked to death. Extermination camps were slightly different – their only purpose was to kill.*

Those selected to die weren't informed of their fate. To prevent panic, they were told they were going to have a shower and were given soap and towels as they were marched into big chambers disguised as shower rooms. With as many as 2000 prisoners packed inside at any one time, the doors were sealed and poisonous gas was poured through the vents. In about 30 minutes, everyone was dead. The bodies were later burnt.

'At last, after 32 minutes, they are all dead... The dead stand like pillars pressed together in the chambers. There is no room to fall or even to lean over. Even in death one can tell which are the families. They are holding hands in death and it is difficult to tear them apart in order to empty the chambers for the next batch. The corpses are thrown out with sweat and urine, smeared with excrement and menstrual blood on their legs. The corpses of children fly through the air. There is no time... Two-dozen dentists open the mouths and look for gold... some of the workers check genitals and anus for gold, diamonds and valuables.'

↳ SOURCE F: *An eyewitness account of a gassing by a Nazi death camp guard, August 1942 (by SS Officer Kurt Gerstein, Belzec, from* Investigating History, *by Neil DeMarco, 2003).*

❗ FACT Anti-Semitism

Anti-Semitism, as hatred of Jewish people is officially known, has been common in Europe for many centuries. Among other things, they have been blamed for the death of Jesus Christ and the outbreak of Black Death in the fourteenth century. At one time or another, they have been driven out of almost every country in Europe and there are few nations today without some record of anti-Semitic violence in their history.

'The children were taken to an enormous ditch; they were shot or thrown into the fire. No one bothered to see if they were really dead. Sometimes one could hear infants wailing in the fire. If mothers managed to keep their babies with them, a guard took the baby by its legs and smashed it against a wall until only a bloody mess remained in his hands. The mother then had to take this "mess" with her to the "bath" [gas chamber].'

↳ **SOURCE G:** *Another eyewitness account.*

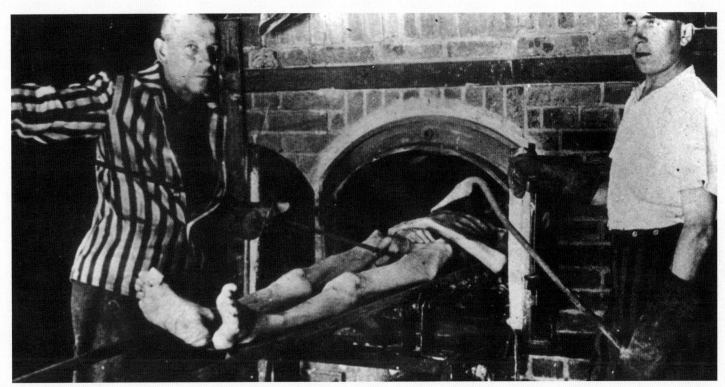

↳ **SOURCE H:**
A photograph of prisoners burning corpses.

Work _____.

1 a What is the difference between a concentration camp and an extermination camp?

b In your own words, explain what happened to Jewish prisoners as soon as they arrived at Auschwitz.

2 a Why did the Nazis tell the Jews they were going for a shower?

b In your own words, describe what really happened in the 'shower rooms'.

3 Look at Source F. The man who witnessed this scene shot himself soon after writing his account.

a Why do you think he committed suicide?

b Is there anything in the source that suggests how the man was feeling about what he was witnessing?

4 Is there any evidence on these pages to show that some Nazis did not consider the Jews to be human beings? Back up your thoughts with evidence from the text or sources.

FACT The Holocaust

The Nazis' attempt to wipe out the Jewish race is often known as the **Holocaust**. However, many Jews object to this term as it means 'sacrifice'. Some prefer to use the word 'churban', which means 'destruction'.

'Among ourselves we can talk openly about it, though we will never speak a word in public... I am speaking about... the extermination of the Jewish people. That is a page of glory in our history that... will never be written.'

↳ **SOURCE I:** *Heinrich Himmler, the man in overall charge of the 'final solution', speaking at a meeting in 1943.*

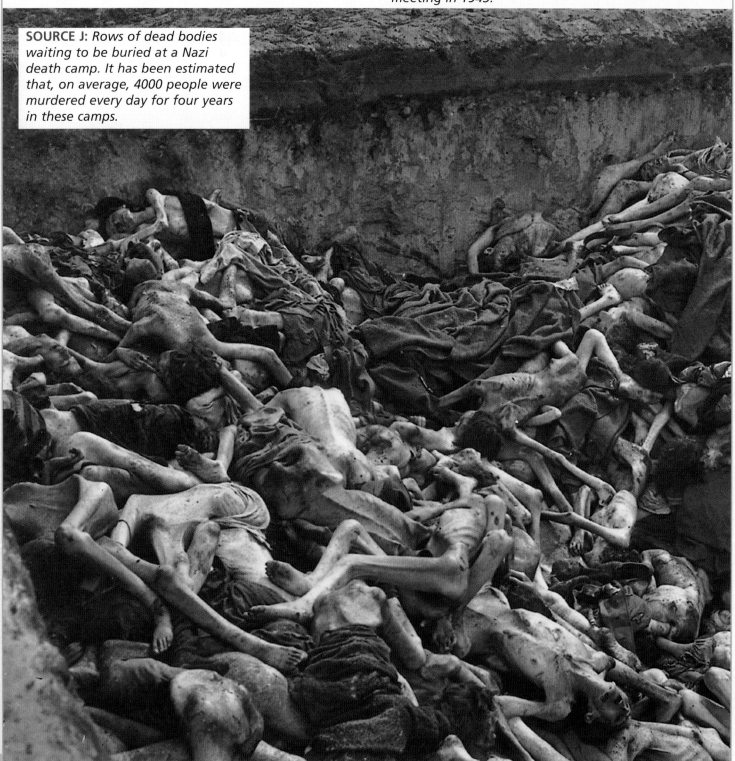

SOURCE J: *Rows of dead bodies waiting to be buried at a Nazi death camp. It has been estimated that, on average, 4000 people were murdered every day for four years in these camps.*

! FACT Rebellion

There were occasional rebellions in death camps. The most famous of all was in Treblinka in 1943. One of the prisoners managed to get into the weapons store where he handed out guns and grenades. After setting the camp on fire, 150 prisoners managed to escape and 15 guards were killed. However, the Nazis soon regained control and all of the escapees were killed. 550 other prison workers were killed in revenge too!

Over six million people, mainly Jews, were killed in death camps like Auschwitz as part of the 'final solution'. When Allied soldiers entered these camps after Germany's defeat in 1945, some were so shocked by what they saw that their hair turned white overnight.

At Dachau death camp, American soldiers killed 300 camp guards who had not had time to run away – the surviving inmates killed 200 more! At other camps, soldiers forced the local German population to walk past the unburied bodies, the gas chambers and the ovens to show them what had been going on so close to their homes. Indeed, thousands of people, not only loyal Nazis, helped with the 'final solution' – ordinary people like railway workers, office clerks, policemen and soldiers. 150 German companies used Auschwitz prisoners as slaves – other firms even competed for the contract to design and build the gas chambers and the ovens in which people were murdered and burnt. As reports and photographs of this mass murder started to make their way around the world in newspapers and on news programmes, a new word – **genocide** – entered the vocabulary of a shocked world. It was hoped that genocide – the deliberate extermination of a race of people – would never happen again!

✚ Hungry for MORE

Rudolf Hess, the man in charge of Auschwitz, escaped from his camp but was captured in 1946. He went on trial with many other leading Nazis later that year. At his trial, he talked about his family and said he didn't like his job. He said he was only following orders. Despite his pleas, he was found guilty of 'war crimes' and sentenced to life imprisonment. As a class, discuss:
• Whether his punishment was fair or not.
• Whether we should continue to hunt Nazi war criminals (some escaped and were never found) and put them on trial, or let the matter drop.

⭐ WISE-UP Words

anti-Semitism
genocide
ghettoes
Holocaust

Work

1 Look at Source I.
   a Who was Heinrich Himmler?
   b Why do you think Himmler wanted people to be secretive about the final solution?
   c Do you think Himmler was proud of his work on the final solution? Give a reason for your answer.

2 **a** Explain what the word 'holocaust' means.
   b Why do you think some people don't approve of the word 'holocaust when describing what happened to Jews during the war?

3 Today, Auschwitz extermination camp is a museum. Many people were against turning it into a museum and wanted it to be pulled down.
   a Why do you think some people wanted Auschwitz destroyed?
   b Do you think we should forget a place like Auschwitz or not? Give reasons for your opinions.

4 **a** What does the word 'genocide' mean?
   b Find out if genocide has ever happened again.

— MISSION ACCOMPLISHED? —

• Can you explain what the word 'genocide' means and when and where else this has occurred in the twentieth century?

United nations?

—————————————— MISSION OBJECTIVES ——————————————

- To be able to explain what the United Nations is and what it does.
- To be able to list some of the successes of the UN.

Towards the end of World War II, Britain, Russia and the USA realised that they had to do something to prevent such a war happening again. They believed that if there was more cooperation between countries, they could club together to stop someone like Hitler before they got too powerful and started a war. They formed the United Nations (UN for short), which is still an important organisation today. So just how do countries get together and cooperate? How do they decide what action to take? And what decisions have they made to improve the lives of people around the world?

UN DECLARATION OF HUMAN RIGHTS

- All human beings are born free and equal.
- Everyone has the right to life, liberty and freedom from fear and violence.
- Everyone has the right to protection of the law without discrimination.
- Everyone has the right to a fair trial and will not be arrested without good reason.
- No one shall be a slave.
- No one shall be tortured or punished in a cruel, inhumane or degrading way.
- Everyone has the right to seek asylum from persecution in other countries.
- Adult men and women have the right to marry, regardless of their race or religion.

SOURCE A: *The UN has a charter or collection of aims, which was first listed in September 1945. All countries must sign the UN Declaration of Human Rights before being allowed to join.*

Security Council

The five most powerful countries at the end of World War II (Britain, France, the USA, Russia and China) formed the permanent **Security Council**. They were joined by ten other countries (temporary members) and meet when it looks like a dispute could turn into a war. They can stop countries attacking each other by:

- asking all UN members to stop trading with them until a shortage of supplies forces them to back away from war
- sending in soldiers – or peacekeepers – to prevent or contain the fighting.

Any decisions need a 'yes' from all five permanent members and peacekeepers are sent from armies of several countries.

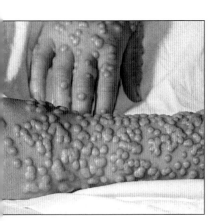

World Health Organization (WHO)

Mounts health campaigns, does research, runs clinics and vaccinates against infectious diseases.

SOURCE B: *One of the WHO's greatest successes was the elimination of smallpox, one of history's biggest killers, through a massive vaccination programme.*

The General Assembly

A sort of world Parliament, with each country having one vote. There were 51 member countries in 1945. By 2000 there were 184.

Secretary General

A key person who manages the UN and speaks on its behalf.

International Labour Organization (ILO)

Tries to protect workers all over the world by improving their conditions, pay, rights and insurance.

Children's fund (UNICEF)

Helps underfed, poorly treated or neglected children throughout the world.

↰ **SOURCE C:** *The logo of the UN. What do you think it means? By 1960, 100 countries were members of the UN. This increased to 127 members by 1970, 154 by 1980 and 184 by 2000.*

International Court of Justice

Based in Holland. Fifteen judges, each from a different nation, settle legal disputes between countries before they lead to war.

Educational, Scientific and Cultural Organization (UNESCO)

Tries to get countries to share each other's films, books, music, sport and scientific discoveries so that they understand each other more and are less likely to fight.

WISE-UP Words

human rights
Security Council

Work

1 Imagine you are representing your country at one of the first meetings of the UN. You are holding a press conference. What would be your answers to these questions?

- Why is this new organisation necessary?
- What is the Security Council and how can it stop one country attacking another?
- Are all nations of the world in the UN?
- How do all countries get a say in UN decisions?
- Why do all countries have to sign the Declaration of Human Rights before being allowed to join the UN?
- People throughout the world are weak and vulnerable after the war – how will the UN help them?

2 Look at Source A. Do you think that some of the rights are more important than others? Explain your answer carefully.

3 a Draw the logo of the UN.

  b Explain what you think the logo means.

MISSION ACCOMPLISHED?

- Could you tell somebody why the UN was set up?
- Can you name one of your human rights?
- Can you list another success of the UN?

Why was there a cold war?

_____ MISSION OBJECTIVES _____
- To be able to explain the reasons why the allies of the Second World War became enemies.
- To understand why it became known as the Cold War.

During World War II, the USA, the USSR and Britain fought together to defeat Nazi Germany and Japan. As the war came to a close, it became clear that the enormous differences these countries shared would be a lot harder to ignore once the fighting had stopped. So just what were these differences? How could allies turn to enemies so quickly? And why did the two sides' armies never go into battle with each other?

Different ways to run a country

By the end of World War II, the USA and the USSR (or Russia as it was often called) had emerged as the two **superpowers** of the world. But the common goal of defeating Hitler had papered over the cracks in their relationship. To begin with, the two countries organised themselves in entirely different ways – USSR was communist, USA was capitalist. Both believed their way was best… and it would set them on a deadly collision course! (See Source B.)

SOURCE A: *American and Russian soldiers meet at the end of World War II. Russian troops had arrived from the east while the Americans arrived from the west and met up around Berlin, Germany's capital.*

SOURCE B: *Communist and capitalist countries are organised very differently. What sort of country do you think you live in today?*

CAPITALISM V. COMMUNISM

HERB'S CARWORKS WHIZ-E TOOLS BUY BURT'S BEER BILL DITT CONSTRUCTION INC. FIDDLER CITY BANK
PRIVATE FIRMS

STATE TRACTOR FACTORY No.4 STATE BUILDING SUPPLIES THE PEOPLE'S BREWERY STATE BANK STATE FOOD STORE No.112
STATE OWNERSHIP

TWO PARTY GOVERNMENT

ONE PARTY GOVERNMENT

SALE LOWER PRICES ½ PRICE SPECIAL OFFER SPRING SALE 25% OFF
FREE ECONOMY

FIXED PRICE 50R. CONTROLLED PRICE 75R. FIXED PRICE 10R. FIXED PRICE 6R.
CONTROLS

GREAT DIFFERENCES IN WEALTH BUT MAJORITY ARE WELL OFF

WEALTH MORE EQUALLY SHARED GENERALLY LESS THAN U.S.A.

Differences over the past

- There was a history of bad feeling between some of the countries that ran back to the First World War. When Russia had a revolution in 1917, Britain and the USA sent troops and supplies to help destroy the new communist government. The Russian leader, Joseph Stalin, had not forgotten this.

- Stalin had been very unpopular in Britain and the USA during the 1930s because of his brutality and because he had signed a peace **pact** with Hitler. It was this pact that brought Britain and France into the war. The '**West**' had not forgotten this.

- Nine out of ten German soldiers killed in World War II died fighting the **Soviets**. The combined deaths of Britain, France and the USA were less than a million. The USSR lost 11 million soldiers and 12 million civilians. Stalin was convinced that the USA and Britain had waited for the Soviet armies to do all the fighting and dying before invading in 1944.

Differences over the future

What to do with war-ravaged Europe quickly caused disagreement. Britain and the USA wanted the countries of Europe – including Germany – to recover fast so they could buy and sell goods with them. Stalin wanted to keep Germany weak and create a 'buffer' of countries that he controlled between the USSR and Germany. Despite several attempts to come to an agreement, Europe became divided in two by what Winston Churchill called an 'iron curtain'. The countries to the west of the curtain became capitalist and had close relationships with the USA. The countries to the east became communist and were controlled by the USSR. Relations between East and West grew worse and worse. Capitalism and communism were in a deadly struggle for control of the world. The Cold War had begun.

SOURCE C:
How Europe was divided after World War Two.

Work

1 In fewer than 50 words, try to explain the differences between capitalism and communism.

2 a List five different reasons why the wartime allies fell out.

   b Which reason do you think was most important? Explain your answer.

Key

— The Iron Curtain

Communist states dominated by the USSR

Other communist states

Areas under Western control

Areas under Soviet control

North Sea

Atlantic Ocean

SWEDEN

NORWAY   FINLAND

DENMARK

EIRE UNITED
      KINGDOM

NETHERLANDS   POLAND
              EAST
BELGIUM   GERMANY

LUXEMBOURG
        WEST
        GERMANY   CZECHOSLOVAKIA

FRANCE

        AUSTRIA   HUNGARY

                  ROMANIA

PORTUGAL ANDORRA   YUGOSLAVIA   *Black Sea*

SPAIN   ITALY   BULGARIA

              ALBANIA   TURKEY

Mediterranean Sea   GREECE

USSR

A 'cold war'

Despite the bad feeling and threats exchanged between the two sides, no actual fighting took place – that is why it became known as the Cold War. If the two sides had sent their armies into battle, it would have become a 'hot war' – just like all the others in history. So why didn't the bullets start flying this time?

A MAD idea

The USA dropped the first nuclear bombs on Japan in 1945 to end World War II. In 1949, the Soviet Union detonated its first nuclear bomb on a test site. Both sides were terrified that the other would soon have more of these horrific weapons than them, so they quickly began **stockpiling** nuclear bombs. They hoped that by having so many, they would put the other side off launching an attack as it would mean the certain destruction of both countries – and the world! This theory became known as Mutually Assured Destruction – or MAD for short.

A close call

Soldiers from the two major cold war nations – USA and USSR – never actually fought directly against each other in over 40 years of tension… but they came very close. In October 1962, for example, the two sides went to the brink of war when an American spy plane saw that Russian ships were taking nuclear missiles to the small Caribbean island of Cuba, just 90 miles from the American coast. Thankfully, after 13 days of unbearable tension, the two countries worked out a deal and the weapons were withdrawn – and the world breathed a huge sigh of relief! However, hostility remained for many years after the Cuban Missile Crisis and the Cold War became a war of nerves, a war of threats and bluffs and of spies and propaganda.

The Cold War thaws

Towards the end of the 1980s the USSR began to struggle to afford its huge army and massive stockpile of nuclear weapons. The Soviet people were very poor and started to make demands to improve their quality of life. The Soviet Union began to collapse. One by one, the countries of Eastern Europe won their freedom from Soviet Control. In 1991, the 15 countries that made up the USSR split up and began to rule themselves. By 1993 the people of Russia had free speech and free elections. The Cold War had come to an end.

WISE-UP Words

pact
Soviets
stockpiling
superpowers
West

SOURCE D: *One hundred nuclear weapons would have guaranteed the total destruction of the world. By the end of the Cold War, the USA and USSR had 40,000 between them. For 40 years, every time the two superpowers fell out, every living thing on the planet faced annihilation.*

Work

1 Explain why the Cold War got its name.

2 In no more than 50 words, explain the theory of Mutually Assured Destruction.

3 What are the dangers of MAD?

4 Do you think MAD was a good idea? Explain your answer carefully and try to think of reasons why World War III was avoided and why the Cold War came to an end.

SOURCE E: *American children were taught to 'duck and cover' under their school desks in the event of a nuclear attack. It would have given no protection whatsoever.*

MISSION ACCOMPLISHED?

• Can you tell someone why the USA and USSR became enemies after World War II?

• Do you know why the Cold War got its name?

Space race

- To be able to explain what the space race was and why it started.
- To come to your own conclusion as to who won the space race.

In the 1950s and 1960s, mankind left the Earth's atmosphere for the first time and began to explore outer space. Enormous amounts of money and resources were spent in trying to send machines, animals and later humans into the inky blackness. So what made space so important all of a sudden? Which countries led the way? And who won the great space race?

A cold war contest

After World War II, the two most powerful nations on the planet were the USA and the USSR. They became known as the superpowers because of their immense military power, raw materials and population. It was these two countries who led mankind's first journeys into space. But rather than work together, they competed fiercely to be the world leader in space exploration. There were two reasons for this:

- The USA and the USSR both had huge numbers of nuclear bombs. This actually prevented them fighting as war would have meant the destruction of the entire world. Instead of competing on the battlefield – like countries normally did – they looked for other ways of proving they were the most powerful country on earth. Space was the perfect alternative battlefield!

- The best way to send nuclear bombs across the world was by intercontinental ballistic missiles (**ICBMs**). In order to cover the huge distances, the missiles had to leave the atmosphere, orbit the Earth, and re-enter the atmosphere over the target. If both superpowers had the technology to send bombs into space – why not send other things? The race was on!

A satellite named *Sputnik*

A **satellite** is an object that orbits another object. The Earth is a satellite of the Sun, and the Moon is a satellite of the Earth. In 1957, the first ever artificial satellite was placed in the Earth's orbit by the Soviet Union. Named *Sputnik*, it was around 50 centimetres in diameter and did little more than send beeps back to earth. It terrified the Americans. If the Soviets could put *Sputnik* in space, they could send a nuclear missile to the United States.

↳ SOURCE A: *The Russian* Sputnik – *the first satellite made by people to be put in space.*

The first space dog

Less than a month after *Sputnik* was launched, the Soviets sent a stray dog from the streets of Moscow into orbit. It was a one-way trip for the dog – named Laika – who died from the extreme heat shortly after leaving the atmosphere. The Soviets kept this quiet but claimed a clear lead in the space race!

The first spaceman

On 12 April 1961, Yuri Gagarin became the first human being to travel into space. The cosmonaut (as the Soviets called their spacemen) made a 108-minute orbit of the Earth on board his *Vostok 1* spacecraft.

The first space walk

On 18 March 1965, Alexei Leonov stepped outside his *Voskhod 2* spacecraft to complete the first space walk in history. Yet another 'first' for the Soviets.

The first man on the moon

On 20 July 1969, the American *Apollo 11* mission delivered astronauts Neil Armstrong and Buzz Aldrin to the surface of the moon. Millions of people around the world watched Armstrong's first historic steps. The USA had at last won a 'first' in the space race – and what a 'first' it was!

↰ SOURCE B: *Landing on the moon.*

↵ SOURCE C: *The USA's* Saturn V *rocket. The space race would have been impossible without technology developed to deliver nuclear bombs.*

Work

1 In your own words, explain why the USA and USSR got involved in the space race. You must include at least two reasons.

2 Who do you think won the space race? Explain your answer very carefully.

3 Why do you think humankind's exploration of space has slowed since the end of the cold war between the USA and USSR? You might want to discuss this as a class first.

➕ Hungry for **MORE**

It wasn't just in space that the USA and USSR tried to prove they were the best. See if you can find out about how they competed in the Olympics and even chess matches!

MISSION ACCOMPLISHED?

• Could you tell someone why the USA and USSR were in such a hurry to explore space? Have you decided who was the space race champion?

103

Did man *really* land on the moon?

MISSION OBJECTIVES

- To decide, based on the evidence in this book, whether you think Neil Armstrong and Buzz Aldrin really landed on the moon.

During the 1950s and 1960s, the USA and the USSR were competing in a frantic 'space race' to be the first to conquer space and put a man on the moon. Both sides were determined to prove that their country and way of life were superior.

American pride was dented in April 1961 by the news that Yuri Gagarin, a Russian astronaut, had become the first human to orbit the Earth. It seemed that Russia had won the **space race**… but not for long! The US President, John F Kennedy, responded by setting what many thought was an impossible target: 'To land a man on the moon and return him safely to earth… by 1970!' Just eight years later, on 20 July 1969, America's *Apollo 11* moon-mission triumphed and Neil Armstrong became the first man to walk on the surface of another world. Millions across earth watched the event 'live' on their TV sets. To many Americans, and other countries of the world, landing a man on the moon was more of an achievement than putting one in space – it showed the greatness of the American way of life and its superiority over the Russians.

↳ SOURCE A: *To those who think the landings were faked, this picture is often used to back up their arguments. They say the photograph is too perfect – it looks like the astronaut posed for it. Some of the other key points made about this picture are listed below.*

- The cameras were mounted on the front of each astronaut's space units (with no auto focus). So why is it such a good picture? Did professional photographers take them in a special studio?
- Why is the flag fluttering? There's no atmosphere on the moon, no breeze at all. A flag wouldn't wave in a vacuum so there must have been a slight wind on the film set.
- Why do the footprints look like they've been set in wet sand? There is no water on the moon to make this happen, so surely the footprints should have disappeared like in the dry sand on a beach.
- And where are the stars? The sky should be full of them!

But as news of the moon landing spread across the earth, another famous story was just beginning. As photographs and film were released, some people began to say the whole mission, including the moon landing itself, was faked. They said that in 1969, Americans didn't have the technology to land men on the moon (and get them back safely) and started to pick apart each and every part of the mission. Even the photograph on this page came under scrutiny (Source A). Some wondered why the photograph was of such good quality. And where are the stars – aren't they meant to be in the background? Sources B and C also point to the fact that the mission was faked.

SOURCE B: *A photograph of a moon rock. Can you see the letter 'C'? The people who think the landings were faked use this photograph to back up their theory that the whole thing was filmed in a TV studio. They suggest that every rock on the 'faked' moon surface was individually labelled, starting at 'A'. This is a close-up photo of rock 'C' (which the people who built the set forgot to turn over!).*

Controversy still rages over this historic event today. Did the Americans fake the landings just to 'get one over' on the Russians? Was it faked in 1969 because the President had promised the American public to put a man on the moon before 1970? Were the moon landings filmed in a TV studio rather than on the moon itself? These pages will ask you to form your opinions on this great debate – was man on the moon in July 1969… or not?

In 2001, a survey in the USA showed that 30% of US citizens believed the 1969 moon landings were faked. It clearly remains a very 'hot topic', not just in the USA, but all over the world. Study these photographs, facts and written sources very carefully. These cover the most controversial areas of the whole topic.

'NASA couldn't make it to the moon, and they knew it! In the late 1950s a study on astronauts landing on the moon found that the chance of success was 0.0017 per cent. In other words, it was hopeless. As late as 1967 three astronauts died in a horrendous fire on the launch pad without even taking off. It was well known that NASA was badly managed and had poor quality control. Yet by 1969 they suddenly put men on the moon. And got them back again with complete success! It's just against all common sense and statistical odds.'

SOURCE C: *Based on an interview by Roger van Bakel with Bill Kaysing published in 1994. Bill Kaysing is famous for writing the book* We Never Went to the Moon, *published in 1974.*

▍▍ PAUSE for Thought
Based on the evidence you have seen so far, what is your opinion? Were the moon landings faked or not?

Now study the following sources of information carefully. The work section will ask for your opinion as to whether the moon landings were faked or not.

'Pictures from astronauts transmitted from the moon don't include stars in the dark lunar sky – an obvious production error! What happened? Did NASA [the US government agency responsible for space travel] film-makers forget to turn on the lights? Most photographers already know the answer: it's difficult to capture something very bright and something else very dim on the same piece of film... astronauts striding across the bright lunar soil in their sunlit spacesuits were dazzling. Setting a camera up properly for a glaring space suit could make the background stars too faint to see.'

⤴ SOURCE D: *From a science website.*

'[The mark on the rock] is not a "C". The photograph is a copy of the original photograph. If you look at the original, taken in 1969, the "C" disappears. This is simply because all it is, is a tiny hair that has got into one of the copies along the way.'

⤴ SOURCE E: *Evidence from a website that tries to prove that the moon landings were not faked,* www.redzero.demon.co.uk/moonhoax/.

'The astronauts received a great deal of training before they left earth; part of this was in the operation of cameras, which were specially designed to be used by the astronauts with their suits on. The *Apollo* astronauts took around 17,000 photographs... and there's plenty of not-so-great ones that NASA have never published... only the best ones were released to the world.'

⤴ SOURCE F: *Further evidence that the moon landings were not faked.*

'The flag isn't waving. It looks like that because of the way it's been put up. The flag hangs from a horizontal rod, which pulls out from the vertical one. In *Apollo 11*, they couldn't get the rod to extend completely, so the flag didn't get stretched fully. It has a ripple in it like a curtain that is not fully closed... it appears to have fooled a lot of people into thinking it waved.'

⤴ SOURCE G: *From a space website,* www.badastronomy.com.

'The Russians were watching the USA space programme like hawks and analysing everything the Americans did. If there was the slightest suggestion that a hoax was happening, the Russians would have been falling over themselves to tell the world about it.'

⤴ SOURCE H: *An answer to the question: 'The first man on the moon: real or fake?' posted on the Internet in 2008.*

⤴ SOURCE I: *The three astronauts of the Apollo II moon misssion: Neil Armstrong, Michael Collins and Buzz Aldrin.*

WISE-UP Words

space race

Work

Now you've had a chance to look through the evidence, it's time to decide whether YOU think the USA put man on the moon in 1969.

1 Find reasons why the USA felt it was really important to put a man on the moon before the USSR. What was the 'space race'? How had the USSR dented American pride in 1961? What had President Kennedy promised and why? Why would the USA want to beat the Russians and put a man on the moon before them?

2 Find evidence that the moon landings were faked. Think about the photographs. What is 'wrong' with some of them? Make notes on the suspicions surrounding the moon landings.

3 Find any evidence that the moon landings were not faked. Can any of the 'errors' on the photographs be explained? Make notes that answer some of the suspicions about the landings from Step 2.

4 Time to make up your mind! Were the moon landings faked? Write a short report for a children's TV programme about the moon landings. In your report, you should express your opinion about the moon landing debate. Remember, you must back up your theory with evidence.

'Beverly Hills, California, USA – detectives are investigating a complaint that retired astronaut Buzz Aldrin punched a man in the face after being asked to swear on a Bible that he had been to the moon... [the man] said he does not believe Aldrin or anyone else has ever walked on the moon.'

↰ SOURCE J: *CNN News, 10 September 2002.*

—MISSION ACCOMPLISHED?—

- Can you recall at least two pieces of evidence that support the claims that man landed on the moon?

- Can you remember two pieces of evidence that support the theory that the moon landing was faked?

BRITAIN ABROAD

This enquiry concentrates on the decline of the world's largest ever empire – the British Empire – focusing in detail on the independence of African colonies and, firstly, on the struggle for freedom of one of Britain's most treasured 'possessions' – India.

1: The 'jewel in the crown'

MISSION OBJECTIVES

- To understand the different factors that contributed to the decline of the world's largest ever empire.

During the reign of Queen Victoria, Britain spent enormous amounts of time, energy and resources conquering foreign lands all over the world. Collectively, the land Britain controlled was known as the British Empire.

By the time of Queen Victoria's death in 1901, land nearly 40 times the size of Britain itself belonged to the British Empire. Britain ruled over 450 million people living in 56 different places – or colonies – all over the world. This amounted to approximately one quarter of the world! Put simply, at the start of the 1900s the British Empire was the biggest empire the world had ever known (see Source A).

Fifty years later, after two world wars, the British Empire was breaking apart. More and more countries wanted nothing to do with Britain. They wanted their chance to run their countries themselves – they wanted their independence. And Britain, still trying to rebuild after World War II, was in no position to stop them. One by one, nearly all Britain's colonies became independent countries and today, Britain's Empire consists of only a few tiny islands! So whatever happened to the British Empire? Let's start by looking at India.

Incredible India

India was one of Britain's largest possessions. It was the colony that many Britons treasured most, calling it the 'jewel in the crown' of the Empire. Even Queen Victoria herself enjoyed the title 'Queen of Great Britain and Empress of India'.

SOURCE A: *A Victorian map of the British Empire from 1886. The colonies are shown in blue. Some of the people (and animals) who lived in the empire are printed around the map.*

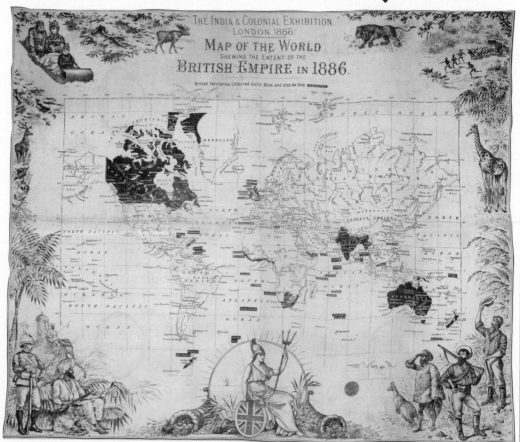

British rule

The British takeover of India was gradual. In the 1700s a group of British businessmen set up the East India Company and began trading with Indian princes for silk, tea and spices. Many of the employees of this company lived in great luxury in India and made huge fortunes. The company even had its own private army, which it used to seize more and more Indian land. In 1857 the Indians rebelled against the British control of their land, but the rebellion was crushed brutally. Two years later the British Government took over the powers of the East India Company and began to rule India directly. A **viceroy** was put in charge of India on behalf of Queen Victoria herself – and was joined by thousands of British soldiers who made sure he was able to maintain control.

Changing a nation

The issue of British control and influence in India has always been controversial and has often been interpreted differently. Some argue that India benefited from British influence in some ways. By 1900 the British had built nearly 50,000 miles of road, as well as railways, schools and hospitals. They built dams to help flood areas and dug nearly 70,000 miles of canal. They also introduced a new legal system and helped settle ancient feuds between rival areas and regions… whether the Indians wanted these things or not!

But India suffered too. British customs were forced on them and local traditions, culture and religions were sometimes ignored. Indian workers were often exploited, the country's raw materials taken back to Britain and native lands were seized… and if there was ever any resistance, the British army usually came down very hard on the rebels!

Size
- Larger than the continent of Europe
- Fifteen times bigger than the British Isles

Population and religion
- 300 million, 1/5 of the population of the world
- 207 million Hindus
- 62.5 million Muslims
- 6 million Sikhs
- Plus millions of Buddhists, Christians and others

Languages
- 15 main languages – Hindi and Pakistani – northern and central areas
- Urdu and Gujarati – west
- Bengali – east
- Tamil – south

Main resources
- Cotton
- Tea
- Iron ore
- Coal
- Rice
- Diamonds

↰ **SOURCE B:** *British India factfile. The present day countries of India, Pakistan, Burma, Bangladesh and Sri Lanka were all included within the borders of British India.*

'Wherever the British go… we replace misery, poverty, cruelty and disorder with peace, justice, wealth, humanity and freedom.'

↰ **SOURCE C:** *The views of Lord Curzon, a former Viceroy of India.*

'Can these thieves really be our rulers? These thieves… import a huge number of goods made in their own country and sell them in our markets, stealing our wealth and taking life from our people. Can those who steal the harvest of our fields and doom us to hunger, fever and plague, really be our rulers? Can foreigners really be our rulers?'

↰ **SOURCE D:** *A leaflet written by Indians who wanted the British out. Who do you think the thieves were?*

↵ **SOURCE E:** *A painting of Lord Curzon's Durbar, held when King Edward VII became King after Queen Victoria's death. A durbar was a large ceremonial meeting and this one was so big that they had to build a railway track five miles long to take people around it. All of the most important people in India attended. It went on for ten days and finished with a Christian church service. The elephants pictured here carry Indian princes and are decorated with fine cloth, gold, silver, diamonds and pearls valued at £100 000 each in today's money!*

Indian independence?

By 1900, many educated Indians started to believe that India should be free from British control. A political group called the Indian National Congress was formed to bring this about, but despite holding meetings and organising demonstrations, the British ignored their demands.

In 1914, Indians fought alongside British soldiers in the Great War (see Source F). India itself gave Britain a huge amount of money, food and materials – and nearly 50,000 Indian soldiers died in the trenches!

In 1919, the British Government responded to Indian demands for a greater say in running their country and made slight changes to the way India was governed. Law-making councils were set up in each province and over five million wealthy Indians were given the vote. However, the British Government, based in London, still controlled taxation, the police, the law courts, the armed forces, education and much more. Whilst some welcomed the changes as a step in the right direction, others were bitterly disappointed. A demonstration in the town of Amritsar in the province of Punjab was put down with severe violence by British troops. The local British commander in charge of the soldiers ordered his men to fire into the crowd – killing 379 Indian men, women and children.

The Amritsar incident was a turning point for the Indian National Congress and its leader, Mohandas Gandhi. He wrote, 'when a Government takes up arms against its unarmed subjects, then it has lost the right to govern'. The Congress, more loudly than ever, demanded an independent India.

⤶ **SOURCE F:** *A picture of Naik Darwan Sing Negi, the first Indian winner of the Victoria Cross, Britain's top bravery medal, in 1914. He was part of an Indian battalion fighting with the British army during the Great War.*

Gandhi

Gandhi, a holy man and a very clever politician, told Indians to do all they could to make life difficult for the British, without using violence. Today, this is called passive resistance. Gandhi called it 'satyagraha', which means 'soul force pure and simple'. He encouraged strikes, demonstrations and boycotts (for example, asking Indians not to buy any goods made in Britain). His most famous protest occurred in 1930 when he began a campaign against the salt tax. At the time, Indians were not allowed to make their own salt – they had to buy it – and it was heavily taxed by the British Government. Ghandi led thousands of Indians to the coast where they began making salt from seawater. All over India, Indians copied Gandhi 's example until, after putting 100,000 people in prison, the British gave in and got rid of the salt tax. By 1935, after many years of non-violent (and in some cases violent) protests, the Government of India Act gave Indians the right to control everything except the army. India, however, was still part of the British Empire and was still ruled by a viceroy. Many Indians, including Gandhi, continued to demand complete independence.

⤶ **SOURCE G:** *A photograph of Gandhi, taken in 1925. Every day he span cotton on a small spinning wheel to encourage people to lead simple lives. He wanted Indians to be proud of their country and realise that they didn't need British rule to survive.*

SOURCE H: *Indian soldiers with a captured German cannon in the Libyan desert in 1943.*

India at war again!

In 1939, when World War II began, India was still part of the British Empire. Like in World War I, thousands of Indians joined up to fight as part of the British Empire force. In total, 2.5 million Indians fought in what was the largest volunteer army in history.

After the war, it was clear that Britain would have to give India its independence. Britain wasn't strong enough to hold on to a country so desperate to rule itself – and the people in Britain, tired of war, weren't keen to see their soldiers trying to control marches and demonstrations that so easily turned to violence!

'How can you even dream of Hindu-Muslim unity? Everything pulls us apart. We have no inter-marriages. We do not have the same calendar. The Muslims believe in a single God, the Hindus worship idols... The Hindus worship animals and consider cows sacred. We, the Muslims, think it is nonsense. We want to kill the cows and eat them. There are only two links between the Muslims and Hindus: British rule – and the common desire to get rid of it.'

SOURCE I: *From a 1944 interview with Mohammed Ali Jinnah, the leader of an Indian political party called the Muslim League. He eventually became Pakistan's first leader.*

But the whole matter of independence was complicated by the increasing violence between Hindus and Muslims. Relations had been bad for a long time, but after 1945, they started to break down completely. If India gained its independence, Muslims didn't want to be ruled by a mainly Hindu government (remember, there were a lot more Hindus in India than Muslims – see Source B). Instead, Muslims wanted a country of their own, made from areas where people were Muslims. They were to name this new country after these areas – P for Punjab, A for Afghanis, K for Kashmir, S for Sind and TAN for Baluchistan. The word PAKISTAN means 'land of the pure' in Urdu.

As violence between Muslims and Hindus continued, the British hurriedly made plans to split India into two countries – India would be for Hindus and Pakistan would be for Muslims. The millions of Sikhs, who felt they didn't belong in either, would have to choose one or the other.

Partition of 1947

On 15 August 1947, Britain stopped ruling India. The whole sub-continent was divided into Hindu India and Muslim Pakistan (itself divided into two parts – see Source J). Immediately there were problems. As it was impossible to make sure that the boundaries were drawn so that all Muslims were in Pakistan and all Hindus were in India, millions now found themselves in the wrong country. As they fled across the boundaries to be in the country of their religion, whole trainloads were massacred by the 'other' side. Nobody knows exactly how many were killed, but some have estimated as many as one million! Then, at the height of this violence and bloodshed, Gandhi himself, the man who had believed in non-violence, was assassinated by an extremist Hindu.

The troubled start for the new, independent nations of India and Pakistan continued. Major differences continue to this day.

The cost of World War II in terms of money, lives and buildings meant that the British Government had to concentrate on rebuilding Britain itself. As the Empire took a back seat, many colonies, like India, under British rule demanded their independence. Today, the British Empire consists of a few loyal islands.

SOURCE J: *How India was divided. Areas where more than half the people were Muslim became Pakistan whilst areas where over half the population were Hindu became India. This left millions in the 'wrong' country. It has been estimated that over 14 million fled to the 'other side' in 1947. Thousands from both religions were slaughtered on the way.* ↱

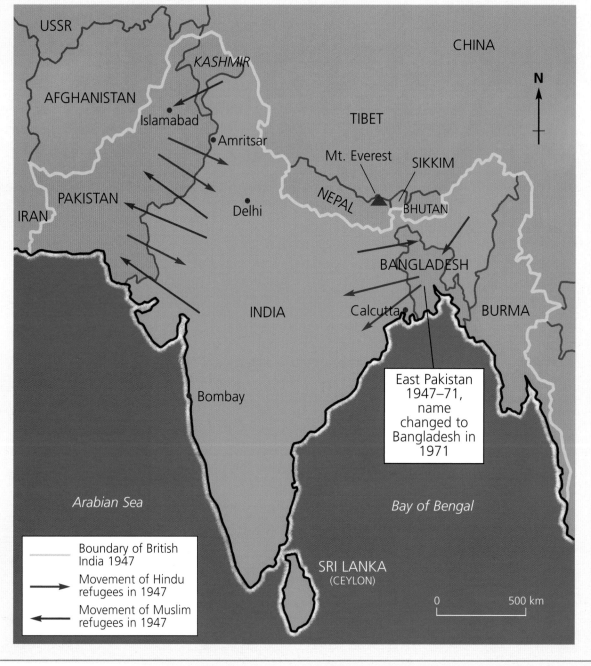

↵ **SOURCE K:**
Partition violence.

! FACT The Raj

The British Raj (or rule) extended over 300 million people. The present day countries of India, Pakistan, Burma, Bangladesh and Sri Lanka were all included within the border of British India.

✚ Hungry for MORE

Find out what's left of the British Empire. Which countries or colonies are still part of the British Empire? Make a timeline showing when different nations gained their independence from Britain. What is the British Commonwealth?

Work

1 This wordsearch contains seven words or names connected with British India. When you find each one, write a sentence about it in your book.

M	U	S	L	I	M	P
L	S	R	O	T	N	Q
V	I	C	E	R	O	Y
S	K	O	F	E	Z	H
T	H	T	N	M	R	I
E	E	T	P	Z	U	N
A	O	O	Q	R	C	D
P	L	N	N	M	I	U

2 a What advantages did the British think they introduced to India?

b What do you think some Indians thought about British rule in India?

3 Look at Source E. In your own words, explain what is going on in the picture.

4 a How did India contribute to the Great War?

b What changes were made to the way the British governed India after the Great War?

c Why were some Indians happy with these changes?

d Why were others disappointed?

e What happened in Amritsar in 1919?

5 Look at Source G.

a Why did Mohandas Gandhi lead such a simple life?

b Why do you think his protest against the salt tax annoyed the British so much?

c Was Gandhi pleased with the Government of India Act? Explain your answer carefully.

6 a Why was India split into two countries in 1947?

b How did Pakistan get its name?

c Why did there continue to be violence between Hindus and Muslims even after India and Pakistan became separate countries?

d What do you think Sikh people disliked about the new countries and borders?

7 Look at Source I.

a Who was Mohammed Ali Jinnah?

b In your own words, explain why Jinnah thought that unity between Hindus and Muslims was impossible.

—MISSION ACCOMPLISHED?—

• Can you sum up, in no more than one hundred words, how India gained its independence from British rule?

Look at Source A carefully. The map shows the huge continent of Africa – and the colours indicate which European nation owned that particular area in 1900. You should quickly notice that almost all of Africa was ruled by seven European nations – Britain, France, Germany, Spain, Portugal, Belgium and Italy.

2: Independence in Africa

MISSION OBJECTIVES

- To understand why Africa became the focus of expansion for several European nations in the 1800s.
- To understand how African nations regained their independence during the twentieth century.

As you can see in Source A, there are a few independent African countries, but most have been taken over or colonised by the Europeans. In fact, between 1880 and 1900 over 80% of Africa was divided up among the European powers. This expansion was sometimes fiercely resisted by local tribes or settlers, but attracted by valuable raw materials such as diamonds and gold and cheap labour, the majority of Africa was 'swallowed up' by the European powers in the 1800s. Britain itself took over control of 16 colonies in Africa, including Egypt, the Sudan, Nigeria, Kenya, Rhodesia (now Zimbabwe) and South Africa. This, combined with other colonies such as India, Australia and Canada, made the British Empire the largest the world had ever known.

Now look at Source D on page 115. Again it shows Africa, but this time it shows the continent at the start of the twenty-first century, in the year 2000. You will notice that there is no key this time showing which European power owns which area. Instead you can see a whole continent of independent countries, not tied or controlled, or ruled by anyone other than themselves. So how was independence achieved?

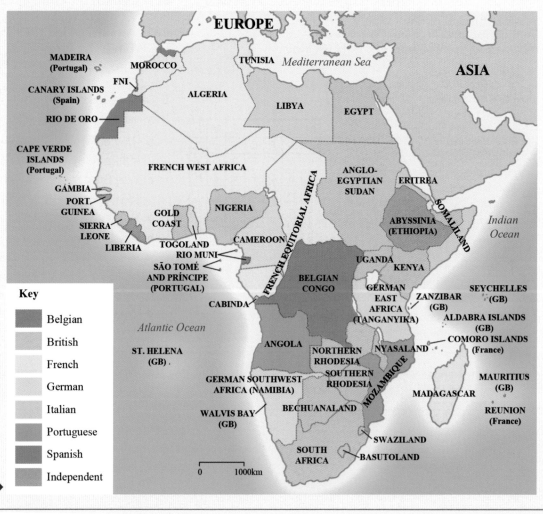

SOURCE A: *Africa in 1900.*

Controlling Africa

As you can see from Source A, there were four main European powers that controlled Africa in the early 1900s: Britain, France, Belgium and Portugal… and each of these countries viewed their colonies differently. Britain thought of itself as a parent – the mother country – helping their colonies to develop. Queen Victoria herself said that Britain's role was to 'protect the poor natives and advance civilisation'. France believed its role was to turn Africans into Frenchmen. Their colonies were run from Paris and treated as part of France. Belgium and Portugal ruled their colonies very harshly and were determined to hold onto them for as long as possible. In general though, all European powers exploited their colonies in some way. They took their raw materials and used the natives as cheap labour. Africans had no say in how their countries were ruled and European settlers banished Africans from the best land and took it for themselves.

When they first came they had the Bible and we had the land. Now we have the Bible and they have the land.

↳ **SOURCE B:** *An African saying.*

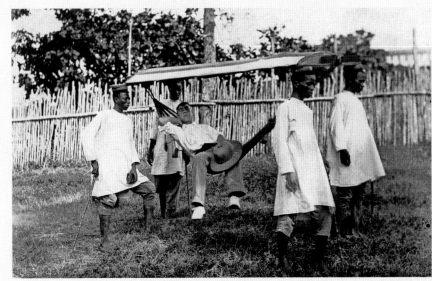

↳ **SOURCE C:**
An amazing photograph showing a white European settler using local men at his colonial mansion in Africa.

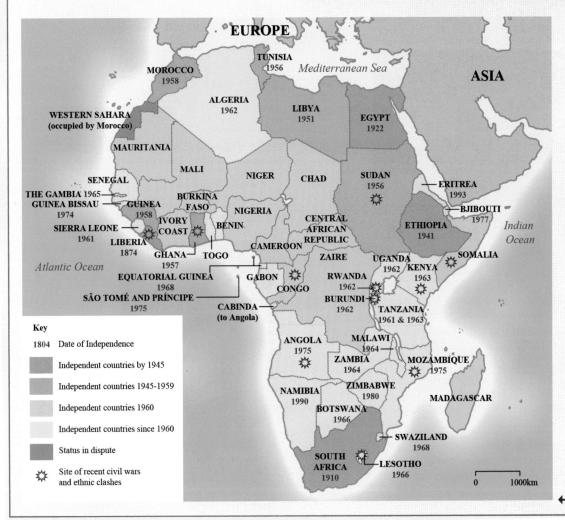

Key

1804	Date of Independence
	Independent countries by 1945
	Independent countries 1945-1959
	Independent countries 1960
	Independent countries since 1960
	Status in dispute
✶	Site of recent civil wars and ethnic clashes

↵ **SOURCE D:** *Africa in 2000.*

The impact of World War II

Some of Britain's colonies – such as Canada, Australia, New Zealand and South Africa – had been running their own affairs for years. Australia, for example, had been part of the British Empire since 1770, but by 1900 it had its own Parliament that was making most of the key decisions about the country. New Zealand became a British colony in 1840, but had gained the freedom to run its own affairs by 1907. In Africa, South Africa had been self-governing since 1910 and Egypt since 1922.

By the end of World War II, more and more colonies were demanding the right to govern themselves. And by 1945 countries like Britain and France no longer had the strength or wealth to hold on to their colonies. Many Africans had fought for Britain and France against Nazi Germany too. They felt they were fighting to defend freedom yet were frustrated that their own countries were not yet free.

When India won its independence from Britain in 1947, it led to a whole host of countries demanding their freedom. In 1957, the first British colony in Africa got its independence when the Gold Coast (as it was known under British rule) became Ghana. Source D on the previous page shows the speed at which independence spread through Africa.

↰ **SOURCE E:** *A jubilant crowd carries Julius Nyerere, premier of Tanganyika (Tanzania), after being granted internal self-government. The following year he was made president on independence.*

The transfer of power

In the British colonies, independence for African nations was achieved fairly peacefully. There were riots in some places like Kenya, but on the whole the transfer of power went smoothly. Newly independent nations like Nigeria, Gambia and Kenya were invited to join the **British Commonwealth**, an organisation of independent, free countries with close cultural, trade and sporting links to Britain.

Elsewhere in Africa some of the other European nations were reluctant to give up their colonies. In Angola and Mozambique, for example, Portugal's determination to hang onto these colonies led to a long war between African and Portuguese soldiers. In Algeria, French forces fought to keep control from 1945, until independence was finally agreed in 1962.

↰ **SOURCE F:** *The Commonwealth Games, once known as the Empire Games, is a sports competition held every four years in one of the former colonies of the British Empire. Athletes from former British colonies are invited to participate.*

SOURCE G: *In recent years there have been several high-profile campaigns and events (such as Make Poverty History and Live 8) aimed at helping some of the world's poorest countries, including many in Africa. Comic Relief, for example, raises millions with its Red Nose Day to fund aid projects all over Africa.* ↱

A new Africa

For many newly independent nations, freedom produced its difficulties as well as its benefits. Some nations, like Morocco, Tunisia and Egypt have developed thriving tourist industries, while others have made good use of raw materials such as rubber, gold and diamonds. However, some countries have seen rivalries between tribes flare up into bloody civil war. This happened in Nigeria in the 1960s, Uganda in the 1980s, and Sierra Leone, Rwanda and Somalia in the 1990s. Many new nations have struggled to create their own systems of government, build up their own industry and trade, and cope with internal divisions. Source H shows some of the problems faced by some of the newly independent African nations in the years after they gained freedom. Yet perhaps the greatest problem the newly independent nations have had to deal with is poverty. Of the 25 poorest countries in the world, 17 are in Africa… and despite offers of loans and aid from richer countries the problems of poverty and long-term debt still remain.

	Country	Ruler	Date of independence	The price of freedom?
	Algeria	France	1962	Independence was achieved only after unrest and an armed rebellion.
	Angola	Portugal	1975	There has been a civil war in Angola since 1975.
	Congo	France	1960	Congo had a civil war after independence and its first president was assassinated.
	Ghana	Britain	1957	Ghana's government has been plagued by rebellion and corruption.
	Kenya	Britain	1963	Kenya was ruled as a one-party state until 1992.
	Mauritania	France	1960	In a military coup, Mauritania's first president was overthrown.
	Mozambique	Portugal	1975	Mozambique suffers from famine and poverty due to civil war, a lack of food supplies and debt.
	Nigeria	Britain	1960	Since independence, Nigeria has been under almost constant military rule.
	Senegal	France	1960	Senegal was ruled as a virtual one-party government until the 1980s.
	Uganda	Britain	1962	A turbulent period led to over a million deaths.
	Zimbabwe	Britain	1980	Zimbabwe won independence after the black majority defeated the white minority. Tension continues.

↳ **SOURCE H:** *African independence, adapted from* DK Pockets World History *by Philip Wilkinson (1996).*

WISE-UP Words

British Commonwealth

Work

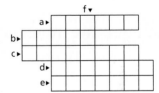

1 a Describe how **one** of the British **or** the French **or** the Belgians **or** the Portuguese ruled their colonies.

 b Why were African colonies such a 'rich prize'?

 c How did World War II change the situation for African colonies?

2 Copy out and complete the word grid below, using clues a–e. When you have correctly completed the grid, a word will be revealed (f). Write a sentence about the word in line f.

Clues:
a) Portuguese colony, independent in 1975.
b) _____ Africa: self-governing since 1910.
c) Formerly Rhodesia.
d) Former French colony.
e) New _____: a former British colony.

3 Explain what is meant by the term 'British Commonwealth'.

4 a In your own words, explain what challenges many African nations have faced since independence.

 b Have **you** ever 'helped out' an African nation? Think carefully – there are lots of ways you may have done.

5 Many historians say that Britain lost its Empire because of its involvement in two world wars. Do you agree with this view? Use the information on these four pages to support your answer.

— MISSION ACCOMPLISHED? —

• Can you explain how an independent Africa was achieved after World War II?

HOW TOLERANT IS MODERN BRITAIN?

Different groups and nationalities have been moving to Britain for hundreds of years, but during the twentieth century there was an increase in the amount of people from all over the world deciding to make their homes in this country. This **migration** had a dramatic effect on British society and way of life – changing everything from the music we listen to, to the way we speak and the food we eat. So just why did people decide to move to Britain? Where in the world did they come from? And how were they treated when they got here?

1: The Empire comes home

MISSION OBJECTIVES

• To be able to explain where Britain's immigrant population moved from.

Britain has attracted people from all four corners of the world – but some areas have provided more immigrants than others.

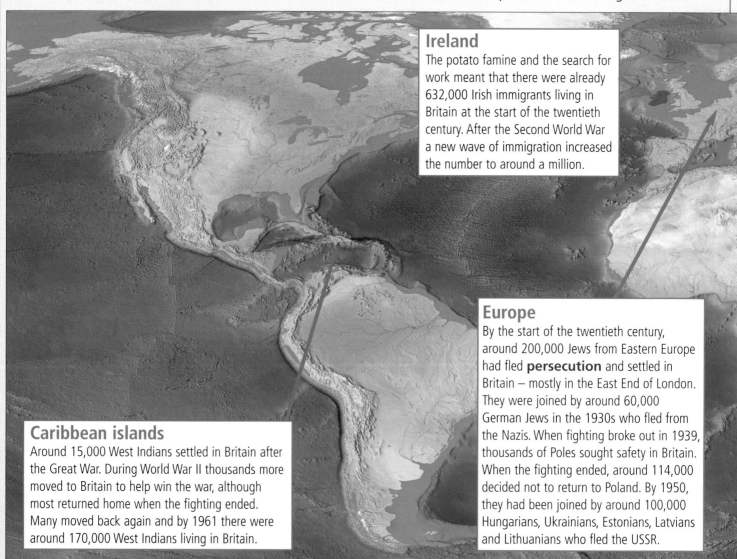

Ireland
The potato famine and the search for work meant that there were already 632,000 Irish immigrants living in Britain at the start of the twentieth century. After the Second World War a new wave of immigration increased the number to around a million.

Europe
By the start of the twentieth century, around 200,000 Jews from Eastern Europe had fled **persecution** and settled in Britain – mostly in the East End of London. They were joined by around 60,000 German Jews in the 1930s who fled from the Nazis. When fighting broke out in 1939, thousands of Poles sought safety in Britain. When the fighting ended, around 114,000 decided not to return to Poland. By 1950, they had been joined by around 100,000 Hungarians, Ukrainians, Estonians, Latvians and Lithuanians who fled the USSR.

Caribbean islands
Around 15,000 West Indians settled in Britain after the Great War. During World War II thousands more moved to Britain to help win the war, although most returned home when the fighting ended. Many moved back again and by 1961 there were around 170,000 West Indians living in Britain.

✚ Hungry for MORE

In recent years, due to the ease and cheapness of travel, the number of people choosing to live and work in another country has greatly increased. That not only means people have been moving to Britain – it means British people have started new lives abroad. See if you can find out what kind of people have moved to Britain in recent years. And find out the number-one destination for Brits abroad.

SOURCE A: *This poster was produced in WWII. It showed all the people of the British Empire – no matter what race, nationality or religion – working together under the same flag.* ↱

TOGETHER

★ WISE-UP Words

migration
partition
persecution

Work

1 Create a bar chart to show the numbers of immigrants that have moved to Britain from different parts of the world.

2 Do you think the British Empire has influenced immigration to Britain? Give reasons for your answer.

3 Look at the poster on this page. In your own words, describe the poster. Also write a sentence or two about the message of the poster.

Cyprus

Cyprus was very poor in the years following World War II and things got worse after Turkey invaded and divided the island in two. Around 70,000 Cypriots left and now call Britain home.

Hong Kong, Malaysia and Singapore

People from the Far East began to move to Britain throughout the 1950s and 1960s. Most came from the poorer areas of the British colony of Hong Kong, and by 1961 there were around 30,000 people from the Far East living in Britain. In 1997, Hong Kong stopped being a British colony and became part of China. Around 50,000 people were given British passports on the 'handover'.

Kenya and Uganda

Many of the people who moved to Britain from East Africa in the 1960s and 1970s were Asians who suffered racism and persecution from Africans. Around 44,000 Kenyan Asians settled in Britain in the late 1960s and 26,000 Ugandan Asians made the move in the early 1970s.

India, Pakistan and Bangladesh

When the 'jewel in the crown' was given independence from Britain in 1947, it split into three countries: India, Pakistan and Bangladesh. This **partition** of India led to fighting and many thousands of people died as whole populations moved across the dividing lines. Some sought safety in the former 'mother country' – Britain. In 1955, there were around 10,000 immigrants from India, Pakistan and Bangladesh living in Britain and trying to improve their standard of living. By 1991, around 1.5 million people from the Indian sub-continent were living and working in Britain.

— MISSION ACCOMPLISHED? —

• Can you name a country that provided migrants from the British Empire?

• Can you name a country that provided Britain with immigrants that wasn't in the British Empire?

On 22 June 1948, a ship named the *Empire Windrush* landed at Tilbury docks in London. On board were 492 passengers – the vast majority of them men – who had come to live in Britain. It was an event that would change British social history forever. So just what made these newcomers special, and what made them move to Britain? How were they treated? And how did they help to change life in Britain?

2: What was so special about the *Windrush*?

MISSION OBJECTIVES

- To explain why some people of the British Empire decided to start new lives in Britain.
- To know what was significant about the *Empire Windrush*.
- To be aware of how the '*Windrush* generation' was treated in Britain.

Moving to the mother country

During World War II, Britain relied heavily on people from all over the Empire to survive the attack from Nazi Germany and Japan. The Caribbean islands had supplied over 10,000 men for Britain's army, navy and air force, and for many of these men, the war was an exciting opportunity full of new sights and experiences. When the fighting ended, they found they had little to celebrate when they were sent back home. Life was very hard in the Caribbean in the 1940s. Jamaica had been devastated by a hurricane in 1944, there was no tourist industry and the price of sugar – the Caribbean's only export – was at an all-time low. For ambitious young men, it was clear that their future lay abroad – under the grey skies of Britain.

Why Britain?

In 1948 Parliament passed the British Nationality Act. This meant that all the people of the Empire – now called the Commonwealth – were British passport holders and were allowed to live and work in Britain. Many of these people had been brought up speaking English, had been named after British heroes and educated to believe in Queen and country. Britain was also very short of workers.

Welcome *Windrush*?

The voyage of the *Windrush* made headlines in Britain before the ship had even landed. Thousands of immigrants from Europe and Ireland had been pouring into the country since the war had finished, but it was the arrival of one ship of English speaking, Christian, British subjects that caused alarm. Newspapers were full of stories of the 'colour problem' that was heading towards Britain's shores and some MPs demanded that the ship was turned around. When the *Windrush* finally docked, the smartly dressed West Indians smiled nervously at the journalists and one of them sang a song called *London's the Place for Me*. Soon, they had all found jobs, and friends and relatives followed in search of work. **Multi-cultural** and **multi-racial** Britain had arrived.

SOURCE A: The first black immigrants after WWII to Britain became known as the 'Windrush generation'.

SOURCE B: Many black people faced prejudice and difficulty finding housing. This led to 'black areas' being created in most of Britain's big cities.

SOURCE C: The NHS, London Transport, the British Hotels Association and the British Transport Commission all encouraged people from the Caribbean to move to Britain.

'I knew a lot about Britain from schooldays, but it was a different picture when you came face-to-face with the facts. They tell you it is the 'mother country', you're all welcome, you're all British. When you come here you realise you're a foreigner and that's all there is to it.'

SOURCE D: John Richards – one of the passengers on the Empire Windrush.

'The second day in England I was offered five jobs. If someone want to leave, let them leave, but I have been here during the War fighting Nazi Germany and I came back and help build Britain. People said that we would not stay longer than one year; we are here, and I and my people are here to stay.'

SOURCE E: Sam King – one of the passengers on the Empire Windrush.

'We appreciate of course that these people are human beings, but to bring coloured labour into the British countryside would be a most unwise and unfortunate act.'

SOURCE F: The General Secretary of the National Union of Agricultural Workers speaking in 1947.

Work

1 Give three reasons why people may have wanted to leave the Caribbean at the end of World War II.

2 Give three reasons why people from the Caribbean may have chosen to move to Britain.

3 Why might people from the Caribbean believe they had a right to live in Britain in the 1940s and 1950s?

4 Read Source F. Was the man who said these words racist? Explain your answer.

5 Why do you think the Windrush caused more alarm in the papers and in Parliament than immigration from Europe and Ireland? Explain your answer very carefully.

6 Was Britain in the 1940s and 1950s a tolerant place? Explain your answer carefully.

Although many in Britain were alarmed by the arrival of people of different religions, cultures and colours, it didn't stop these people building new lives and making their homes here. At first the immigrants were often treated like strange outsiders, but gradually, over the years, they have become an important part of, and have made a large contribution to, British society and culture. In fact, it is hard to imagine what life in Britain would be like without the influence of immigration. So just what changes have immigrants made to British society? How has their arrival helped the people of Britain? And does this mean that modern Britain is a tolerant place?

3: Immigration nation

―――――― MISSION OBJECTIVES ――――――
- To be able to explain how immigration has affected life in Britain.

Cultural contribution

SOURCE A: John Lennon and Paul McCartney are the most successful singer-songwriters in the history of the world. They were born in Liverpool, but both had Irish grandparents who had moved to England in search of work.

SOURCE B: George Michael has sold over 100 million records and is one of Britain's most successful singers. Born in London, his real name is Georgios-Kyriacos Panayiotou and his father moved to Britain from Cyprus in the 1950s.

SOURCE C: Immigration from the West Indies has had a huge influence on British music. Bands such as UB40, The Specials (above) and Madness used the reggae sounds of Jamaica – brought to Britain by Caribbean immigrants – to produce records that were hits all over the world. In recent years, the music of India and Pakistan has started to have an increasing influence on the British music scene.

SOURCE D: The Notting Hill Carnival in London is the second largest street festival in the world. It was started in 1964 by the area's large Caribbean community to celebrate their culture. It is now a major national event that attracts up to two million visitors of all backgrounds every year.

Hungry for MORE

Many of Britain's greatest Olympians have been either immigrants or the descendants of immigrants to Britain. See if you can find out more about the achievements and backgrounds of Daley Thompson, Linford Christie, Kelly Holmes and Christine Ohuruogu.

SOURCE F: *England's cricket team has included many players of different racial backgrounds for a long time. In recent years they have been captained by Nasser Hussain (who was born in India to an Indian father and English mother) and Kevin Pietersen (who was born and raised in South Africa).*

SOURCE E: *Britain's sporting teams – especially England's – have benefited from immigration for many years. Viv Anderson became the first black player to represent England at football in 1978 and Paul Ince became the first to captain his country in 1993. Since Anderson's debut, over 60 black players have appeared for England.*

! FACT Say what? Immigration has even influenced the English language. Look below at just a few everyday words that have been absorbed from other cultures:
Arabic: sofa, alcohol, sugar
Turkish: coffee, yoghurt
Gaelic: slogan, trousers
Hindi: bangle, shampoo, pyjama

Getting better

Many people see the National Health Service as one of Britain's greatest achievements. It means that everybody gets healthcare if they need it – not just if they can afford it. But it may not have been possible without the help of immigrants. In 2008, of the 243,770 doctors who worked for the NHS, 91,360 trained abroad before moving to work in British hospitals. Thirteen per cent of nurses were born outside the UK and, for the last ten years, half of all the other vital NHS positions have been filled by people who qualified abroad.

A changing diet

Immigration has completely changed what people in Britain eat. In 1957, there were only 50 Chinese restaurants in the whole country. By 1970, there were over 4000, and now there is one in almost every town and village in the country. The food brought by immigrants from India, Pakistan and Bangladesh has been even more popular, and the curry now rivals the Sunday roast and fish and chips as Britain's national dish. Chicken Tikka Masala is the country's best-selling ready meal and 'going for a balti' has become a weekly event for millions of Britons. It is now such a part of life in Britain that a song called *Vindaloo* became an anthem for the England football team!

Hungry for MORE

Many things that people consider to be 'typically British' are in fact the result of immigration to these islands. See if you can find out more about the origins of Marks and Spencer, Tesco, ice cream vans and Punch and Judy shows.

Work

1 a Describe how immigration has affected British:

healthcare • diet • sport • music

b For each category, explain if you think the effect of immigration has been positive (a good thing) or negative (a bad thing).

2 Do you believe that modern Britain has been open to new ideas and change? Do you believe modern Britain is a tolerant country? Explain your answer carefully.

MISSION ACCOMPLISHED?

- Could you tell someone three ways in which immigration has affected British society?
- Have you decided if modern Britain is a tolerant place?

The Rosa Parks story

MISSION OBJECTIVES

• To understand the significance of the Montgomery Bus Boycott in the Civil Rights Movement.

In 1863, President Lincoln ended slavery in the United States. From then on, it was illegal to own, buy or sell another human being. Yet, despite their freedom, many black Americans continued to be treated as second-class citizens. Racist US laws meant that black Americans were not allowed to use the same schools, the same park benches, cinemas or swimming pools as white people. They weren't even allowed to drink from the same water taps! These were known as 'segregation laws'. It seemed as if black Americans were free, but not equal.

In Montgomery, a town in the southern state of Alabama, a local law said that black Americans could not sit on the front seats of buses. On Thursday evening, on 1 December 1955, a 42-year-old black woman named Rosa Parks got on the bus to go home after a long day's work in a shop. She sat down in the 'whites only' section. When asked to move, she said 'no'. Her refusal began a chain of events that changed a nation – how?

Thursday 1 December 1955

Rosa Parks gets on the bus after a long day at work. She sits in the last row of seats in the 'whites only' section. After two or three stops, the 'whites only' section begins to fill up. The driver orders Rosa to move!

The angry bus driver puts on the emergency brake, leaves the bus and returns with a policeman. Rosa is arrested (see Source A).

⤶ **SOURCE A:** *A photograph taken shortly after Rosa's arrest. She is being fingerprinted for police records.*

'There comes a time when people get tired. We are tired of being segregated and humiliated, tired of being kicked about. There will be no threats and bullying. Love must be our ideal. Love your enemies, bless them and pray for them. Let no man pull you so low as to make you hate him.'

⤶ **SOURCE B:** *Martin Luther King Junior speaking on the first day of the bus boycott.*

Friday 2 December 1955

The next day, a meeting of black community leaders is held to discuss what to do about Rosa's arrest. They agree to call a **boycott** of all city buses, starting on Monday 5 December. A popular new local church leader called Martin Luther King Junior is chosen to lead the protest. Later that evening, Rosa appears in court and is fined $14 – her lawyer says he will appeal to the highest court in the land.

April 1956

Some of the white people in Montgomery begin to threaten anyone involved in the boycott. Protesters receive threatening phone calls and property is vandalised. Then a bomb explodes at the house of the boycott leader, Martin Luther King Junior. Luckily, no one is hurt but supporters of the boycott are furious and ready to fight. Calmly, King tells them not to fight – he believes that 'non-violent protest' is the best way to achieve equal rights.

Monday 5 December 1955 onwards...

To many people's surprise, no member of the black community travel on any buses on Monday morning. This continues for days, then weeks, then months! Soon the bus companies start to lose money – 75% of their passengers are black – and the white owners of town centre shops complain because the protesters are shopping closer to home rather than travelling into the centre to buy their goods.

13 November 1956

The bombing only makes the protesters more determined. Finally, almost one year after Rosa refused to give up her seat, America's Supreme Court rules that the bus law is illegal. It is scrapped. The next day, Rosa and King board a city bus together… and Rosa takes a seat right at the front!

Work

1 a What were segregation laws? Give at least three examples in your answer.

b Write down at least five words or phrases that might describe your feelings if you suffered as a result of segregation laws today.

2 Look at Source B.

a Who was Martin Luther King Junior?

b Rewrite Source B in your own words.

c Finish this sentence: 'By reading Source B, I get the impression that Martin Luther King Junior was…'.

3 Write a short play about the events in Montgomery during 1955–6. Make sure you include: segregation laws, Rosa Parks on the bus, the meeting about the boycott, the first day of the boycott and the end of the bus law. You might want to work in groups to do this task. Why not act out your play for the rest of the class? Your teacher might even video you!

Martin Luther King Junior and his followers continued to organise marches, boycotts and demonstrations wherever local laws discriminated against black Americans. One year, Martin Luther King Junior himself travelled 780,000 miles and made 208 speeches campaigning for equal rights. These people were called '**civil rights** protesters' because they called for the same rights as ordinary white civilians. In 1961, they organised a famous 'freedom ride' from Washington to New Orleans. Using Rosa Parks' example, protesters travelled on a series of buses and on each one, they sat in the 'whites only' section.

Sometimes they organised 'sit-ins' where they refused to leave a 'whites only' restaurant until they were seated. First started by black students at a Woolworth's food counter in 1960, 70,000 other people had tried similar protests all over America by 1961.

Throughout the whole civil rights struggle, King insisted on peaceful protest and urged his followers not to fight back when attacked: 'We must meet violence with non-violence,' he said.

SOURCE C: *One of the February 1957 covers of* Time, *the USA's largest-selling weekly magazine. It shows a picture of Martin Luther King Junior and, if you look carefully, you can see a photograph of the Montgomery Bus Boycott in the bottom left-hand corner.*

'I have a dream that one day this nation will rise up and live out the true meaning of its creed [beliefs]... that all men are created equal. I have a dream that one day my four little children will live in a nation where they will not be judged by the colour of their skin but by the content of their character. I have a dream. When we allow freedom to ring from every town and every hamlet [village], from every state and every city, we will be able to speed up the day when all God's children, black and white, Jews and Gentiles [non-Jewish people], Protestants and Catholics, will be able to join hands and sing in the words of that old Negro spiritual, "Free at last! Free at last! Great God Almighty, we are free at last!"'

SOURCE D: *The words of Martin Luther King, 28 August 1963.*

↵ **SOURCE E:** *Martin Luther King making his famous 'I have a dream' speech in Washington.*

WISE-UP Words

activists
boycott
civil rights
segregation

Work

1 a Why were Martin Luther King Junior and his followers called 'civil rights protesters'?

b What other methods, apart from the Montgomery Bus Boycott, did civil rights protesters use in the campaign to gain equal rights?

c What was Martin Luther King Junior's attitude to violent protest?

d Suggest reasons why Martin Luther King Junior did not want to use violence.

2 a Write a sentence or two about:
i) The Civil Rights Act, 1964
ii) The Voting Act, 1965.

b In what way is the USA still divided?

c If the USA is still divided, does that mean that Martin Luther King Junior was a failure? Explain your answer carefully.

3 Look at Source D.

a In your own words, try to sum up Martin Luther King Junior's 'dream'. What was his dream for the future?

b What is your dream for the future? Write your own speech, using Martin Luther King Junior's as your inspiration.

On 28 August 1963, King spoke to 250,000 people at a massive rally in Washington and gave one of the most famous speeches in history (see Sources D and E). As a result of the pressure from King and other civil rights **activists**, the American Government finally began to change the law. The Civil Rights Act of 1964 made racial discrimination illegal. A year later, the Voting Act gave equal rights to all black and white people throughout the USA.

But despite the great strides made in the area of civil rights, laws cannot change people's minds. In many ways, the USA remains a divided society today. King himself was shot dead by a white racist in 1968 and King's dream of a peaceful, multi-racial society is far from reality. Individual black Americans – lawyers, sports stars, musicians, doctors – have enjoyed glittering careers but at the start of the twenty-first century, the average black family earned just about half the wage of an average white family. But King's dreams still live on.

! FACT Black is beautiful

Not all black people supported Martin Luther King Junior – they disagreed with his non-violent approach. The most famous of these was Malcolm X, who adopted the Muslim religion because he felt it was one that non-white people could feel was their own. One of his most famous followers was the world heavyweight boxing champion Cassius Clay, who changed his name to Muhammad Ali, a Muslim name. He felt that Clay was a slave name given to his ancestors by slave owners who brought them from Africa. Ali was well known for saying, amongst other things, 'I'm black and I'm proud'.

——MISSION ACCOMPLISHED?——

• Can you write a paragraph that explains the significance of the Montgomery Bus Boycott?

Why is there conflict in the Middle East?

————————————— MISSION OBJECTIVES —————————————
- To understand why the Middle East is so important to different religious groups.
- To remember how and why the state of Israel was established.

Look at Source A. This dramatic photograph was taken in June 2002 in Jerusalem, a significant and troubled city in the heart of the Middle East. It shows the graphic aftermath of a Palestinian suicide bomber's successful attempt to blow up a bus full of Israeli passengers. In total 19 Israelis were killed and 50 were injured. Sadly images like this have been all too common in recent years. Indeed newspapers, magazines and news programmes are often dominated by stories from the Middle East. But who exactly are the Palestinians, and who are the Israelis? What are the origins of the troubles between them? And why has the Middle East been the centre for so much conflict in the twentieth century?

↵ **SOURCE A:** *The aftermath of a Palestinian suicide bomb attack in 2002 on a Jerusalem bus that killed at least 19 Israelis and wounded 50.*

Look at Source B. This region of land is known as the Middle East. It is mainly desert but large areas of land near to rivers or by the sea are very fertile and good crops can be grown. The Middle East is also the source of 60% of the world's oil – a vital resource in today's modern society. But, for many years, this whole area has seen lots of conflict, invasion, war and terror campaigns. So what are the causes of the problems in the Middle East?

SOURCE B: *The Middle East.* ↘

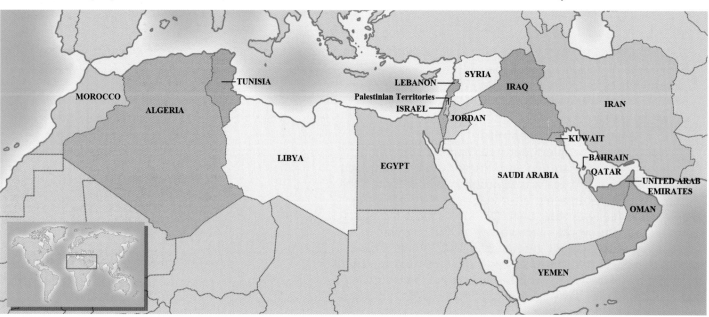

The 'hot spot'

Much of the conflict centres around a small, disputed territory called Palestine… or Israel, depending on who you support in the dispute. This region stretches from the Mediterranean Sea to the River Jordan and the Dead Sea (see Source B). It is a fertile area that contains Jerusalem – a holy city for three of the world's most important religions: Judaism, Christianity and Islam.

	Country	Pop. (in millions)	Capital	Language	Religion	Life Exp M	Life Exp F
	Algeria	33	Algiers	Arabic, French	Sunni Muslim	70	72
	Lebanon	3.8	Beirut	Arabic	Islam/ Christianity	70	74
	Iraq	27	Baghdad	Arabic/ Kurdish	Islam/ Christianity	57	60
	Iran	71	Tehran	Persian	Islam	69	72
	Syria	19	Damascus	Arabic	Islam	71	75
	Libya	6	Tripoli	Arabic	Islam	71	76
	Saudi Arabia	26	Riyadh	Arabic	Islam	70	74
	Tunisia	10	Tunis	Arabic/French	Islam	71	75
	Jordan	6	Arabic	Arabic	Islam	70	73
	Kuwait	3	Kuwait City	Arabic	Islam	75	79
	Egypt	75	Cairo	Arabic	Islam	67	72
	Qatar	0.6	Doha	Arabic	Islam	71	76
	United Arab Emirates	3	Abu Dhabi	Arabic	Islam	76	81
	Morocco	32	Rabat	Arabic/ Berber/French/ Spanish	Islam	67	72
	Yemen	21	Sanaa	Arabic	Islam	59	62
	Israel	6.7	Jerusalem/ Tel Aviv	Hebrew/ Arabic	Judaism/ Islam	77	82
	Bahrain	0.75	Manama	Arabic	Islam	72	76
	Palestinian Territories	3.8		Arabic	Islam	71	74
	Oman	3	Muscat	Arabic	Islam	73	76

⌐ SOURCE C: *Information on Middle East nations and territory.*

WISE-UP Words
Zionism

Jews versus Romans

At the time of Jesus Christ, Jews had lived in Palestine for a long time. But the area was part of the Roman Empire and was controlled by the Romans – and the Jews hated this. In fact, the Jews rebelled against the Roman rule twice (in AD66–73 and 132–135) and were defeated both times. After the second rebellion, Jews were ordered to leave Jerusalem and all Jewish religious customs were declared illegal. As a result, lots of Jews left Palestine altogether and began to settle elsewhere. However, many Jews dreamt of a return to Palestine, the place they regarded as their homeland. This belief is called **Zionism**.

Here come the Christians and the Muslims

For many centuries after the Jews left, Christianity dominated the area and Jerusalem became a very important city for Christians. After all, Jesus Christ was born in nearby Bethlehem and had been killed and buried in Jerusalem.

But Jerusalem soon became a very important city for followers of Islam too. Many believe that their great leader, the prophet Mohammed, had gone up to heaven from Jerusalem and millions of his Arab Muslim followers began to settle there. As a result, both Christians and Arab Muslims wanted Jerusalem to belong to them. Indeed, during the Middle Ages, there were great battles between Arab Muslims and Christians over control of Jerusalem (remember studying the Crusades?). Gradually though, Palestine came under the control of Arab Muslims and was part of a huge Islamic Empire that dominated the whole region.

Enter the Turks

But Palestine changed hands once again in the 1500s when it became part of a huge Turkish Empire, ruled by Turks from Turkey. It remained under Turkish control until the 1900s. Most Arabs living there hated Turkish rule.

Palestine and the Great War

Turkey was on Germany's side during the Great War, and when Turkey lost the war, Palestine was taken away from them and given to Britain to look after. At this time Palestine contained about 90% Arab Muslims and 10% Jews.

Jews and Arabs in Palestine

From 1918 onwards, the British allowed Jewish immigration into Palestine while at the same time promising to protect the rights of the local Arab population. In fact, between 1920 and 1930, about 100,000 Jews went to live in Palestine. And when Hitler came to power in Germany and began picking on Germany's Jews, thousands more moved into Palestine to escape the Nazis. Between 1933 and 1936, 170,000 Jews moved into Palestine.

Indeed, by 1940, 40% of Palestine's people were Jews – and now some Arabs were getting afraid of being outnumbered in what they regarded as their own country!

In an attempt to prevent trouble between Jews and Arabs the British introduced a quota system, restricting Jewish immigration into Palestine.

The Holocaust

During World War II, the Nazis tried to kill as many Jews as they could, mainly in death camps dotted around Nazi-occupied Europe. By the end of the war, about six million had been killed.

When Hitler and the Nazis were defeated and the true horrors of the death camps were shown to the world, many began to think that Jews should be given their own homeland where they could be safe from persecution. Some thought that more Jews should be let into Palestine but the British stuck rigidly to the quota system. Soon tension increased in Palestine. Arabs and Jews clashed – and both blamed the British for not sorting out the problem. A terror campaign against the British even started. Arabs blamed the British for letting in too many Jews while the Jews blamed the British for not letting in enough!

SOURCE D: *A photograph of death camp survivors who had been held captive in Auschwitz (Poland). When asked, many said they wanted to settle in Palestine.*

A new nation

Soon after World War II, the United Nations suggested separating Palestine into two countries – one Arab and one Jewish (see Source D).

The Arab leaders said no to the plan, arguing that the Jews had no claim at all on the land they considered their own. But the Jewish leaders accepted the plan and announced that Israel was a new nation in the world! The President of the USA gave his support to the new state.

Immediately, war broke out between the new state of Israel and the Arabs. And the Palestinian Arabs were helped by their Arab neighbours – Egypt, Syria, Jordan and Iraq. Over the next 15 years, there were four major wars between Israel and its neighbours!

War in the Middle East

As soon as the Jewish state of Israel came into existence in 1948, it was attacked by a Palestinian army. Other Arab nations such as Egypt, Syria, Jordan and Iraq helped Palestine. But although Arab forces outnumbered the Israelis, they were badly organised and the Jews began to drive the Arab armies back. In fact by 1949 Israeli forces controlled much of Palestine except for two areas – the Gaza Strip and the West Bank. Hundreds of thousands of ordinary Palestinian Arabs fled the land that Israel now held and became refugees in the Gaza Strip, the West Bank or neighbouring Muslim countries such as Egypt, Syria and Jordan. Many of these people and their children have remained in refugee camps ever since. In 1967 the Gaza Strip and West Bank were captured by Israel too! Source E outlines in detail the continued conflicts in this area.

↳ SOURCE E: *The United Nations' plan to divide Palestine. Note that Jerusalem was to be an international city under UN control.*

War	Date	Information
Arab-Israeli War	1948–49	Palestine refuses to recognise the new state of Israel and invades. The Palestinian Arabs are helped by other Muslim nations such as Egypt, Jordan, Syria and Iraq. But the war goes badly for Palestine. Many Palestinians flee as refugees to neighbouring Muslim nations.
Suez crisis Second Arab-Israeli War)	1956	Tension builds between Israel and the neighbouring Muslim state of Egypt whose leader had vowed to return the ancient area of Palestine to the Arabs. Eventually war breaks out and United Nations forces enter the war zone as peacekeepers.
The Six-Day War	1967	Tensions continue between Egypt and Israel. Eventually war breaks out again when Israel launches a surprise attack on Egyptian territory, including many of the areas where Palestinian refugees live.
Yom Kippur War	1973	Egypt and Syria attack Israel and an 18-day war leaves the conflict undecided. A peace treaty is eventually signed at Camp David in 1979.

↳ SOURCE F: *Middle East conflicts.*

Terrorists or freedom fighters?

By the 1960s, many Palestinians were getting increasingly frustrated at not having their own state. They were angry at Israeli control of land they regarded as their own. They formed lots of groups, the best known of which was called the Palestinian Liberation Organisation (PLO).

Some of the groups were terrorist organisations and launched attacks on Israeli Jews. American cities, citizens and aircraft were often targets because they blamed the USA for backing Israel. Amongst their most shocking terror acts was the hijacking and blowing up of three aeroplanes in 1970, and in 1972 Israeli athletes competing at the Olympic Games in Germany were assassinated.

⤺ SOURCE G: *A photograph of one of several Palestinian terrorists who invaded the Olympic Village at the 1972 Games in Munich and took Israeli hostages from their Olympic team. Look carefully and you will see him wearing a white mask covering his head on one of the balconies. The men at the bottom of the photograph are German Special Forces agents disguised in athletes' team suits. Nine members of the Olympic team eventually died.*

Many Palestinians say their suicide attackers are the only way of fighting the Israeli occupation of their land. Israel has responded by attacking the areas where they believe the suicide attackers are sheltering, such as the Gaza Strip and the West Bank.

↵ SOURCE H: *One of the most common terrorist tactics used by Palestinians against Israel is the suicide bomber. The bombers aim to kill and injure as many people as possible so often target shopping centres, restaurants and buses. This is a photograph of two suicide bombers taken before an attack.*

The search for peace

By 1993 Israel still occupied all of the Gaza Strip and West Bank… and the Palestinians wanted them out. The terror attacks continued by Palestinians who felt that terrorism was their only way of driving Israeli troops out. Eventually, after long negotiations, the two sides signed an historic agreement called the Oslo Accords with US President Bill Clinton. The idea was based on the theory of 'land for peace'. This meant that Israeli forces would gradually withdraw from the areas they occupied, provided that there was peace in the area. A Palestinian Government was also created to govern Palestinians living in the Gaza Strip and West Bank.

However, both sides continued to disagree on many things, and they both distrusted each other on nearly every issue. In 2000 violence broke out again. Hundreds of Palestinians and Israelis were killed in serious fighting, including many children. The Israeli army went back into some of the areas that it had previously handed over to Palestine. They argued they needed to do this to stop the suicide attacks, while the Palestinians said the Israeli leaders just wanted to stop the Palestinians ruling themselves. Israel even built a huge concrete wall around the West Bank to stop Palestinian suicide bombers travelling into Israeli cities. Palestinians say the barrier cuts into land they claim to be Palestinian and stops farmers from getting to their land. It seems that the difficulties in the Middle East – especially between Israelis and Palestinians – are set to continue.

↥ SOURCE I: *President Clinton with Israeli PM Yitzhak Rabin and Palestinian leader Yasser Arafat, 1993. Arafat extended his hand first, while Rabin needed some encouragement from Clinton to shake hands. Rabin was assassinated by an extremist Israeli in 1995, who thought he was an enemy of the Jewish people.*

Work ‿‿‿‿‿‿.

1 a In your own words, explain what is meant by the term 'Middle East'.

   b Why do you think the city of Jerusalem has been the centre of so much conflict in the Middle East?

2 a How did the Jewish people come to be such a small minority in Palestine in the years up to 1918?

   b What is 'Zionism'?

   c How did Palestine become a largely Arab Muslim country in the years up to 1918?

3 a Draw this puzzle into your book and fill in the answers to the clues.

Clues:
1) Yom _____ War of 1973 between Egypt, Syria and Israel.
2) Looked after Palestine after the Great War.
3) _____ Accords: a 1993 peace deal between Israel and Palestine.
4) New Jewish state in 1948.
5) Religion of vast majority of Middle East nations.
6) Gaza _____.
7) Jewish religion.
8) Rulers of Palestine AD 66–73 and 132–135.
9) 1956 crisis.

   b Now read down the puzzle (clue 10). Write a sentence or two about this word.

4 Look at Source G carefully.

   a In your own words, explain what has happened.

   b Why do you think Palestinian terrorists targeted Israeli athletes taking part in the Olympic Games, rather than any other sports competition?

   c Why do you think Palestinian terrorists have used such violent terror tactics over the years?

▌**FACT** Israel and Lebanon

Lebanon is to the north of Israel and contains many different religious groups, including Palestinian refugees. In the 1970s and 1980s there was a civil war in Lebanon and during this time Israel invaded South Lebanon to prevent Palestine attacks across its northern border. An armed Lebanese group – Hezbollah – was set up to oppose the Israeli invasion. And when the Israelis left South Lebanon in 2000, tension and conflict still remained between Lebanon and Israel.

——MISSION ACCOMPLISHED?——

- Can you outline why the Middle East has been the source of so much conflict in the twentieth century?

What is 'terrorism'?

MISSION OBJECTIVES

• To understand what is meant by the word 'terrorism' and how terrorists operate in today's world.

On the morning of 11 September 2001, 19 terrorists hijacked four American passenger planes. After taking control, the hijackers flew two of the aircraft straight into two of the tallest buildings in New York City – the twin towers of the World Trade Center, two skyscrapers containing thousands of office workers.

A third plane with 64 passengers on board was flown into the Pentagon building in Washington, the headquarters of the US army, navy and air force. Half an hour later, the fourth plane crashed in a field near Pennsylvania, not far from Washington. Many experts believe it was heading for the White House, the home of the US President. The fourth flight never made it because some of the 38 passengers fought with the hijackers to stop them reaching their target.

The US President, George W Bush, was visiting a school when he heard of the attacks. In a statement a few hours later, he said that 'a national tragedy has occurred today. Two aeroplanes have crashed into the World Trade Center in a terrorist attack on our country.'

But what exactly is **terrorism**? How, when and where have terrorists attacked in the past? And how, if at all, can terrorists be stopped?

↵ SOURCE A: *The front page of* The Sun *newspaper from 12 September 2001. The photo shows the second plane hitting the World Trade Center.*

'Today our fellow citizens, our way of life, our very freedom came under attack in a series of deliberate and deadly terrorist attacks. These acts of mass murder were intended to frighten our nation into chaos and defeat. Thousands of lives were suddenly ended by evil, despicable acts of terror... our military is powerful and it is prepared. The search is under way for those who committed this evil act. We will make no distinction between the terrorists who committed these acts and those who harboured them.'

↳ SOURCE B: *Part of President Bush's television statement, read out on the evening of 11 September 2001. What do you think the final line of his speech means?*

So what is terrorism?

Terrorism is the use of violence and intimidation for political reasons. Terrorists want to change the way governments and politicians behave by using threats, fear and bloodshed – in other words, terror. Terrorists don't usually represent a large proportion of the population so never get enough support for their ideas by normal peaceful methods. Instead, they try to frighten people into behaving the way they want.

SOURCE C: *A timeline of events on 11 September 2001. In total, over 3000 people died in the attacks.* ↱

Hijacked planes

1 American Airlines Flight 11 hijacked after taking off from Boston with 92 people aboard. Hits first tower.

2 United Airlines Flight 175 from Boston to Los Angeles also hijacked. Hits second tower.

3 American Airlines Flight 77 seized en route from Washington to Los Angeles. Hits Pentagon.

4 United Airlines Flight 93 from Newark to San Francisco crashed near Pittsburgh.

New York

8.45am

Hijacked plane hits World Trade Center.

8.55am

Second plane hits southern tower.

10.07am

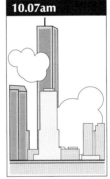

Southern tower collapses.

10.27am

Northern tower collapses.

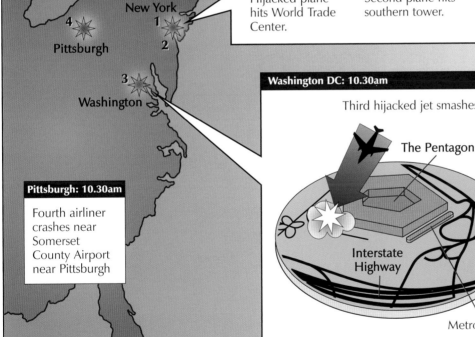

Pittsburgh: 10.30am

Fourth airliner crashes near Somerset County Airport near Pittsburgh

Washington DC: 10.30am

Third hijacked jet smashes into the Pentagon

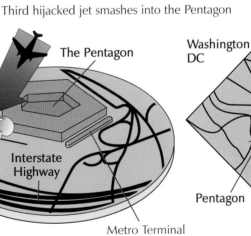

The Pentagon

Interstate Highway

Metro Terminal

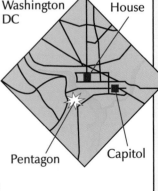

Washington DC

White House

Pentagon

Capitol

Work

1 Why do you think the terrorists chose as their target:
- The World Trade Center • The Pentagon • The White House?

2 a In your own words, explain what is meant by the word 'terrorism'.

b What is a 'terrorist'?

3 a Make your own timeline of events for the terrorist attacks on the USA on 11 September 2001.

b Why do you think many people criticised the American government's security services after the attacks?

Why is the USA targeted?

The attacks on the World Trade Center and the Pentagon in September 2001 were two more in a series of attacks by one of the world's most famous terrorist groups, al-Qaeda. This mysterious group's members, led by a millionaire Saudi Arabian named Osama Bin Laden, are all followers of Islam but have very strict, extremist beliefs that are different from Muslims living in Britain. They believe they are fighting a holy war, or **jihad**, against enemies of their religion.

The USA, in particular, is seen as one of al-Qaeda's greatest enemies. They dislike the USA because they believe Americans interfere too much in the Middle East, the area around the eastern Mediterranean Sea including Kuwait, Iran, Iraq, Israel, Syria, Jordan, Saudi Arabia and so on. The Middle East is the source of 60% of the world's oil. In today's modern world, oil is essential, especially for nearly all forms of transport. American cars, trucks and trains as well as homes and factories all need this oil – as a result, the USA is very interested in what happens in this area.

For many years, the USA has kept battleships and built airbases in some Middle Eastern countries, most notably Saudi Arabia. Not just al-Qaeda but many other countries find the American presence in the Middle East threatening. Al-Qaeda also targeted the USA because they believe they helped enemies of Islam, like Israeli Jews, during wars against Muslim nations in the Middle East. Al-Qaeda want American influence out of the Middle East and are prepared to use terrorism to either frighten the USA into leaving or anger them so much that the US starts a holy war against all Muslim states. This, al-Qaeda hope, will end with final victory for Islam.

! FACT Osama Bin Laden

- Born in 1957, seventeenth son of a very rich family.
- Grew up in Jeddah, Saudi Arabia.
- Has more than 50 brothers and sisters.
- Al-Qaeda (which means 'the base') set up in 1989 in Afghanistan to fight people who were seen as enemies of Islam.
- Has used his money to run his global terror network.

↰ SOURCE D: *Until the 11 September attacks, al-Qaeda had mainly used car bombs. Other attacks include a bombing of the World Trade Center in 1993, killing six, and bombings of the US embassies in Kenya and in Tanzania, killing 234 people. This photograph shows rescue workers helping victims after the 1998 bombing in Kenya.*

Terrorism has been used for many, many years to try to achieve a wide variety of different aims and objectives. Sometimes the terrorists have political causes – they say they represent a group that want their own country, for example – whilst other terrorists have religious causes like al-Qaeda. More often than not though, terrorism is used for a mixture of religious and political reasons.

Work

1 Write a sentence or two to explain the following terms:

extremist • jihad • al-Qaeda

2 a What do you think is meant by the term 'anti-American'?

b Why is al-Qaeda so anti-American?

How do terrorists attack?

Terrorists use a variety of methods to cause death, destruction and disruption. They include:

Bombs Bombs can be hidden in busy places, on trains, buses and even planes. A timer is usually used to set off the explosion when the bomber has left the area.

Car bombs A car or van packed with explosives is also a common terrorist weapon.

Chemical attack Poison gas can sometimes be used. In Tokyo, Japan, 12 people were killed in 1995 when a nerve gas called sarin was released on the city's underground train system. In 2001, a killer disease called anthrax was used as a terror weapon in the USA. Anthrax bacteria, in the form of white powder, was sent through the US mail system.

Hijacking Terrorists can take control of boats, planes and buses. They use the passengers as hostages or use the vehicle as a weapon. Source E shows hijacked airliners burning at Dawson's Field, Jordan, in 1970.

Letter bomb Explosives in an envelope or parcel that blow up when it is opened. This is a common method used by extreme animal rights groups.

Mortar bomb A bomb fired through a metal tube or pipe. It flies only a short distance (around 50–200 metres) but can be made cheaply. The IRA used mortar bombs to attack 10 Downing Street, the home of the Prime Minister, in 1991.

Suicide bomb Explosives are attached to the bomber's body. They approach their target and explode the bomb. Palestinian terrorists are best known for this.

SOURCE E: *Palestinian terrorists took over these three airliners – two American, one Swiss. They targeted American planes because they felt the USA always helped out Israel, a country that occupies land that the Palestinians claim is their own. Palestinian terrorists argued that they have to use terrorism as they have no country to fight from. They wanted their own country – Palestine – and wanted land that Israel occupies. Terrorist acts continue today in this area of the Middle East.*

Can we stop them?

Stopping terrorists is not easy. Remember that their reasons for committing terrorist acts are just as established as our determination to stop them. However, many methods have been tried!

1 Hunt them down

This is hard to do. Many terrorists have remained hidden for many years, despite great efforts to find them. There are always more volunteers to take the place of any who are caught or captured.

2 Attack people who help terrorists

This is a commonly used method. In 2001, American troops, helped by other nations including Britain, invaded Afghanistan. The Government there had allowed al-Qaeda to set up training bases for many years. This tactic makes it harder, but not impossible, for terrorist groups to operate.

3 Prevention

Security has been even stricter at airports since the 11 September attacks. In this country, the public have always been on their guard and asked to report any 'suspicious packages' to the police. Stations, city centres and any public places are very hard to guard all the time.

4 Negotiation

One answer is to involve the terrorists in discussions about their beliefs, concerns and activities. This has been tried several times, with some success. However, this is the most unpopular solution because to many, it looks like the terrorists have won!

WISE-UP Words

jihad
terrorism
terrorist

SOURCE F: *The bombed-out remains of a London bus after the terrorist attacks in London on 7 July 2005. Three young men, members of al-Qaeda, blew themselves up on London tube trains, whilst a fourth exploded his bomb on this bus in Woburn Place. In total, over 52 people were killed and 700 injured.*

Work

1 In your own words, explain the different methods used by terrorists to cause death, disruption and destruction.

2 Why have there been many years of conflict in the Middle East between Israelis and Palestinians?

3 a List each of the methods used to try to stop terrorists.

b Which method do you think could be most effective in stopping terrorism? Give reasons for your answer.

MISSION ACCOMPLISHED?

- Can you explain how terrorists operate and what efforts have been used to stop them?

CAN YOU GET JUSTICE IN MODERN BRITAIN?

Crime and punishment has always been one of the 'big' issues. The state of the country's prisons, the number of police 'on the street', and some of the more daring robberies and grisly murders have always sold newspapers and dominated television news programmes. So what changes in law and order have we seen in the twentieth century? Has the crime rate increased during the last one hundred years, for example? And have the **types** of crimes being committed and the way they are punished changed in any way in more recent years?

1: Crimewatch UK

MISSION OBJECTIVES

• To understand some of the key changes in law and order in the twentieth century.

A crime wave?

Look at Source A. It shows a selection of 'law and order' stories from some of Britain's national newspapers. It clearly shows that 'crime and punishment' is one of Britain's hottest issues. Look at Source B – it might give you an idea as to why law and order gets so much news coverage.

BIKES PROJECT HIT BY THEFT AGAIN

COUPLE TELL OF BURGLARY ORDEAL

MAN SHOT DEAD

WEEKEND OF VIOLENCE ON STREETS

↖ SOURCE A: *A selection of newspaper headlines from recent years.*

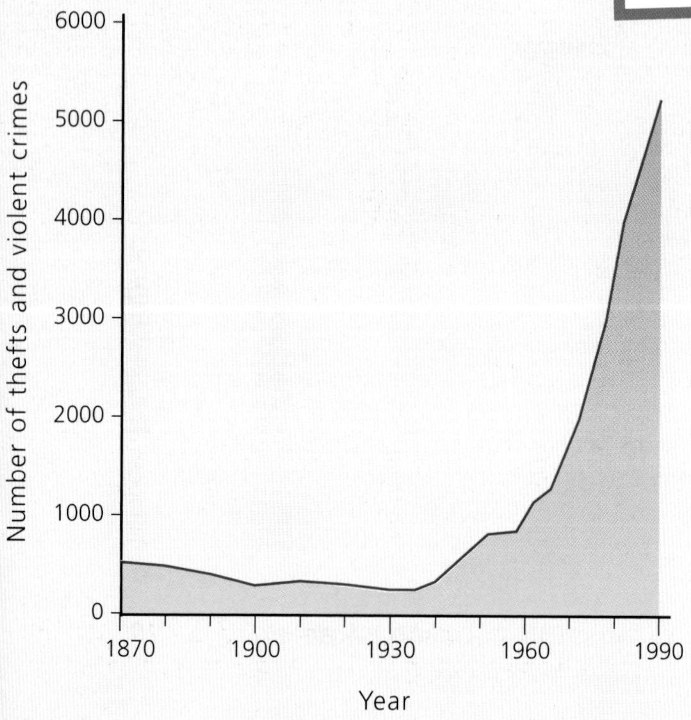

↵ SOURCE B: *This graph shows all the crimes known to police per 100,000 of the population between 1870 and 1990. The graph has even been adjusted to take the rising population into account! It is easy to see that, according to these figures, the crime rate has increased dramatically, especially since about 1950.*

Graph: Number of thefts and violent crimes (y-axis: 0 to 6000) against Year (x-axis: 1870 to 1990).

Now look carefully at Source C. This shows the numbers of murders, burglaries and thefts known to police between 1900 and 1996. But do the figures tell the whole story?

Date	Murder/Manslaughter	Burglary	Theft
1900	312	3812	63,604
1910	291	6499	76,044
1920	313	6863	77,417
1930	300	11,169	110,159
1950	315	29,834	334,222
1960	282	46,591	537,003
1970	393	190,597	952,666
1980	620	294,375	1,463,469
1996	681	1,101,000	2,280,000

⮠ SOURCE C: *The numbers of murders, burglaries and thefts known to the police between 1900 and 1996.*

Sources B and C are based on *recorded* crimes; these are crimes that people have reported by going into, or phoning, a police station. But these sorts of statistics are problematic! For example, not all people report crimes, so the real figures could be even higher. A survey in the 1980s even suggested that there were 12, yes, 12 times more cases of vandalism than were actually reported!

New crimes

Some analysts put the increase in crime in the twentieth century down to factors such as new technology. Invent computers, for example, and you have computer crimes such as 'hacking'. Invent credit cards and you have card fraud and identity theft. Mobile phones have caused a huge increase in attacks on 11–16-year-olds between the hours of three and five o'clock as they walk home from school with their mobile phone pressed to their ear, oblivious to the fact that someone wants to steal it!

However, the most startling impact that new technology has had on crime statistics must be the invention of the motor car. Suddenly, you have lots of new crime associated with it – car theft, speeding, drink driving, joy riding, driving without insurance and tax and so on. In fact, in 2005, there were 4,350,000 car crimes, including the theft of over 214,000 cars. Car theft is now one of the country's biggest crime categories – and one of the police's biggest headaches.

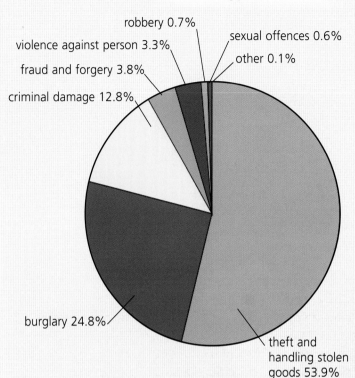

robbery 0.7%
violence against person 3.3%
fraud and forgery 3.8%
criminal damage 12.8%
sexual offences 0.6%
other 0.1%
burglary 24.8%
theft and handling stolen goods 53.9%

⮠ SOURCE D: *The types of crimes committed in the late twentieth century.*

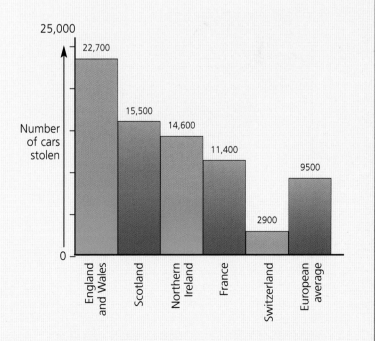

25,000

Number of cars stolen

22,700 — England and Wales
15,500 — Scotland
14,600 — Northern Ireland
11,400 — France
2900 — Switzerland
9500 — European average

0

⮠ SOURCE E: *Number of cars stolen per 100,000 of the population in different countries in 2000.*

Catching criminals

The twentieth century saw major advances in the technology used to catch criminals. Police took advantage of all sorts of special equipment in order to put criminals behind bars – fingerprinting (1901), bicycles (1905), police cars (1919), two-way radios or walkie-talkies (1923), breathalyser machines (1967), right up to DNA technology from the 1980s onwards.

SOURCE F: *Police officers today use all the latest technology available. This armed officer is 'on patrol' at one of Britain's airports.*

! **FACT** Safe or unsafe?

A 1997 survey of 11 countries showed one in three Brits felt unsafe out alone at night, compared to one in four Americans, one in four French people and one in ten Swedes! A similar survey found that in Britain, elderly people felt they were most at risk from violent crime – however, the under 30s are 13 times more likely to be the victim of a violent crime than an older person.

Punishing crime

Up to the nineteenth century, criminals were usually treated as worthless, sinful people who got what they deserved in rotten prisons. As the century wore on, there was more of a belief in reforming criminals and the prisons in which they served their sentences. In the twentieth century, a whole host of reforms greatly changed the way prisoners were punished. Look carefully at Source G. It shows the gradual change in prisoner punishment.

1907: Probation introduced – an alternative to prison. Criminals reported once a week to the police station. If they didn't re-offend, there was no further punishment.

1914: Longer to pay fines – this meant that people who had been fined could take longer to pay rather than be sent to prison.

1937: First 'open prison' – trusted adult prisoners were sent to these 'prisons without bars' to serve out their sentences.

1962: Birching (whipping) was stopped.

1965: Capital punishment (hanging for murder) was abolished.

1967: Parole introduced – prisoners were released early if they had behaved in jail.

1972: Community service introduced – criminals could be sentenced to help out on community projects instead of spending time in jail.

1999 onwards: Electronic tagging – a type of probation. Criminals, upon release from prison, wear an electronic bracelet that allows the police to know where they are at any time.

SOURCE G: *Some key dates in the history of punishment.*

Young criminals

Many special measures affecting younger criminals have been introduced since 1900. The first borstal – a juvenile prison – was opened in Kent in 1902, followed by many others. These were replaced by Youth Detention Centres for under 21s in 1983. In 1933, the age of criminal responsibility was raised to the age of eight, and then raised further to ten (1963) and then 14 in 1969. Also in that year, specialist juvenile courts, supervision and care orders were introduced as a way of reforming and helping young offenders.

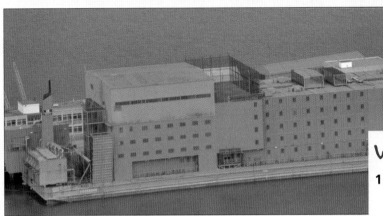

SOURCE H: *A prison ship, used as a solution to overcrowded prisons. This one was moored off the Dorset coast and held 500 prisoners.*

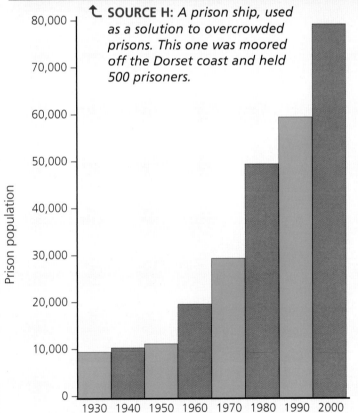

SOURCE I: *Britain's rising prison population. In the 1980s, Britain had the fourth highest proportion of prisoners in Europe, with the prison population growing at a rate of 350 prisoners a week. More prisons have been built since 1990 and even 'private prisons' have opened, run by companies on behalf of the government.*

Problematic prisons

During the 1980s and 1990s, some of Britain's prisons were filled to bursting point. Prison staff shortages meant that in some places, prisoners were spending 23 hours a day in their cells with no education programmes and little exercise. There were riots in some prisons, notably in Strangeways Prison in Manchester in 1990. One solution to overcrowding was the use of prison ships, last used in the 1800s. This one, pictured in 1997, was moored off the Dorset coast and held 500 prisoners.

Work

1 a In general terms, what has happened to the crime rate in the twentieth century?

b Can you suggest reasons for this?

2 a What do you think is meant by the term 'new crime'? Give examples in your explanation.

b In what ways has the invention of the motor car contributed to the increased crime rate?

3 a Make a list of as many recent TV crime programmes, TV dramas, films – even soap opera storylines – relating to crime.

b You probably didn't struggle to think of lots of suggestions to put in your list. Why do you think crime is such a popular feature on our TV screens?

4 Match up the dates on the left with the correct events on the right. Make sure the dates on the left are in the correct chronological order.

1907	electronic tagging started
1901	probation system began
1965	first 'open prison' set up
1999	breathalyser tests first used
1919	fingerprinting introduced
1967	police cars first used
1902	capital punishment abolished
1937	first 'borstal' was opened

5 a What is a 'prison ship'… and why were they reintroduced?

b Think carefully. Can you suggest your own reasons to help deal with the rising prison population? You may want to discuss solutions as a class.

—— MISSION ACCOMPLISHED?——

- Can you outline five key changes in law and order in the twentieth century?

As you may know from your previous studies in history, religion – especially Christianity – has had an enormous influence on Britain's development. It has been involved in every area of British life and has helped shape our laws, politics, language and everyday customs. Over recent years, Christianity has been joined in Britain by many other religions. But despite the historic importance of Christianity and the arrival of other **faiths**, many people claim that religion in Britain is on the decline. So how many people today consider themselves to be religious? Why do some people believe that religion's influence is fading? And just how religious is modern Britain?

1: A secular state?

MISSION OBJECTIVES

- To be able to define the word 'secular'.
- To be able to explain why some people believe that the influence of religion is fading.
- To decide if modern Britain is a religious place.

If something has nothing to do with religion, it is often called **secular**. For example, while Christmas and Easter are religious holidays, bank holidays are secular. In the 2001 census over three-quarters of the British population said they belonged to a religion, with around 72% declaring themselves Christian. In recent years, more and more people have started to claim that Britain has become a secular state, meaning that religion has little or no influence on how we live our lives or run the country. But what makes them say this? What is their evidence? And what evidence is there that indicates they're wrong?

Adherents		% pop.
Christian	42,079,000	71.6
No religion	9,104,000	15.5
Muslim	1,546,626	2.7
Hindu	552,421	1.0
Jedi Knight	390,000	0.7
Sikh	329,358	0.6
Jewish	259,927	0.5
Buddhist	144,453	0.3

↳ SOURCE A: *2001 census results.*

Does the census make sense?

The reason why there is such a debate over the importance of religion is because both sides dispute the statistics. Those who argue that Britain is secular claim that although people may say they are Christian, they don't ever attend church or even believe in the religion. Those who argue that Britain is still a Christian country say that people exaggerate how low church attendance is. They also argue that just because someone doesn't go to church, it doesn't mean that they aren't Christian. Look through the sources and see what you think.

'There are 900 mosques and 150 Hindu temples in Britain; along with 365 synagogues, 250 Sikh gurdwaras, 160 churches with Caribbean origins and 20 Buddhist houses. There are dozens of parishes for the Greek, Russian and Serbian Orthodox churches, while London's own Catholic churches are full of the Spanish, Portuguese, Polish, Italian and Filipino faithful.'

↳ SOURCE B: *Extract from* Bloody Foreigners – the story of immigration to Britain *by Robert Winder (2004).*

↳ SOURCE C: *Many churches no longer attract worshippers, so have been given new uses. This one is a pizza restaurant and many others have become bars, shops and apartments.*

'For a thousand years, Christianity penetrated deeply into the lives of the people, enduring Reformation, Enlightenment and industrial revolution... Then, quite suddenly in 1963, something very profound changed the character of the nation... The British people since the 1960s have stopped going to church, have allowed their church membership to lapse, have stopped marrying in church and have neglected to baptise their children. Meanwhile, their children stopped going to Sunday school, stopped entering confirmation and rarely, if ever, stepped inside a church to worship in their entire lives.'

⤵ SOURCE D: *Adapted from* The Death of Christian Britain *by Callum G. Brown, 2001.*

⭐ **WISE-UP** Words

faith
Jedi
secular

'"Are we a pagan country?" asked James Lansdale Hodson in 1946. "Few of my friends go to church and I read in a report of the Archbishop's committee that 90% of our people never attend church. The church each week has five million attendances; the cinemas have 40 million."'

⤵ SOURCE E: *Extract from* Austerity Britain 1945–51 *by David Kynaston (2007).*

' "In 1952, when the Queen came to the throne, it was very much a Christian society. The Prince of Wales will become head of a nation which is multi-faith. The Prince has said that he wants to be seen as a defender of all religious faiths and not just the Anglican church," said Vernon Bogdanor, Professor of Government at Oxford University.'

⤵ SOURCE F: *This story appeared in the* Daily Telegraph *on 14 Nov 2008 after Prince Charles declared he would like the title 'Defender of the faiths' when he became King. Ever since Henry VIII, the monarch has had the title 'Defender of the faith'.*

❗ **FACT** Use the force!
During the 2001 census, an Internet campaign was started to get people to declare their religion as 'Jedi' – the fictional religion from the Star Wars films. As a result, 390,000 Britons were officially recorded as being Jedi Knights – more than were recorded as Sikh, Jewish or Buddhist!

Work

1 Define what the word secular means in one sentence.

2 **a** Look at Source A. Create a bar chart based on the census results.

   b Does the information provided by the 2001 census indicate that Britain is a secular country? Explain your answer.

3 What evidence is there in the other sources that Britain has become secular?

4 Look at Source B. Describe the effect that immigration has had on religion in Britain.

5 Is modern Britain a religious place?

___ **MISSION ACCOMPLISHED?** ___

• Can you tell someone what the word secular means?

• Do you know why some people believe that Britain is a secular country?

• Have you decided if modern Britain is a religious place?

A united Europe

MISSION OBJECTIVES

- To be able to explain why the countries of Europe have cooperated more and more in the second half of the twentieth century.
- To be aware of which countries belong to the European Union and when they joined.

During the first half of the twentieth century, Western Europe was devastated by the two most horrific wars that the world had ever seen. During the second half of the twentieth century, Europe witnessed peace, increased wealth and close cooperation. So just why was Europe suddenly so peaceful? Just how closely do the countries of Europe cooperate? And which countries are members of the European Union?

Europe in ruins

Wars between European nations – particularly between Germany, France and Britain – had been raging on and off for centuries. At the end of World War II, the leaders of Europe saw that things had to change. They had an idea that if they put aside differences in language, culture and history, they could work together and wars between them would be unthinkable. Rather than compete as rivals, they could work together to increase wealth and ensure peace. This vision of a united Europe – that is as closely linked as the United States of America – has gradually evolved over the decades. Today, hundreds of millions of Europeans now share the same currency, vote in European elections and live under the same laws and regulations.

The evolution of the European Union

1950s
In 1951, six countries joined their iron and coal industries together to form the European Coal and Steel Community (ECSC). That way, they could never build up their armies on their own. In 1957, the Treaty of Rome was signed, which renamed the group the European Economic Community (EEC) and paved the way for greater **cooperation**.

1960s
The Common Agricultural Policy was signed, which meant that all farmers in the EEC are paid the same for their produce. In 1968, the EEC began to trade with other countries as a single state – the biggest trading bloc in the world.

1970s
The success of the EEC attracted other countries and it expanded to include three more members. In 1979, the European Parliament was elected by EEC citizens. At first it could just advise, but now it can pass laws that apply in all member countries.

1980s
Three more members joined the EEC and a '**single market**' was created. This meant that goods, services, money and people could move freely between all 12 EEC countries.

1990s
The Maastricht Treaty was signed, which renamed the community the European Union (EU). All countries agreed to extend cooperation even further – including **foreign affairs**. Another three countries became members and the EU agreed to accept more members in the future.

2000s
On 1 January 2002, 12 member countries adopted the **Euro** as their **currency**. Three hundred million Europeans now carried the same coins and notes in their pockets. In 2004, ten more countries joined the EU, joined by another two in 2007. It is planned that more European countries will follow.

▌▌PAUSE for Thought

Cooperation between EU members is increasing more and more – to the point where there might one day be a European army or police force. Some people don't agree with this and there is a UK Independence Party that campaigns for Britain to leave the EU. Why do you think some people are against the EU increasing its power?

↳ **SOURCE A:** *The EU flag.*

★WISE-UP Words

cooperation
currency   Euro
foreign affairs
single market

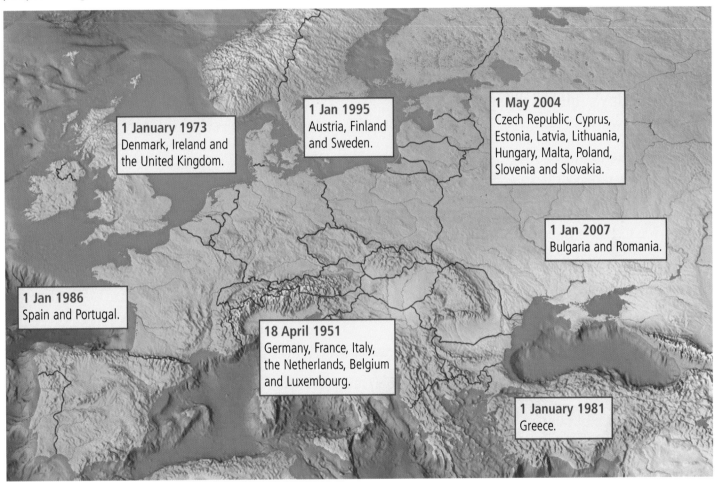

1 January 1973
Denmark, Ireland and the United Kingdom.

1 Jan 1995
Austria, Finland and Sweden.

1 May 2004
Czech Republic, Cyprus, Estonia, Latvia, Lithuania, Hungary, Malta, Poland, Slovenia and Slovakia.

1 Jan 2007
Bulgaria and Romania.

1 Jan 1986
Spain and Portugal.

18 April 1951
Germany, France, Italy, the Netherlands, Belgium and Luxembourg.

1 January 1981
Greece.

↳ **SOURCE B:** *The European Union has grown steadily since it was formed in 1951.*

Work ——————.

1 a Explain why many Europeans wanted to increase the cooperation between countries in the 1950s.

b Has their plan for Europe worked? Explain your answer.

2 a List the original six member states who joined in 1951.

b List the countries that joined in the 1970s.

c List the countries that joined in the 1980s.

d List the countries that joined in the 1990s.

e List the countries that joined since the year 2000.

f How many members does the EU have in total?

3 What do you think have been the three most important developments in the evolution of the EU? Explain your choices.

▌**FACT** A divided Europe?

Many people from the poorer countries in the EU have moved to the wealthier ones to work. This has caused racial tensions in some communities when large numbers of people who speak a different language and have a different culture have settled and opened businesses.

—— MISSION ACCOMPLISHED? ——

• Could you tell someone why the EU was formed?

• Can you list five member countries and when they joined?

A shrinking world

————————————MISSION OBJECTIVES————————————
- To be able to explain how and why the world has 'shrunk'.
- To decide which invention has been most important in creating the 'global village'.

Throughout the twentieth century, people claimed that the world was shrinking at an alarming rate. In reality of course, it was exactly the same size in the year 2000 as it was in 1900. So what did people mean when they spoke of a shrinking world? What developments caused it to shrink? And which invention do you think has been the most important in creating today's 'global village'?

The lives of billions of people have been completely transformed by modern technology. Journeys that once took weeks now take hours and, where it used to take months to exchange messages across the world, it can now be done with the click of a mouse. People now travel – both inside their own countries and abroad – more than ever before, and inventions such as cinema, television and the Internet mean that cultures and ways of life are copied and shared the world over. The result has been the creation of the '**global village**', where people separated by thousands of miles can still work and communicate and interact with each other instantly. This has given many people the impression that the world is getting smaller.

Ocean liner: In 1900 it took five days to travel from Britain to the USA.

Aeroplanes: The first powered flight was carried out in 1903 by the American Wright brothers. Amazing advances were made in **aviation** during the following century. It now takes a few hours to reach the USA and low-cost flights mean international travel is experienced by millions.

Satellites: Thousands of satellites have been put into orbit around the world since 1957. Television signals are beamed up and 'bounced' back to receiving dishes on earth. This allows 'live' news and sports events to be seen as they happen – thousands of miles away.

Cars

By 2030 there will be 1.2 billion cars in use in the world. The Ford Motor Company first made the car affordable to the common man in the early 1900s and fast, multi-lane roads (motorways) started to appear all over the world. This shortened journey times and allowed people and goods to travel over longer distances.

The microchip

The invention of the microchip in the 1950s revolutionised human communications. They are the 'brains' of computers and mobile phones that allow instant communication anywhere in the world. Information that used to fill rooms of libraries and be held in one location can now be put on a data storage device that fits in your pocket and taken anywhere.

The mobile phone

Mobile phones first became available in Britain in 1985 but their use really took off in the late 1990s. It is estimated that over 40 million people in the UK now use a mobile phone – with that figure rising all the time. They are now much more than just telephones, allowing users to record, send and receive video images across the world. They are also an increasingly popular way of using the Internet.

The Internet

The World Wide Web was invented by British scientist Tim Berners-Lee in the late 1980s and early 1990s. He developed the idea of 'hypertext' so he could share his research across a single computer network. People then used this technology to make websites that could be accessed from anywhere in the world. The Internet was born and has changed the way businesses operate and people live their lives.

The television

The television became extremely popular throughout the world in the second half of the twentieth century. It has enabled people to see historic events and horrific disasters from the comfort of their living room – no matter where in the world they have taken place. The television has also exposed people to the different cultures, sights and wildlife of the world without them having to travel anywhere.

WISE-UP Words

aviation
global village

Work

1 In your own words, explain how the world 'shrank' in the twentieth century.

2 a Place the following developments or inventions in what you think is the correct order of importance:
 – the microchip
 – the satellite
 – cheap jet travel
 – the television
 – the Internet
 – the car
 – the mobile phone.

 b Explain why you have put them in the order you have.

 c Now write a sentence about each development or invention.

⬆ SOURCE A: *Tim Berners-Lee's Internet has completely changed the way millions of people live and do business.*

MISSION ACCOMPLISHED?

- Could you tell someone how the world has 'shrunk'?
- Have you decided which invention was most important in 'shrinking' the world?

The McDonald's story

MISSION OBJECTIVES

- To be able to explain how and why McDonald's developed.
- To understand some of the arguments for and against multinationals like McDonald's.

Most people in Britain will have heard of a company called McDonald's. In fact, on a global scale, billions of people all over the world will have heard of McDonald's. Indeed, it is one of the global success stories of the twentieth century with more than 23,000 restaurants in 109 countries serving food and drink to 38 million customers daily!

McDonald's is what we call a multinational company – that is, a huge moneymaking business that offers products and services that are identical throughout the world to customers. The presence of these companies' 'logos' or 'brands' promises the same product whether it is purchased in Birmingham, Boston, Beijing or Bucharest. The rise in power and status of multinational companies such as McDonald's, Coca-Cola, Nike and Disney is an example of what is known as globalisation; a term used since the 1960s to refer to the spread of these brands all over the globe.

So how did McDonald's restaurants begin? What makes them so successful internationally? And is everyone happy about global success stories like McDonald's?

The beginning of a 'food empire'

McDonald's is a huge billion-dollar multinational restaurant chain and one of the world's most famous 'global brands'. There are restaurants all over the world willing to sell you a Big Mac or a Happy Meal. McDonald's is such a familiar sight in nearly every major city centre that you may be forgiven for thinking that McDonald's has always existed. Yet despite its size and popularity, McDonald's was only founded in the middle of the twentieth century by two brothers… neither of whom was called Ronald! The following story outlines their success story:

1

In the 1940s, two brothers named Maurice and Richard McDonald opened a BBQ restaurant in California, USA.

They sold all sorts of food, including chicken, steak, hot dogs, hamburgers, French fries, milkshakes and Coca-Cola.

2

Their restaurant was like hundreds of others. Food was prepared in a 'central hub' and cars parked in the order bays.

But in 1948 the brothers got fed up of this style of restaurant and unveiled plans for a new one.

3

The brothers planned to open a 'hamburger bar' offering only a limited menu of hamburgers, cheeseburgers and drinks.

The food was prepared on a sort of assembly line, with one worker cooking the burger, another sorting out the bun, and so on.

4

The new 'revamped' restaurant opened on 12 December 1948 and Richard McDonald cooked the first hamburger!

The assembly line system meant the food was cooked quickly.

5

Over the next few years the restaurant went from strength to strength.

The brothers stuck to their rigid formula – the limited menu of burgers, French fries, Coca-Cola and milkshakes were made quickly and sold cheaply!

6

In 1954 a salesman named Ray Kroc managed to persuade the McDonald brothers to buy eight of his milkshake machines for their restaurant.

While in the restaurant, Kroc was amazed at how the staff prepared the food orders in seconds.

7

Kroc asked the brothers if he could open up several other restaurants, each selling the same food and drink in the same way as in the first one.

Kroc would run the others, but they would share out any profits. The restaurants would buy lots of Kroc's milkshake machines as part of the deal, of course.

8

The first one of the new McDonald's restaurants opened just north of Chicago on 15 April 1955.

On the first day the restaurant made $366.12; a lot of money in 1955.

9

In 1959 the one hundredth McDonald's restaurant was opened.

Most new restaurants had thin yellow arches at each end of the building, similar to the original one in 1955. They were later joined together to form the famous 'golden arches'.

10

Ray Kroc had plans to massively expand the business and open McDonald's restaurants all over the world... but the McDonald brothers weren't interested.

In 1961, Kroc offered the brothers $2.7 million to 'buy them out'. They accepted and Kroc began running the whole business.

11

In order to expand the business, Kroc introduced something known as **franchising**.

This meant that anyone who wanted to open a McDonald's restaurant had to pay Kroc around $1000 for the honour of doing so, and then 1.9% from the profits of the restaurant. He would then pass 0.5% onto the McDonald brothers.

12

The 'franchise method' proved very successful. An ordinary businessperson would buy a building site and then pay McDonald's to build the restaurant. They then bought the food to cook from McDonald's, but the businessperson kept around 98% of the profit.

By 1963 there were over 500 restaurants, most of which were franchises.

13

In 1963 McDonald's sponsored an American children's TV show called *Bozo the Clown*.

The actor who played the clown was hired to appear at McDonald's restaurants and soon McDonald's thought the company could do with their own clown... Ronald McDonald was born.

14

In 1968 McDonald's best-known burger was born – The Big Mac.

A franchisee named Jim Delligatti invented it in his restaurant.

15

Another franchisee named Herb Peterson invented their first breakfast product – the McMuffin – in 1973.

He was looking to increase morning sales and came up with the idea when he realised that people didn't particularly enjoy eating burgers and fries at breakfast time.

16

The Happy Meal first appeared in 1972.

Specialist clubs all over the world collect the toys and boxes... and some of the older toys fetch thousands of dollars!

17

Britain's first McDonald's restaurants opened in London in 1974.

Today, McDonald's has spread to five continents.

18

The success of McDonald's continues. The first McDonald's in China opened in 1992. It is now the largest food chain in the world supplying food and drink to nearly 40 million people a day.

A recent survey placed the 'golden arches' logo as one of the most recognised logos in the world... even more recognised than the Christian cross!

Not such a Happy Meal

Despite its worldwide success, McDonald's is not without its problems and controversy. In recent years McDonald's has come under attack from protesters who feel that they are just one big moneymaking organisation who value profits above anything else. There have been criticisms over the treatment of workers, the amount of packaging they use and some concerns over the healthiness of their foods.

They have also come under attack from environmentalists who claim that large areas of rainforest have been cut down to provide space for the millions of cows they need to produce the beef for their burgers. McDonald's have always insisted that they get their beef from lots and lots of smaller farms – and there is not one huge 'McDonald's herd' that requires millions of acres of rainforest to be cleared!

❗ FACT Global responsibility

Some argue that globalisation has contributed to a growing sense of global responsibility. They say big multinational companies are now doing more than ever to combat developing-world poverty and conserve the environment. They argue that large organisations like Disney, McDonald's, Tesco and Nike have the power, money and status to make real differences on a global scale when they campaign on certain issues.

↰ SOURCE A: *In recent years there have been anti-globalisation riots that have targeted multinational companies such as McDonald's, Nike and Starbucks. Protesters are concerned that when these big companies make a profit, it is often at the expense of poorer countries who supply cheap labour and raw materials.*

❗ FACT Hamburger history

The McDonald brothers *did not* invent the hamburger. Many places claim to have invented it; perhaps the most famous being Hamburg in Germany. The story goes that a chef named Otto Kuasw in Hamburg in the 1890s used to make a snack consisting of ground-up beef sausage in batter, served between two pieces of bread and topped with a fried egg. This became the favourite snack of American sailors who used to visit the German port of Hamburg – and brought the 'hamburger', as they called it, back to the USA.

Work

1 Write a sentence or two about the following terms:

   a multi-national

   b globalisation

   c franchising

2 Write down reasons why you think global companies such as McDonald's have received:

   a criticism

   b praise

3 Each of the following people have contributed in some way to the success of McDonald's:

   a Maurice and Richard McDonald

   b Ray Kroc

   c Ronald McDonald

   d Jim Delligatti

   In your opinion, which one has contributed most to the success? Give reasons for your answer.

4 Each of the following dates are important in McDonald's history:

   1973; 1959; 1961; 1955; 1968; 1963; 1974; 1948; 1954; 1972

   a Write each date on a separate line in chronological order.

   b Beside each date, write down what happened in that year.

─ MISSION ACCOMPLISHED? ─

• Can you explain how and why McDonald's developed?

• Do you understand some of the arguments *for* and *against* multinationals like McDonald's?

A century of change

MISSION OBJECTIVES

- To be able to compare the Britain of 1900 to the Britain of 2000.

Queen Victoria died over one hundred years ago, in the first month of 1901. She left behind a country that was powerful, proud and very optimistic about the future – after all, the British navy was bigger than any other two countries' navies added together; Britain sold more goods and made more money than any other nation and the British Empire was the largest empire the world had ever known! But Britain itself was a divided nation. Despite advances in health, medicine, work and living conditions, millions of Brits still suffered in terrible poverty, while others lived a life of luxury.

Over a century later, Britain was a very different country. The Empire had gone; its navy was only just inside the world's top ten and it had dropped to the fifth largest trading nation. Two world wars had left Britain a lot weaker – and other countries had become much more powerful in the meantime, particularly the USA and Japan. But the country itself was far less divided and more equal than in 1901. For example, all adults had the vote (women hadn't been able to vote until 1918), and great efforts had also been made to fight poverty and improve housing, healthcare and local communities. In fact, a survey in the year 2000 showed that 74% of Brits were happy with their lives! This was one of the highest percentages of all European nations. Clearly then, the last 100 years has been a century of change. So just how much has Britain changed?

The 'average family'

Towards the end of the twentieth century, the average British family consisted of mum, dad and two children… but things were changing! In 2001, more couples were getting divorced than at any other time in history, while the number of children raised by just one parent had jumped to 25%. A further one out of every three births took place outside marriage, compared to one out of every nine in 1980! Indeed, many said that at the end of the twentieth century there was no such thing as an 'average family'!

In 1900, the average British family was made up of a mum, dad and four children. Divorce was virtually unknown and if an unmarried girl became pregnant she and her family would be condemned to a life of shame.

Oh baby

Out of every 1000 babies born in 1900, 125 died before they reached the age of one. By 2000, that number had reduced to six deaths per 1000. In 2000, four babies per 1000 died before the age of one in Japan; seven per 1000 in the USA, but 69 per 1000 in India.

How long have I got?

If a person born in 2000 reached the age of one, they could expect to live to the age of 78 if they were female and 73 if they were male. However, in 2000, one person in four still smoked, despite the fact that smoking causes cancer and, very worryingly, one in six children were obese. The three most common causes of death in 2000 were heart disease, cancer and respiratory (breathing) problems. There was one doctor per 667 people in Britain in 2000 compared to one per 313 people in Germany, one per 435 in the USA and one per 32,500 in Ethiopia.

In 1900, the three most common causes of death were respiratory diseases, such as pneumonia and bronchitis, heart problems and tuberculosis or TB (you get your TB jab to prevent this now!). If you reached the age of one in 1900, you could expect to live to the age of 53 if you were a man and 56 if you were a woman. What other vaccinations or 'jabs' do you get to prevent disease today?

Religion

Christianity, as it had been for centuries, remained the predominant religion. In 2001, there were over 40 million Christians, making up nearly three-quarters of the population. This included the Church of England, Church of Scotland, Church of Wales, Catholics, Protestants and all other Christian groups. People with no religion formed the second largest group, accounting for 15% of the population. Muslims were the largest religious group after Christians (see Source A).

Look at what I've got!

Between 1900 and 2000 there were massive changes in what was called **consumer goods** ownership – these are often items that people *could* live without, but chose to buy in order to make their lives better. For example, in 1900 there was only one car for every 880 people – in 2000, there was one car for every three people. And 66% of people now owned a mobile phone, compared to 0% in 1900… because mobile phones didn't even exist then!

Getting older

Britain's population is getting older. As recently as 1950, only 10% of Britain's population was over 60 – in 2000, over 21% was! Put simply, better medical care and a 'safer Britain' meant that people were living longer. And, in their old age, Brits are usually looked after by pension money, and benefits from the Government and the NHS… in 1900, older people had to rely on family, savings or charity!

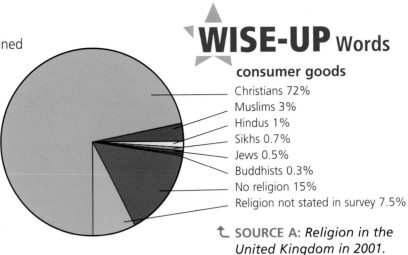

WISE-UP Words

consumer goods

Christians 72%
Muslims 3%
Hindus 1%
Sikhs 0.7%
Jews 0.5%
Buddhists 0.3%
No religion 15%
Religion not stated in survey 7.5%

↰ SOURCE A: *Religion in the United Kingdom in 2001.*

School and work

The average children of 2000 would attend school from the age of five to sixteen. They would be taught a Government-set National Curriculum covering a wide range of subjects using the latest computer technology to help them (they still used books though!).

In 1900, pupils only had to go to school until the age of 12. They would all be taught the basics – Reading, wRiting and aRithmetic (the three Rs), but boys would be taught slightly different things (sports, woodwork and science) to girls (cooking, sewing and singing) for part of the day! Why do you think this happened?

Work

1 a Draw two spidergrams. One should be called 'Britain in 1900' and the other should be called 'Britain in 2000'. Surround each spidergram with facts and figures about Britain at these times.

b Write a paragraph about the changes that took place in Britain between 1900 and 2000.

c Of all the changes mentioned in your paragraph, which do you think was the most important? Give reasons for your choice. See if other people in the class agree with you.

d When would you have rather lived: 1900 or 2000? Again, give reasons for your choice.

2 a In 2000, a survey showed that 74% of British people were happy with their lives and proud to be British. Why do you think so many people were proud to be British?

b Are you proud of Britain or not? Give reasons.

c Which of these words describe the country you would like to live in: free, caring, peaceful, safe, powerful, rich, fair, poor, equal, respected, religious, classless, clean?

d Which words do you think best describe Britain today – can you add some of your own?

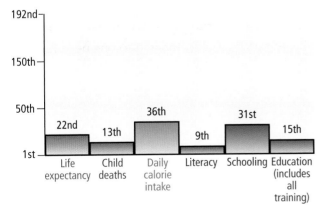

↰ SOURCE B: *A 2000 world ranking chart. This records Britain's position in the world (out of 192 countries) in several different categories.*

MISSION ACCOMPLISHED?

• Can you remember five major changes that have taken place in Britain in the last one hundred years?

Have you been learning? 3

TASK 1 Possessive apostrophes

In this task, you will learn about apostrophes to show possession (belonging).

- *The attack belonging to <u>one</u> terrorist*
  ➜ *The terrorist's attack*
  (Rule: In singular words, write the apostrophe <u>before</u> the s)

- *The attack belonging to <u>two or more</u> terrorists*
  ➜ *The terrorists' attack*
  (Rule: In plural words, write the apostrophe <u>after</u> the s)

a Write out these sentences, adding the apostrophe in the correct place in the second half of the sentence.

  i)   The plan belonging to the Commander
       ➜ The Commanders plan

  ii) The speech belonging to the leader
       ➜ The leaders speech

  iii) The weapons belonging to the soldiers
       ➜ The soldiers weapons

  iv) The land gained by the winners
       ➜ The winners land

  v)   Mussolini was an ally of Hitler
       ➜ Hitlers ally was Mussolini

  vi) The property belonging to the Jews
       ➜ The Jews property

  vii) The nuclear submarines belonging to America
       ➜ Americas nuclear submarines

  viii) The bombs belonging to the terrorists
       ➜ The terrorists bombs

b Still working in your books, work out whether these are singular or plural. Write S or P for each. The first has been done for you.

  i)   Queen Victoria's son | S |

  ii) Italy's army | |

  iii) The soldiers' food | |

  iv) Russia's land | |

  v)   The winners' decisions | |

  vi) Hitler's house | |

  vii) The rebels' punishment | |

TASK 2 An exercise in propaganda

a Write a full detailed definition of the word 'propaganda'.

b Read the propaganda stories below about alleged German atrocities (cruel acts that broke the 'rules' of war) during World War II.

> French children were machine-gunned by German soldiers when they conquered France. Their mothers were killed too.

> German prison camp guards refused to give captured and wounded soldiers any medical treatment or water.

> Germans used the corpses of Allied soldiers. The fat was turned into oil and the bones were mixed up with rotten vegetables for the pigs to eat.

> Thousands of innocent civilians were killed when German submarines sank passenger ships early in the war.

> Priests all over Belgium and Holland who refused to ring their church bells to celebrate the Germans taking their town were killed and hung on the bells.

> German bomber planes deliberately targeted schools and hospitals on their bombing raids over Britain.

i) Despite there being little proof of any of these atrocities actually being committed, some of these stories appeared in British newspapers during World War II. Why do you think the British Government was so keen to advertise these allegations?

ii) Imagine you work for the Government as their official propaganda war artist. Using a plain sheet of A3 or A4 paper, design a propaganda poster to suit one of the six stories that could be displayed in a British newspaper during the war.

TASK 3 Spot the mistakes

Here are ten sentences. Each sentence has two errors. One is a spelling mistake; the other is a factual error. When you have spotted each mistake, write the sentence out correctly.

a Hitler's top secret plans for the invation of Britain in September 1940 was called 'Operation Snow Leopard'.

b The RAF pilots who fought in the Battle of Britain became known as 'The Fighters' after Winston Churchill honoured their victory with the speech 'never in the feild of human conflict was so much owed by so many to so few'.

c As soon as World War II broke out, thousands of schoolchildren were moved away from the places most likely to be bomed by the enemy. This was known as evaporation.

d During World War II, American and British ships dropped nearly three million tons of bombs on 131 German citys. This killed nearly one million men, women and children and made eight million people homeless.

e The Nazi decision two kill every Jew in Europe was known as their 'first solution to the Jewish problem'.

f Even after Germany surrendered, the Japanese continued to fight. At 8:15am on 6 August 1955, the USA dropped the world's first nuclear bomb on the Japanese city of Hiroshima. Free days later, another was dropped on Nagasaki.

g The bomb on Hiroshima killed 80,000 people instantly. In total, 70,000 of the city's 780,000 buildings were totally distroyed.

h The League of Nations was set up after World War II in order too prevent future wars and conflict. It continues to aim to improve living and working conditions, health, children's welfare, education and much more.

TASK 4 Which way?

There are always at least two ways of looking at any event. Look at the ten headlines that could have appeared in newspapers between 1900 and 2000. There are five events.

a Pair up the headlines so that you have one biased for the event and one biased against it. Then write down what the five events were.

b For each event, write an unbiased headline.

c Choose any one of the five events and write your unbiased news story about it.

   i)   Germans elect new leader – war hero to run country

   ii)   World's greatest ship launched today

   iii)   Watch out – they've got the vote now!

   iv)   McMenace

   v)   Unsinkable! Don't be fooled

   vi)   A Nazi piece of work

   vii)   America unleashes billion dollar death bombs

   viii) McDonald's – a twentieth century success story

   ix)   At last – women gain equal political rights

   x)   Nuked! Japan defeated

Glossary

Abdicate Run away or resign from a formal position (for example, a monarchy).

Activists People acting to bring about change (for example, political or social).

Alliances Different sides, for example in war.

Allies People on the same side, for example in war.

Anti-Semitism Prejudice against Jews.

Appeasement Trying to keep another nation happy by doing as it asks.

Area bombing Bombing whole towns and cities to make sure that everything was destroyed.

Armistice Ceasefire.

Arms race A race between countries to build up the biggest army.

Assassinate Kill a public figure (for example, a politician or monarch).

Assembly line An efficient manufacturing process in which each person has just one job to do.

Aviation The area of aeroplanes and flight.

Bolt Part of a firearm. When pulled back, it prepares the rifle to be fired by pushing the cartridge into the chamber.

Bomber A heavy plane designed for dropping bombs.

Boycott Refuse to use.

British Commonwealth A group of independent, free countries with close links to Britain.

Brittle Easily fractured/broken.

Called up Conscription (see below).

Censored Controlled/banned.

Civil rights Some of the most important human rights.

Civilians People who are not in the armed forces.

Communism A theory that everyone in society should be equal and everything should be shared.

Communist Someone who believes in communism.

Concentration camps Hitler's prison camps.

Concrete bunker A bunker built under the ground of trenches and reinforced by concrete.

Conscientious objectors Men who refused to join the army because they believed that war was always wrong.

Conscription Being forced to join the army by the Government.

Consumer goods Non-essential items that improve people's lives.

Cooperation Working or acting together.

Court martial Military court.

Cowardice Being scared; a lack of courage to face danger.

Currency The type of money used.

Death toll The number of people who died during a particular event or time.

Democracy A form of government where the majority of the people in a country hold the power to decide who rules.

Desertion Running away or abandoning something, for example the army.

Dictatorship A form of government where a country is entirely controlled by one person.

Duckboards Wooden boards placed on the ground of trenches to stop people from sinking in the mud.

Dugouts Rooms dug out of the back walls of trenches.

Eugenics The scientific study of how to improve races.

Euro The currency used in much of the European Union.

Evacuation Leaving a place – in the Second World War, over one million people who lived in areas most at risk from bombing were moved to safer places.

Faith Religious belief.

Far East The countries of East Asia.

Fascism A type of dictatorship started by Benito Mussolini in 1919.

Fighter A type of plane, for example the Hurricane.

Fire step A raised platform on which soldiers stood to look and fire over the top of trenches.

Firestorm An intense fire that creates its own wind system.

Flappers Fashionable young American women in the 1920s.

Foreign affairs Issues to do with international relations and national interests in foreign countries.

Franchising Licensing out a business to someone else (the licenser will take some of the business profits).

Front An area where two armies meet each other.

Führer 'Supreme leader' in German; Hitler's name for himself.

Gas bell Rung in trenches during the Great War to warn troops to put on gas masks.

Genocide Deliberate extermination of a race of people.

Gestapo Hitler's secret police force.

Ghettos Separate areas outside cities where Jews were forced to live.

Global village The name given to the fact that people living thousands of miles apart can communicate with each other instantly through technology.

Globalisation The spread of business all over the world.

Hereditary Passed on from parents to children.

Holocaust A name for the Nazis' attempt to wipe out the Jewish race.

Hull The body of a ship.

Human rights The basic rights and freedoms to which all humans should be entitled.

Hurricane A fighter plane used by the RAF during the Second World War.

ICBMs Intercontinental ballistic missiles; used to carry nuclear bombs across large distances.

Incendiary Capable of causing fire.

Indoctrinated Brainwashed into thinking in a particular way.

Jedi The fictional religion from the Star Wars films.

Jihad The Islamic word for 'holy war'.

Kamikaze Japanese suicide bombers.

Long-term cause A reason that has built up over several years.

Luftwaffe The German air force.

Magazine The part of a rifle in which bullets are stored.

Maiden First, for example a ship's maiden voyage is its first journey.

Martyr Someone who is killed for a cause in which they believe.

Mass-produce Make identical items on a very large scale.

Migration Moving from one country to another.

Multi-cultural Many different cultures existing together.

Multinational Many different nationalities existing together.

Multi-racial Many different races existing together.

Munitions Weapons and ammunition. Thousands of women worked in munitions factories during the Great War.

Pact A formal agreement between nations; a treaty.

Pardon Forgiveness of a crime.

Partition Division.

Pearl Harbor A US naval base in Hawaii that was attacked by the Japanese towards the end of the Second World War.

Periscope An instrument for observation, consisting of two mirrors and a tube. It was used by troops during the Great War to see over the tops of trenches without risk of being shot.

Persecution The regular mistreatment of one group of people by another group.

Precision bombing Used at the beginning of the Second World War; attempting to hit specific targets.

RAF Royal Air Force – Britain's air force.

Rationing Limiting the amounts of food and fuel that could be bought.

Rearmament Building up armed forces and increasing stocks of weapons.

Reforms Changes made to improve something.

Satellite An object that orbits another object.

Secular Of the world; not religious.

Security Council One of the main parts of the United Nations; responsible for maintaining international speech.

Segregation Separation of different racial groups.

Shells Large bullets that are fired over long distances.

Short-term cause A recent reason.

Single market Where goods, services, money and people can move freely between different countries.

SOS A distress signal.

Soviets The people of the USSR.

Space race The competition between the USA and the USSR to put the first man on the moon.

Spitfire A plane used by the RAF during the Second World War.

Stalemate Deadlock.

Sterilised Made unable to have children.

Stockpiling Hoarding/saving up weapons.

Suffragettes A group of women, led by the Pankhursts, who campaigned to win the vote for women – unlike the Suffragists, their tactics consisted of 'deeds not words'.

Suffragists A group of women who campaigned to win the vote for women by peaceful methods such as petitions and marches.

Superpowers The most powerful states/countries in the world.

Swastika An ancient symbol that was adopted by the Nazis.

Terrorism Committing acts of violence in an attempt to force people to agree to demands.

Terrorist A person who carries out terrorism.

Total war War that affected the whole country – not just the soldiers fighting, but the people back at home.

Transatlantic Across the Atlantic Sea.

Treaty A contract between countries.

Triple Alliance The alliance made up of Germany, Austria-Hungary and Italy at the beginning of the Great War.

Triple Entente The alliance made up of Britain, France and Russia at the beginning of the Great War.

Types Kinds.

Viceroy A British ruler in India.

'West' The countries to the west of the 'iron curtain' in Europe.

Zionism The belief that Jewish people should return to live in Palestine.

Index